Conflict Resolution in the High School

This project was made possible by the generous support of the William and Flora Hewlett Foundation, the Lippincott Foundation of the Peace Development Fund, the CarEth Foundation, the W. Alton Jones Foundation, and many individual donors.

Conflict Resolution in the High School: 36 Lessons
by Carol Miller Lieber with Linda Lantieri and Tom Roderick

Editors: Eden R. Steinberg and Caroline Chauncey
Text Design: Sonali Gulati, Linda Lecomte, and Jeff Perkins
Cover Design: Lorraine Karcz

Lieber, Carol Miller
ISBN-10 0-942349-11-3
ISBN-13 978-0-942349-11-5

Inquiries regarding permission to reprint all or part of *Conflict Resolution in the High School* should be addressed to: Permissions Editor, Educators for Social Responsibility, 23 Garden Street, Cambridge, MA 02138.

"Classroom Management Checklist" is reprinted with permission of Quest International from Lions-Quest *Working Towards Peace* (2nd edition) " 1995 by Quest International.

"Getting to the Heart of It" is adapted with permission from *I am Lovable and Capable* by Sidney B. Simon (Chesterfield, Mass.: Values Press, 1991). Send for a catalog of other strategy books from Values Press, P.O. Box 556, Chesterfield, MA 01012.

"Pride and Prejudice" is excerpted from *A Gathering of Heroes: Reflections on Rage and Responsibility*, by Greg Alan-Williams © 1994. Reprinted by arrangement with Academy Chicago Publishers.

"Anger Mountain," "Feeback Sandwich," and "Haves and Have-Nots" are adapted with permission from *Dealing With Differences* by Marion O'Malley and Tiffany Davis (Chapel Hill, N.C.: Center for Peace Education, 1995).

"Why Use I-Statements?" is adapted with permission from Carol Miller Lieber and Rachel Poliner, Educators for Social Responsibility, 1996.

"Soap and Water" by Anzia Yezierska from *How I Found America: Collected Stories of Anzia Yezierska* © 1991 by Louise Levitas Henriksen. Reprinted by permission of Persea Books, Inc.

"More About Power" is adapted from the work of Jinnie Spiegel, RCCP National Center, New York, N.Y.

"Anti-Semitism at Sports Event Stirs Sharon," by Kate Zernike and Shirley Leung, is reprinted with permission from the *Boston Globe*, February 19, 1996.

"Target, Bystander, and Ally Cards" are reprinted from *Creating a Peaceable School: Confronting Intolerance and Bullying*, a curriculum developed by Nancy Beardall. The cards were created by Nancy Beardall and Ravitte Gall.

"Crossing Cultures: A Simulation Game" is adapted from *Games by Thiagi: Diversity Simulation Games*, by Sirasailam Thiagaragjan, Ph.D. © 1995. Adapted by permission of the publisher, HRD Press, Amherst, MA (413) 253-3488.

Material on pp. 33-42, 44, 55-60, 71-78, 91-98, 127, 140, 161-166, 179-194, 203-208, and 231-232 is adapted with permission from *Resolving Conflict Creatively: A Draft Teaching Guide for Secondary Schools* © ESR Metropolitan Area, 1990.

 This book is printed on recycled paper.

Conflict Resolution
in the High School

36 Lessons

by Carol Miller Lieber
with Linda Lantieri
and Tom Roderick

esr

EDUCATORS
for
SOCIAL
RESPONSIBILITY

23 Garden Street
Cambridge, MA 02138
(617) 492-1764

Contents

Acknowledgments 7

Introduction 9
How This Guide is Organized 9
The Principles of the Peaceable
    Classroom 10
Options for Lessons 11
Implementing the Curriculum 13

Preparing to Teach
This Curriculum 19
A Three-Minute Guide to Conflict
    Resolution 19
Before You Begin Teaching This
    Curriculum 20
The Limits of *Conflict Resolution
    in the High School* 20
Creating a Classroom Environment for
    Teaching Conflict Resolution 21
Classroom Management Checklist 23
Teaching and Learning Strategies 24
Assessing Student Learning 28

Lesson 1
Getting to Know
Each Other 33
Paired Interviews 34
Opinion Continuum 34
Find Someone Who... 36

Lesson 2
Establishing a Positive
Learning Environment 37
Getting to the Heart of It 38
Line Cards 41

Lesson 3
Making Group
Agreements 43
Group Agreements 44

Lesson 4
Working Together as a Group 47
Machine Building 48

Lesson 5
Diversity in the Classroom 49
Checking Out Perceptions 50
Checking Out Assumptions 50
Perception Cards 52
Checking It Out 53

Lesson 6
Communication:
What's the Big Deal? 55
Back-to-Back Drawings 56
Demonstration of Poor Listening
    in a Discussion 57
Blocker Cards 59

Lesson 7
Active Listening 61
Nonverbal Attending Skills 62
Paraphrasing 62
Reflecting Feelings 63
Extended Active-Listening Practice 63
Thoughts and Feelings 65
Feelings Vocabulary 66
It's Easier For Others To Talk When I... 67
Listening Triads Feedback Sheet 68
Conflict, Violence, and Peacemaking:
    What's Your Opinion? 69

Lesson 8
How Do We Experience Conflict? 71
Conflict Microlab 72

Lesson 9
Exploring the Nature
of Violence 75
Microlab on Violence 76

Defining Violence Activity 76
Defining Violence Handout 78

Lesson 10
Exploring the Nature of Conflict 79
Webbing Conflict 80
Brainstorming What's Positive About
Conflict 80
Pair-Share About a Conflict You've
Experienced 81
Survey About Conflict and Me 82

Lesson 11
**Responding to Conflict: What Do
We Do?** 83
Conflict Styles Skits 84
Conflict Cards Activity 84
Conflict Styles Skits Handout 86
Six Conflict Resolution Styles 89
Conflict Cards 90

Lesson 12
**How and Why Does Conflict
Escalate?** 91
Exploring Conflict Escalation 92
Triad Role-Plays 93
Conflict Synectics Cards 95

Lesson 13
**"Reading" and Understanding
Feelings** 99
Feelings Charades 100
The Feelings Bull's-Eye 100
The Feelings–Motivation Connection 100
"Pride and Prejudice" 102
Feelings Cards 104
Closing Cards 106

Lesson 14
All About Anger 109
Anger Triggers 110
The Anger Mountain Activity 110
Responses to Anger and Cooling Off 111
Responses to Anger Role-Play 112
Anger Mountain Handout 114
Anger Reducers 115

Lesson 15
"You" Messages And "I" Messages 117
Assertion, Aggression, and "I" Messages 118

Turning "You" Messages into "I" Messages 119
"I" Message Skits 121
Ingredients of an "I" Message 122

Lesson 16
**Getting What You Need
Using "I" Statements** 123
Assertive "I" Statements 124
Assertiveness Triads 125
Why Use "I" Statements? 126
Five Steps For Sending Assertive
Messages 127
Assertiveness Triad Scenario Cards 128

Lesson 17
Defusing Someone Else's Anger 129
Introduce Defusion 130
De-escalation Role-Plays 130
Role-Play Scenario Cards 131
De-escalating Conflict 132

Lesson 18
Giving and Receiving Feedback 133
Criticism vs. Feedback Exercise 134
Giving and Receiving Feedback
(Mini-Lecture) 134
Criticism, Praise, Or Feedback?
Activity 135
The Feedback Sandwich 136
Criticism, Praise, or Feedback?
Handout 137

Lesson 19
Point of View 139
Old Woman/Young Woman 140
Introduction to P.O.V. 140
Soap and Water Activity 141
"Soap and Water" 142
What Do You See? 147
Points of View 148

Lesson 20
**Positions and
Underlying Needs** 149
Definitions of Positions
and Interests 150
Positions and Interests Role-Play 151
Getting to the Interests Activity 151
Sibling Dispute Script 152
Getting to the Interests Handout 153

Lesson 21
Win-Win Problem-Solving 155
Kisses 156
Win-Win Problem-Solving and
  Role-Play 157
Case Studies 158
Win-Win Problem-Solving 159

Lesson 22
Negotiation, Mediation, and
Arbitration 161
Defining Negotiation, Mediation,
  and Arbitration 162
Negotiation Microlab 164
Negotiation Skills Web 164
The "-Ate" Processes of Peacemaking 166

Lesson 23
Group Negotiation Practice 167
Group Negotiation 168

Lesson 24
Interpersonal Negotiation 171
Demonstration of Interpersonal
  Negotiation 172
The Negotiation Process Step by Step 172
Negotiation Triads 172
The Negotiation Process 174
Feedback Checklist 175
Negotiation Triad Conflicts 176

Lesson 25
Introduction to Mediation 179
Review the Definitions of Mediation
  and Arbitration 180
Mediation: Discussion and Demonstration 180

Lesson 26
Mediation Practice 183
Review the Mediation Process 184
Fish-Bowl Role-Play (optional) 185
Mediation Practice 185
The Mediation Process 187
A Skillful Mediator... 189
Mediation Role-Plays 190

Lesson 27
Cultural Sharing 193
Identity Shields 194
Cultural Sharing Microlab 194

Lesson 28
Understanding Power 195
Haves and Have-Nots 196

Lesson 29
More About Power 199
The Four I's of Oppression Activity 200
The Four I's of Oppression Handout 202

Lesson 30
Understanding Stereotypes,
Prejudice, and Discrimination 203
Stereotypes 204
Prejudice Web 204
Discrimination 205

Lesson 31
Names Can Really Hurt Us 207
Microlab on Prejudice and Discrimination 208
Names Can Really Hurt Us 208

Lesson 32
Diversity and Conflict 209
How Do Differences Cause Conflict
  to Escalate? 210
De-escalating Conflicts Based on
  Difference 210
Diversity and Conflict at School 210
Diversity on the Conflict Escalator 211
Diversity and Conflict Scenarios 212

Lesson 33
Interrupting Prejudice and
Stopping Verbal Abuse 213
Pair-Share on Interrupting Prejudice 214
Guidelines for Interrupting Prejudice
  and Verbal Abuse 214
Interrupting Prejudice Role-Plays 216

Lesson 34
From Being a Bystander to
Taking a Stand 217
Targets, Bystanders, and Allies 218
Rotation Stations 219
"Anti-Semitism at Sports Event Stirs Sharon" 220
Target, Bystander, and Ally Cards 222

Lesson 35
How Can People
Make a Difference? 227

Introduce the "Making a Difference"
Project   228
"Making A Difference" Project
Presentations   229

Lesson 36
I Can Make a Difference   **231**
Affirmation Gifts   232
Appreciation Exercise   232

Infusing Conflict Resolution
Into the Standard Curriculum   **233**
Infusing Conflict Resolution Concepts   233
Infusing Conflict Resolution Skills   247
Infusing Instructional Strategies for a
Peaceable Classroom   254
Infusing Thematic Units on Conflict and
Cooperation   255

Additional Activities   **259**
Tinker Toys:
A Communication Exercise   260
Building Blocks of Cooperation   265
We All Belong to Groups   269
Peacemaking and Peacemakers   274
Security in Your Life   278
Letting Go of Labels   288
Crossing Cultures:
A Simulation Game   295
Taking Action on a
Community Problem   303

Appendix A
Gathering Activities   **309**
Anger Ball-Toss   309
Concentric Circles   309
Feelings Check-In   310
Feelings Echo   310
Go-Rounds   310
Group Clap   310
Group Juggling   310
Guessing Box   311
"I'd Like to Hear ..."   311
"I Got What I Wanted ..."   311
"I Like My Neighbors Who ..."   311
Initials   311
I Represent Conflict   311
Mirroring   312
Name Game with Motion   312
New and Good   312

Nonverbal Birthday Line-Up   312
Putting Up a Fight   312
Something Beautiful   312
Standing Up   312
Strong Feelings   313
What Color is Conflict?   313
"What Would You Do ...?"   313
What's Important in a Friend?   313
"When I'm in a Conflict ..."   313
Whip   313
"You Like, I Like ..."   313

Appendix B
Closing Activities   **315**
Appreciation   315
Closing Connections   315
Encouragement Cards   315
Feelings Check-In   316
Goodbye/Hello   316
Go-Rounds   316
Group Yes!   316
"If I Had a Wish ..."   316
"I Used To ...."   316
Rainstorm   316
Telegram   317
Closing Quotes   317

Appendix C
Grouping Strategies   **321**
Matching Activities for Forming Pairs   321
Forming Groups of Three, Four, or
More   321
Grouping Strategies Based on Academic
Content   322

Appendix D
Guidelines for Role-Plays   **323**
What is Role-Playing?   323
Types of Role-Plays   323
Role-Play Techniques   323
Role-Play Rules   323
The Teacher's Role   323
Questions for Processing the Role-Play   324
Facilitating Role-Plays   325

Appendix E
Sample Infusion Lesson   **327**
Overview and Research   328
Opinion Walk-About   329
From Win-Lose to Win-Win   329

Appendix F
Course Assessment Questionnaire   **331**

Appendix G
Related Resources   **333**

About the Authors   **335**

About ESR   **337**

Acknowledgments

Developing and implementing conflict resolution curricula and programs for high school students presents a wide range of challenges. In our work with high schools we have witnessed how this kind of learning empowers young people, makes schooling more personally meaningful, and creates more positive relationships between and among adults and adolescents. Nevertheless, asserting that this work is important for all high school students is a risky business that often challenges faculty to rethink their teaching practices and question how their schools can be structured to better support both academic achievement and the emotional and social development of young people. For these reasons our deepest thanks go to high school principals and teachers around the country who have committed themselves to making conflict resolution and intergroup relations education a significant part of their school cultures.

This guide was truly a collaborative effort, fusing the thinking and practice of colleagues from ESR Metropolitan Area in New York City, ESR's Resolving Conflict Creatively Program National Center, and Educators for Social Responsibility in Cambridge, Mass. In particular, we owe a great debt to the pioneering work of ESR Metropolitan Area, whose staff developed the first conflict resolution and intergroup relations programs for alternative high schools in New York City.

We could not have written this guide without the personal and professional support of our executive director, Larry Dieringer. Under Larry's leadership, ESR has continued to commit time and resources to broaden and deepen our work with high school staff and students.

We want to thank all of our colleagues, in our home offices and around the country, who work with Educators for Social Responsibility. We consider ourselves to be very lucky to work with such dedicated and talented individuals. In particular, we would like to thank:

- our editors, Eden Steinberg and Caroline Chauncey, who made the editing process a pleasurable one and who tackled the many publication details with sensitivity and perseverance;

- the director of publications and communications, Laura Parker Roerden, for putting this project on an already full publications plate and seeing it through to its completion;

- Sonali Gulati, Jeff Perkins, and Linda Lecomte for making the words come to life through their design of the book;

- ESR's program staff, especially Zephryn Conte, Mary James Edwards, Jane Harrison, Janet Patti, and Jinnie Spiegler, whose thinking about high school work guided this project and whose feedback made this a better book;

- Peggy Ray, for her work on *Resolving Conflict Actively: A Draft Teaching Guide for Secondary Schools*, the source of several key lessons in this curriculum;

- Rachel Poliner, whose clear-eyed passion for working with secondary teachers always provides new insights and unflagging encouragement;

- William J. Kreidler, whose book *Conflict Resolution in the Middle School* set a standard for this project and whose heart nurtures the spirit we bring to this work.

Finally, we would like to thank Shelly Berman, an early founder of ESR, whose work in the field of social responsibility continues to inform our thinking about young people and schooling. In some measure, we hope this guide furthers ESR's primary mission—to provide young people with tools and skills to participate actively in ways that make this world a more just and peaceful place for everyone.

Introduction

Conflict is a natural and essential part of living. Yet we usually perceive conflict as a negative phenomenon rather than as an opportunity for change and growth. Through training and practice, both students and teachers can build a repertoire of skills to manage and resolve interpersonal conflict in positive ways. Conflict resolution education emphasizes systematic thinking about conflict and provides us with tools and strategies that can help us respond skillfully and creatively to conflicts and differences of all kinds.

Adolescents often experience conflict without a clear understanding of its sources. Many adolescents also lack the means to solve their problems effectively and nonviolently. Young people rarely have an opportunity to learn a systematic way of thinking about conflict or a practical process for handling conflict that can become integrated into their everyday experience.

Conflict Resolution in the High School gives students the opportunity to learn how to resolve their differences peacefully and helps them develop effective ways of living and working together. This guide emphasizes making personal connections to the skills and concepts of conflict resolution. This personal perspective involves providing regular opportunities for self-reflection through observation, writing, reading, and discussion. Learning about conflict becomes a way of learning more about ourselves.

If we want students to use peacemaking skills in their own lives, we, as teachers, must strengthen our commitment to model and practice these skills on a daily basis in our classrooms and communities. We hope this guide can be a starting point for you and your students to build more peaceful relationships and a more peaceful world.

How This Guide is Organized

Conflict Resolution in the High School is divided into the following sections:

Introduction

The goal of the Introduction is to help you understand how the curriculum is organized, the principles on which the curriculum is based, how to use the lesson plans, and how best to implement the curriculum.

Preparing to Teach This Curriculum

This section suggests ways to create an environment for teaching conflict resolution, teaching and learning strategies, and methods to assess student learning.

36 Skill Lessons

This is the core of the curriculum. The lessons introduce students to a body of essential conflict resolution concepts and skills.

Infusing Conflict Resolution into the Standard Curriculum

This section outlines several infusion methods along with practical suggestions for infusion lessons and units.

Additional Activities

These activities extend and deepen the concepts and skills taught in the 36 skill lessons. Many of these activities require multiple periods and are highly active and interactive.

Appendices

These include lists of gathering and closing activities, a course assessment questionnaire for students, suggestions on forming groups for activities, guidelines for leading role-plays, and resources for learning more about conflict resolution.

The Principles of the Peaceable Classroom

This curriculum is based on a model that is used in all conflict resolution materials developed by Educators for Social Responsibility. We call this model the Peaceable Classroom. The Peaceable Classroom is a caring classroom community based on the following principles:

Building Community—Creating a safe and nurturing environment in which everyone participates and everyone belongs.

Mutual Respect—Nurturing mutual respect among students and teachers as the starting point for creating a positive and effective learning environment and reducing adversarial relationships.

Affirmation and Acceptance—Finding ways to affirm the dignity and value of each person in the classroom. Helping students accept each other's strengths, needs, and idiosyncrasies.

Appreciation for Diversity—Exploring individual and cultural diversity in ways that help young people move from tolerance to genuine regard, appreciation, and acceptance of people who are different from themselves. Becoming allies with others to counter bias and interrupt and reduce prejudice. Helping build positive intergroup relations.

Personal Connections—Creating ways to link personal stories, perspectives, and experiences to learning activities and outcomes. Developing personal relationships with each other and making time to stay connected.

Caring and Effective Communication—Encouraging active listening, assertiveness, and open, honest dialogue. Allowing time for students to disagree respectfully and hear other points of view.

Emotional Literacy—Allowing time for expressing and responding to feelings appropriately. Developing the capacity for empathy through perspective taking and the inclusion of multiple points of view. Learning ways to manage emotions constructively. Utilizing affective dimensions of learning to encourage, inspire, and motivate.

Cooperation and Collaborative Problem-Solving—Using cooperative learning and collaborative problem-solving in ways that make each person's contribution integral to achieving the goals of the group.

Managing and Resolving Conflict—Helping young people to develop a "toolbox" of strategies and skills that help them prevent, manage, and resolve conflicts constructively and nonviolently. Developing effective negotiation and mediation skills.

Shared Decision-Making—Using a variety of decision-making processes in the classroom. Helping people affected by the decision to consider the consequences and implications of choices before making a responsible judgment.

Democratic Participation—Participating in nonadversarial dialogue and using controversy constructively. Encouraging open-mindedness and the right of everyone to be heard. Practicing the arts of compromise and consensus.

Social Responsibility—Acting on your concerns in ways that make a positive difference for yourself and others. Developing the convictions and skills to shape a more just and peaceful world.

Safe and Caring Classrooms

We believe that this curriculum works best in a safe and caring classroom. In a safe classroom all students participate and all students feel that they belong. They know that their individual and cultural differences will be accepted and valued as much as the things that they share in common. Teachers show students that everyone counts by balancing the emphasis on individual achievement with a commitment to the well-being of the whole classroom community.

In safe classrooms students feel comfortable expressing their feelings and concerns. They know that they can make mistakes without being ridiculed, deal with their differences constructively, and disagree respectfully. Students seem more likely to risk stretching themselves intellectually and socially when they know that they can practice new skills and receive helpful feedback on their progress. We notice that teachers who practice "partnership learning" through shared goal-setting and assessment, joint decision-making, and joint planning, seem to reduce adversarial, "us vs. them" relationships that are so common in secondary schools.

The activities in this guide work best in a classroom where each student can develop his or her own voice and where listening to peers matters as much as listening to teachers.

A Student-Centered Learning Process

Recent learning research tells us that children "actively construct their own knowledge in very different ways, depending on what they already know or understand to be true, what they have experienced, and how they perceive and interpret new information."* This curriculum emphasizes a student-centered approach that follows students' thinking and concerns in ways that build on their own knowledge and connect their own life experiences to what's happening in the larger society.

Most students learn best when we use an active, experiential teaching approach. Students are more inclined to listen to instructions and retain information if they know that they will be expected to "do something" with it. We also know that students are more willing to read, write about, and discuss "what other people say" if they also have time to discuss their own ideas, opinions, and experiences. In this curriculum, students have opportunities both to work in groups and to try things out by themselves. We need to ensure that students who are "watchers" get to act and perform while students who are "hands-on learners" have opportunities to think and reflect.

Options for Lessons

The lessons in *Conflict Resolution in the High School* are designed to be both easy to teach and easy to adapt. Each lesson plan contains a one-page overview, a series of activities, and handouts for students.

The Workshop Approach

The lessons were designed with two teaching approaches in mind. You will need to decide which approach you want to use. The first is called the "Workshop Approach" and was developed by the Resolving Conflict Creatively Program. (The Resolving Conflict Creatively Program, an initiative of Educators for Social Responsibility, is one of the nation's largest and longest-running school-based programs in conflict resolution, violence prevention, and intergroup relations.) Teachers using the Workshop Approach use the following structure for lessons:

---

* Linda Darling-Hammond, "Reframing the School Reform Agenda," *Phi Delta Kappan*, June 1993.

1. A short gathering activity to bring the class together

2. Reviewing the agenda

3. The main activities

4. An evaluation of, review of, or response to the lesson

5. A short closing activity to end the lesson on a positive note

The Workshop Approach builds community in the classroom and, once students are used to it, helps them engage with the content in a personal and affective way, which is more likely to lead to behavioral change than a heavily cognitive approach.

Lessons take more time with the Workshop Approach, and some of that time is spent on what seem to be "non-academic" activities. Both teachers and students may need to get used to the kind of personal sharing that the Workshop Approach uses.

The Standard Lesson Approach

The other option is the Standard Lesson Approach, which uses this structure:

1. Reviewing the agenda

2. The main activities

3. An evaluation of, review of, or response to the lesson

The Standard Lesson Approach gives more time for the lesson content because the gathering and closing activities are eliminated. However, by sacrificing the community-building activities used in gathering and closing, the discussion may not be as rich and the behavioral change may be less enduring.

We urge you at least to try the Workshop Approach. It reflects our belief that conflict resolution is best taught in the context of a caring community. The gathering and closing activities are thoroughly classroom-tested. Students enjoy them, and we think you will too.

Timing

Each skill lesson takes approximately 50-55 minutes. Many of the lessons in the Additional Activities section require more than one class period.

Four Pathways For Skill Building

If you need to limit the number of lessons you will teach, you may want to select one of the four curriculum pathways presented here. Each pathway includes a series of lessons and can be taught as a self-contained unit.

Building Community and Creating a Peaceable Classroom—Lessons 1-5, 8, 23, 27, 36.

Conflict Resolution and Problem Solving—Lessons 7-17, 19-26, 32.

Diversity and Intergroup Relations—Lessons 5, 27-34.

Emotional and Social Learning—Lessons 6, 11-19, 34-36.

Linking Lessons to Key Conflict Resolution Skills

You may find yourself in a situation where you'd like to teach a specific skill out of sequence or by itself. For instance, you might want to focus on point of view or perspective taking early in the year, knowing that you will want students to use this skill throughout the year. Here is a short list of the key skill lessons:

Active Listening—Lesson 7

Conflict Styles—Lesson 11

Conflict Escalation—Lesson 12

Reading and Understanding Feelings—Lesson 13

Anger Management—Lesson 14

Assertion and "I" Messages—Lessons 15 and 16

De-escalating Conflict—Lesson 17

Point of View and Perspective Taking—Lesson 19

Positions and Interests—Lesson 20

Win-Win Problem-Solving—Lesson 21

Negotiation—Lessons 22, 23, and 24

Mediation—Lessons 25 and 26

Implementing the Curriculum

A variety of methods can be used to implement *Conflict Resolution in the High School*. These methods include:

- cross-graded families
- a required mini-course
- an elective course
- a volunteer teaching cadre
- ninth grade orientation
- block scheduling
- health education
- an advisory period

Descriptions of each of these methods along with their strengths and limitations are presented in the chart that begins on the following page. Whichever approach you use, keep in mind while planning implementation that it may take up to a year to make any needed adjustments in the school schedule or in teaching responsibilities.

Implementation Models

Name and Description	Strengths	Limitations
	Cross-Graded Families	
"Family groups" are formed that include approximately 12 to 15 students from different grade levels (all grade levels are represented in each group). Each group includes up to two adult advisors. Both teaching and nonteaching staff can be included as advisors. Groups typically meet regularly for a specified length of time. Some schools create an annual family group calendar that includes a combination of 50-minute sessions, hour sessions, half-hour sessions, and special activities and events. Students stay with their "family" throughout high school.	• Family groups can be the most effective way to personalize education for all students. • Students and staff share a common language and experience. Everyone is involved, including non-teaching staff, creating a strong sense of community. • High schools rarely create initiatives that involve staff across departments and across roles. Family groups create an opportunity for diverse staff to meet and plan together on a regular basis. • Because students do not receive letter grades, they may feel they can explore interpersonal conflicts and problems more freely. • Older students can mentor younger students. • Students and teachers have an opportunity to form nonjudgmental, non-adversarial relationships.	• Several people are required to organize this approach. • Planning is required to ensure an engaging experience for all ages. • The staff will need to agree on how to redistribute instructional minutes and faculty preparation and meeting time. • It is likely that some faculty will never be comfortable with the idea of family groups.

Implementation Models (continued)

Name and Description	Strengths	Limitations
Required Mini-Course		
The curriculum is taught in a nine-week course that is part of a rotation with other required mini-courses such as health and computers. All students rotate through the course, taking a different mini-course each quarter.	• Several teachers can teach the course each quarter and can team up for planning. • By teaching the same mini-course several times during the year, teachers tend to develop a high degree of skill and confidence about the material. • The course is institutionalized. It becomes part of the formal school program. If the teacher who develops the course leaves, the course continues.	• Other faculty and staff may feel no commitment to supporting conflict resolution education.
Elective Course		
The curriculum is used as basis for a quarter- or semester-long elective course that typically meets for several sessions each week.	• Students choose to take the class and are likely to be motivated. • Teachers responsible for an elective course tend to develop a high degree of skill and confidence about teaching the material. • Courses are usually long enough to allow for real depth.	• The course may reach only a few students, depending on how often it's offered. • Other faculty and staff are not directly involved and may not feel committed to supporting conflict resolution education.

Implementation Models (continued)

Name and Description	Strengths	Limitations
	Volunteer Teaching Cadre	
Various staff members volunteer to be part of a teaching cadre. Volunteers weave direct skill instruction into their courses. They might choose to teach one lesson a week or to develop units that integrate direct skill instruction with infusion activities related to their subject areas. (See the section on curriculum infusion for more information and ideas.) The cadre develops its own leadership as people share ways they are using this curriculum in their classrooms.	• As the cadre works together, members can develop a high degree of skill and confidence about teaching this material. • There is flexibility in who teaches the material, so the cadre can find the best match of skills and interests among them. • If cadre leaders are identified, they can coach and support other cadre members, helping them develop appropriate lessons in their content areas.	• Cadre volunteers must agree to make direct skill instruction a significant part of their course curriculum. • Other staff members may feel less involved and less supportive of a conflict resolution program. • The cadre leader will need training in order to help other team members match conflict resolution skills and objectives with the curriculum standards in various subject areas. • It is essential to schedule cadre meetings to plan, share ideas, and assess the program.
	Ninth Grade Orientation	
The curriculum is used during the first quarter as an orientation for incoming ninth graders as a way to help these students acquire the tools they need for a healthy and productive high school life.	• This model builds community through a common experience that is shared by all ninth graders at the beginning of their high school experience. • Teachers in other content areas are more likely to infuse conflict resolution into their subject areas if all students have had a common learning experience.	• Other topics such as study skills are often taught in ninth grade orientation, leaving less time for conflict resolution. • This may be the only experience students will have with conflict resolution, so they may gain only a superficial understanding.

Implementation Models (continued)

Name and Description	Strengths	Limitations
Block Scheduling		
Teachers involved in English and social studies block courses take responsibility for teaching significant sections of this curriculum. Teachers in various other departments identify specific units they will teach at various grade levels.	• Every student has a common experience every year. • English and social studies teachers can deepen the experience by developing infusion activities.	• Not all teachers may be interested or prepared to teach this material. • Planning is essential: if it is not specified who teaches the curriculum and when, it may not be taught at all.
Health Education		
The curriculum is used as a conflict resolution unit during health class.	• Every student is exposed to the material. • Health teachers are often already familiar with the concepts and instructional strategies of the curriculum. • Students often feel comfortable participating in health class discussions.	• The health curriculum is often overloaded already. • The time period allotted for the curriculum may be limited to as little as one or two weeks. • Other faculty and staff are not directly involved and may not feel committed to supporting conflict resolution education.

Implementation Models (continued)

Name and Description	Strengths	Limitations
	Advisory Period	
The curriculum is used as the basis for conflict resolution focus in an advisory period. Nearly all faculty members are responsible for advisory groups.	• All students are exposed to the material. • Many teachers are responsible for delivering the material; many staff members become familiar and confident with the material. • This model builds community through a common experience.	• The curriculum must be adjusted to fit in short blocks of time, typically 20 to 25 minutes. • There is a need to be selective with topics and lessons, using only those that most staff members can teach comfortably. • It is difficult in such a short time to do sequenced skill building. • Often the purpose of the curriculum must change, focusing on building community, problem solving, and developing more positive relationships.

Preparing to Teach
This Curriculum

A Three-Minute Guide to Conflict Resolution

In this curriculum we define conflict as a dispute or disagreement between two or more people. This working definition covers most types of interpersonal conflict—from an argument in the hallway to a war between two nations. Sometimes these disagreements are problems that need to be solved. Conflict resolution is solving the problems created by conflict situations.

Conflict resolution is an umbrella term. It covers everything from sitting down and talking things out to a sock in the nose to running away and hiding. So we need to put some parameters around what makes for "good" conflict resolution. By our definition, good conflict resolution has three qualities:

- it is nonviolent;
- it meets some important needs of each person involved;
- it maintains—and can improve—the relationship of the people involved.

Of course, you don't always get "good" conflict resolution, but this is our aim both for adults and young people.

There are three key concepts that underlie all conflict resolution education. First, conflict is a normal and natural part of life. It is not going to go away, nor would that be desirable. Without conflict, there is no growth or progress. Without conflict, there is stagnation. The goal of conflict resolution is to use conflict for its constructive and positive aspects, not its destructive ones. In a high school, this means using conflict as a learning opportunity.

Second, conflict is not a contest. In a contest, only one person is the winner. Everyone else loses. In conflict resolution we aim for what is called the Win-Win resolution, where both parties are winners. Winning in a conflict means getting what you want or what you need.

Third, there is no one way that is the right way to handle all conflict situations. Basically, there are six ways to handle conflict, and each of them is appropriate in some situations and inappropriate in others.

- Directing/Controlling—"We're doing it my way and that's that."
- Collaborating—"Let's sit down and work this out."
- Compromising—"Let's both give a little."
- Accommodating—"Whatever you want is fine."
- Avoiding—"Let's skip it."
- Appealing to a Greater Authority or a Third Party—"Let's get some help."

The key to successful conflict resolution is to know when to use which style. For example, as teachers, there are many times when being directive is the most appropriate and the most efficient way for us to handle conflicts. There are also times when avoiding the conflict completely is the most sensible course. And there are times when we want to collaborate and the other party isn't willing. The trick is not to get stuck in one or two styles and use them inappropriately. Conflict resolution is about expanding our options and increasing our skills—and our students' skills—as peacemakers.

Before You Begin Teaching This Curriculum

- Read the guide and be sure you understand what you are going to teach. You will also find that reading other adult resources on conflict resolution will enrich your teaching of *Conflict Resolution in the High School*. There is a list of such books in appendix G.

- Think about personal anecdotes or experiences that you might share with students in the course of class discussion. These not only give you an opportunity to model how to share personal experiences, they can also be powerful teaching tools as students listen to your real-life experiences.

- Practice the skills in your daily life: this will give you a deeper understanding of the skills, and it will give you greater insight into just how long it can take to master some of these social skills. In addition, you will probably get some pointed or amusing stories to share with your students.

- Note the teaching strategies that are unfamiliar to you. Some of the strategies in this curriculum, such as discussions, may be like old friends. Others, such as microlabs, may be completely new. A complete list of teaching strategies along with their descriptions can be found later in this chapter.

- In the course of discussions students may share information that is inappropriately personal. Know your school's policies on discussing such issues and know what your obligations are if you suspect a student is a victim of some kind of abuse. There are certain legal obligations you have in such situations, and your school system may have its own policies as well. Know the "chain of command" in your system—find out to whom you must report what.

- Check with the school nurse and the guidance counselors about what resources exist in the school and in the community to help young people deal with problems. These can include mental health agencies, shelters for homeless or abused young people, government agencies, and others.

- You may want to modify some activities to make them more appropriate for your students. You know the needs of your students, so don't hesitate to make the modifications you feel are necessary.

- Plan time for students to reinforce their learning through decorating the room. For example, students can create posters or bulletin board displays on conflict resolution themes. Invite students to look for quotes or articles on any of the themes of the Peaceable Classroom.

The Limits of *Conflict Resolution in the High School*

Students will learn a great deal about resolving conflict from *Conflict Resolution in the High School*, but it is important to have realistic expectations about what the curriculum does and does not do.

- *Conflict Resolution in the High School* was developed and tested to meet the needs of average, mainstreamed students. Students with severe behavioral or emotional difficulties will need interventions that are beyond the scope of this guide.

- *Conflict Resolution in the High School* can be an important part of a school's violence prevention strategy, but it is not sufficient to be the whole of it. Every school should have a school safety plan, and every staff member and student should know the plan. There should be clear procedures and policies about weapons, racial incidents, sexual harassment, and other types of crises.

- *Conflict Resolution in the High School* does not directly address weapons, sexual harassment, child abuse, drug use, gang violence, or domestic violence. However, this curriculum will enhance efforts to address those topics.

Creating a Classroom Environment for Teaching Conflict Resolution

Students may never have experienced the types of activities that are in *Conflict Resolution in the High School*. Part of ensuring the success of the curriculum rests in creating an emotionally safe and caring classroom environment for students as they engage in these activities and discussions. Below are some important guidelines for creating such an environment. (See also the Classroom Management Checklist on p. 23.)

- Set the ground rules together by making group agreements. This is described in Lesson 3. Making group agreements increases students' sense of ownership over the rules and their commitment to keeping them. If you have already established group agreements with your students, review them and discuss possible additions or changes before you do any other activities in this guide. Regularly revisiting group agreements is a good idea. Check in after three or four weeks and ask the students:

  1. Are the agreements working?

  2. Does the classroom feel like a safe and productive place?

  3. Are there additions or changes that should be made?

  You may need to have your students respond to these questions privately on a piece of paper instead of in front of the whole class.

- Whatever agreements you and the students establish, be sure to make the following non-negotiable policies clear to students:

  1. Everyone has the right to pass. No one will be forced to do anything that makes him or her uncomfortable.

  2. Everyone has the right to privacy. Even though there are activities that ask students to share personal experiences, they should share only those they are comfortable discussing publicly.

  3. Everyone has the right to be treated with respect, which means no laughing at serious statements and no putting people down.

  4. Everyone has the right to confidentiality. Things that students share in the course of discussions should stay in the classroom. They should not be "passed around" to the rest of the school.

- Don't assume that students will know the difference between appropriate and inappropriate behavior. Because the teaching style and activities of *Conflict Resolution in the High School* are often very different from what students may be used to, they might assume that "anything goes." You'll need to tell students explicitly what does not "go." For example, at ESR our policy is that young people should not swear or use curse words in school. However, when students are doing role-plays about real-life conflict situations they might assume that it's all right to swear. You need to let them know that it's not. In fact, we suggest beginning every role-play session with a quick review of what is acceptable and what is not.

- When teaching the lessons, be sure everyone understands the task at hand. Begin by simply asking if everyone understands what they will be doing. It often helps to write the goal of the activity on the board and to ask for a volunteer to review the assignment.

- Put students in groups that include people they do not know well. For other ideas about assigning students to groups, see appendix C.

- Keep an eye on groups to be sure everyone is participating and that they are solving problems as they arise. As much as possible, let groups solve their problems themselves.

- After every group activity, encourage students to evaluate how they did. Ask each group to identify what they did well and what they could do better next time. Another useful set of debriefing questions is:

    1. Did everyone participate?

    2. Did anyone have an idea that was ignored?

    3. Did anyone lead? Was that helpful?[*]

---

[*] ESR thanks Rachel Poliner for contributing this set of debriefing questions.

Classroom Management Checklist*

In setting up the physical environment in my classroom, I:

- ❏ Arrange the room to reflect a student-centered approach.
- ❏ Arrange seating so students can see one another.
- ❏ Make sure bulletin boards and displays reflect the ethnic and racial diversity of my students.

In establishing a comfortable climate, I:

- ❏ Learn students' names and use them often.
- ❏ Give some attention to each student.
- ❏ Avoid playing favorites.
- ❏ Model all of the ground rules.
- ❏ Focus on students' positive qualities and praise their efforts.
- ❏ Set tasks that are within students' capabilities.

In leading a lesson, I:

- ❏ Make sure I'm prepared.
- ❏ Make sure students are ready to learn and have put away unrelated work.
- ❏ Write the session purpose on the board.
- ❏ Ask questions throughout the lesson to check for understanding.
- ❏ Give clear instructions and model tasks when appropriate.
- ❏ Give guided practice before asking students to apply new skills or knowledge.
- ❏ Respond promptly to their assigned work orally or in writing.
- ❏ Use closure questions to help students evaluate their learning.
- ❏ Make homework assignments and/or notebook entries.

In managing discipline, I:

- ❏ Encourage students to discuss solutions rather than blame others.
- ❏ Enforce the ground rules consistently.
- ❏ Handle problems quickly and discreetly, treating students with respect and fairness.
- ❏ Share my reactions to inappropriate behaviors and explain why the behaviors are unacceptable.
- ❏ Talk outside of class with students who continue to disregard the group rules.

* Reprinted with permission of Quest International from Lions-Quest *Working Towards Peace* (2nd edition) © 1995 by Quest International.

Teaching and Learning Strategies

Brainstorming

Brainstorming is a process for generating ideas that fosters creative thinking. The teacher proposes a topic or question and lists students' responses on the board or on chart paper. The idea is to generate the maximum number of solutions for consideration.

Here are some guidelines for brainstorming:

- All ideas are accepted; every idea will be written down.
- There should be no comments, either positive or negative, on any of the ideas presented.
- Say anything that comes to mind, even if it sounds silly.
- Think about what others have suggested and use those ideas to get your brain moving along new lines.
- Push for quantity.

Card Sorts

To help students organize and clarify content information, you can have them sort and rank cards with information related to the topic you are teaching. Here are two examples:

1. Make up sets of cards listing a series of possible titles for a book, story, or play that the group is studying. Each card in the set lists a different title for the same work. Divide students into groups and give each group a set of cards. Ask each group to choose the best title and the worst title. Have them defend their choices to the class.

2. Make up sets of cards listing a series of historical events--for instance, events leading up to the Civil War or important milestones in the life of Frederick Douglass. Ask groups to arrange the cards in chronological sequence or rank them from least important to most important.

Cooperative Learning Groups

This technique involves students and teachers in both creative and critical thinking. It is also a good format in which to begin working on negotiation skills. Students form groups of five or six and work on solving a particular problem. It is important to set clear goals for the group and to establish constraints on what they can or cannot do. (Limiting resources can stimulate creative thinking.) Ask the group to pursue the following sequence of steps: describing the problem in detail; gathering information and assessing the steps necessary to solve the problem; generating possible solutions; choosing the best available solution; and devising a plan to implement it. Make sure they divide their time appropriately between planning and implementing solutions. Encourage each group member to ask, "Am I contributing my fair share to the task? Have I encouraged other group members to contribute?" It may be helpful to assign group members certain roles, such as recorder and reporter.

Concentric Circles

Concentric Circles give students a chance to share with a variety of partners. Divide students into two equal groups. Ask one group to form a circle facing outward. Then ask the other group to form a second circle around that one, facing inward. Each person in the inner circle should be facing a partner in the outer circle. Tell students that they will each have about 45 seconds to share with their partners their responses to a question you will pose. All pairs of partners will speak simultaneously. Identify whether the inside partners or the outside partners will speak first. After the first partner has had a chance to share, signal that the other partner should begin speaking. When both partners have answered the question, ask students to move one, two, or three spaces to the right and pose another question to the group. Have students change partners for each new question.

Conflict Dialogues/Journal-Writing

Students can explore conflict through writing activities that demonstrate their understanding of fundamental conflict resolution concepts. For example, they can write scripts that illustrate how historical figures or fictional characters escalated or de-escalated conflict and then rewrite the dialogue so that the individuals are able to come to some agreement. Students can also take a second look at conflicts they have experienced and write journal entries about how they would respond differently if they could replay the situation.

Concept Synectics (Making Metaphors)

Teachers and selected students act out or physically represent a particular concept for the class, using only their bodies or simple props that can be made from poster board, tape, string, and markers. You may want to select volunteers and practice the demonstration with them ahead of time, or divide the class into groups of four or five and give each a concept to present to the rest of the class. This can be fun and even silly; it helps students grasp the essence of a concept, particularly those covered in algebra, geometry, physics, chemistry, ecology, and economics.

Drawing

Integrating art into lessons in all areas of the curriculum enables students to use their creativity. Examples include creating a group picture, paired drawings where two students hold on to the same drawing tool and create a picture together, or "trust" drawings, in which one student holds the drawing tool and closes her eyes while the other student leads her hand.

Fish Bowl

A Fish Bowl is one way to engage the entire class in whole-group dialogue. This technique is especially useful when emotions are heated or when students bring different perspectives to a controversial topic. It facilitates a kind of sustained, focused listening that is seldom witnessed in a high school classroom.

Invite five to seven students to begin the conversation. Ask them to make a circle with their chairs in the middle of the room. Try to ensure that this group reflects diverse points of view on the issue.

Ask everyone else to make a circle of chairs around the fish bowl, so that you have a smaller circle within a larger circle. Only people in the fish bowl can speak. As the process continues, other students may have a turn to speak.

Here's one way to facilitate a fish bowl:

1. The facilitator asks a question and invites students in the fish bowl to speak to the particular topic or question in a "go-round." Each student in the fish bowl speaks to the question without being interrupted.

2. Then the facilitator designates a specific amount of time for clarifying questions and further comments from students in the fish bowl.

3. After 15 minutes or so, invite students from the larger circle to participate in the fish-bowl conversation. A student who wants to speak can tap a student in the fish bowl on the shoulder and move into that student's seat in the fish bowl. The other student must move to the outer circle.

4. Continue using this same procedure with additional questions.

Go-Rounds

A Go-Round gives every student a chance to respond to a statement or question. In Go-Rounds students are seated in a circle (if possible). Circles greatly facilitate open communication, especially when the teacher joins the group. This structure places everyone on an equal footing. In addition, everyone in the group can look directly at the person who is speaking. This encourages students to pay good attention to one another and contributes to building cohesion in the group. You can have everyone in the room speak even if the group is not arranged in a circle, but communication is more effective if everyone can see the person who is speaking.

Introduce the topic of the Go-Round in the form of a statement or question. Students then take turns responding, going around the circle. A person always has the right to pass when it's her turn to speak. After everyone has spoken, you can go back to someone who has passed to see if he has thought of something he wants to contribute. The topic can be a general one that most students will be able to comment on (for example, "What was something you enjoyed about yesterday's lesson?") or it can be a way to introduce or review the content of the lesson.

Go-Rounds provide opportunities for self-expression, listening to others, and remembering what was said. Often those who find it difficult to speak in groups will speak in a Go-Round, even if given the option to pass. Go-Rounds are especially useful for sharing feelings and experiences.

Microlab

As the name suggests, a microlab is a kind of laboratory where participants can examine their own and others' experiences in the intimacy of a small group. It is designed to maximize personal sharing and active listening. In groups of three or four, students take turns responding to questions. Each person has a specified period of time to respond. When one student is speaking, other students do not interrupt or ask questions and give the speaker their full attention. When introducing microlabs, remind students about the importance of confidentiality. What is shared in a microlab should not be repeated outside the classroom.

Opinion Continuum

This technique allows students to express their own attitudes and opinions and, most important, to realize that it is okay to hold a different opinion from others in the class. To begin activities using this technique, a line is drawn on the board or on the floor with "Strongly Agree" at one end, "Strongly Disagree" at the other, and "Unsure" in the middle. The teacher reads a statement and students position themselves along the line to indicate their opinions. Students can then be invited to explain their positions.

Pair-Share

This technique enables multiple, simultaneous conversations among students, rather than a one-way conversation between the teacher and the group. It is similar to Concentric Circles, except that students stay with the same partner throughout the series of questions. Students share responses to a question in one of two ways: 1) one student focuses on practicing listening skills while the other partner speaks; then partners switch roles; 2) students engage in a dialogue with each other and agree on a response.

"Popcorn-Style" Sharing

In this technique a set amount of time (usually about four minutes) is allotted for the whole group to share ideas on a topic. Free expression of ideas should be encouraged in a nonjudgmental atmosphere. The sharing is "popcorn style," meaning that rather than going around a circle one by one, students are welcome to voice their opinions in a random order. There is no pressure for students to share if they don't wish to.

Role-Plays

Role-plays help to develop students' perspective-taking skills. In this technique, participants assume roles and act out situations in front of the class. They are given new names (names of students currently in the class should not be used) and they stay in character for the duration of the role-play. (See appendix D, "Guidelines for Role-Plays," for more information).

Role-Play Variation: Back-to-Back

In this dramatic variation of a role-play, pairs of students stand back to back. (It may be helpful to designate one student as Person A and the other as Person B for the purposes of giving instructions to the group.) On your signal, they turn and face each other and role-play a situation. Person A is the first to speak.

Rotation Stations

This technique allows students to brainstorm responses to a series of questions in a small group. Write questions or problems on large sheets of newsprint. Post the questions in different areas around the room. Divide the class into groups of four and ask each group to stand at one of the stations. Give each group two minutes to brainstorm two or three responses to the question or problem. Students can write their responses on the paper. Then ask each group to move to the next station and work on another question.

Webbing

This technique gives students the opportunity to visually connect various aspects and levels of a particular topic. This technique can also be used at the beginning of a unit to help the teacher to gauge students' level of familiarity with and understanding of a topic. The key word or concept is placed in the center of the diagram. Students then suggest words and ideas that they associate with that word or concept. These associated words are added to the diagram, branched off from the center. Related ideas are clustered together.

SAMPLE WEB ON "CONFLICT"

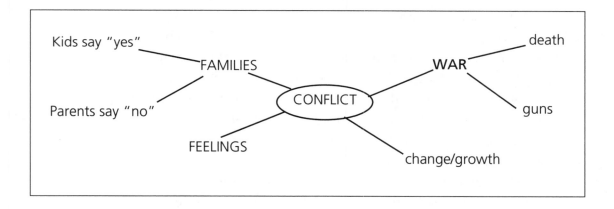

Assessing Student Learning

Before the start of any learning activity, high school students are likely to ask, "Are we getting a grade on this?" One of the challenges in this work is to develop a variety of meaningful ways to assess students' learning.

Assessing Learning Within a Lesson

All of the skill lessons in *Conflict Resolution in the High School* list objectives. Through direct questioning, class participation, and discussion, you should be able to get a sense of whether or not your students are grasping the concepts and key ideas of each session. Each lesson in this guide also contains a section entitled "Checking Out What We've Learned." This section provides specific ways to evaluate student learning in the context of each individual lesson.

Grading Students

Whether you're teaching several lessons, a longer unit, or a quarter or semester course, you might want to consider using a combination of these grading criteria in your class.

__% Class Participation

1. Developing Participation Criteria

   Taking cues from agreements that you have established in class with students, you might develop a list of specific behaviors and attitudes that indicate active participation in class. This list might include:

   - participating in role-plays
   - raising thoughtful questions and making comments that help you and the class reach a deeper understanding of an issue or topic of discussion
   - taking a leadership role in carrying out an activity
   - giving helpful feedback about class activities and experiences
   - participating in debriefing and discussion of lesson activities
   - taking on various roles and responsibilities in small-group activities
   - sharing personal reflections with others in small and larger groups
   - helping to set up activities, distribute materials, and clean up
   - giving words of encouragement to other students
   - laughter and good humor
   - showing appreciation for other students' contributions
   - participation in problem solving when issues and concerns arise that affect the group and the class
   - willingness to volunteer when help is needed
   - ability to focus on a task and complete it
   - sharing responsibility within a group, encouraging all students within the group to participate
   - taking a risk to try out things that are new and challenging
   - friendliness toward other class members
   - positive energy when the group needs it
   - taking turns recording and documenting small-group work
   - ability to work effectively with different students
   - showing patience with students who may approach an activity differently

- writing thoughtful reflections when written responses are part of a class activity
- listening to others without interrupting
- respecting other people's privacy and comfort zones
- willingness to ask questions or admit confusion
- ability to shift gears from one activity or one way of working to another
- speaking openly and honestly to make others aware of a concern or problem
- being on time for class
- being able to stop and come to closure of an activity when time is up

2. Teacher Feedback and Assessment

You might want to type the above list on a sheet that you can duplicate, so that you have a participation log sheet for each student. Jot down observations of specific behaviors on each student's log sheet that give you a snapshot of their participation skills. This snapshot can be a vehicle for giving students personal feedback throughout the class. It can also serve as a starting point for setting goals and checking in on how students are meeting chosen goals, and it can be used when you have conferences with individual students about their participation grades.

3. Student Self-Assessment

Students can also use the criteria list to assess their participation in a number of ways:

- Identify the participation strengths that you already bring to class
- Identify ways to participate that will be challenging for you
- Set goals for what you want to do better
- Reflect back on ways that your participation in class has changed and how those changes have affected how you think and feel about the class and your peers
- Write about one way that you've participated in class that has made a positive difference—something you've done or said that has helped make the class a better learning community for everyone
- Choose one of the "Principles of the Peaceable Classroom" to write about (listed in the Introduction), sharing how your participation has helped make that principle a reality in the classroom

4. Group Assessment

Keep reviewing and assessing how well the group is keeping agreements you've made together, inviting students to suggest ideas that can help the group with particular agreements that are hard to keep consistently.

Using the "Principles of the Peaceable Classroom" as a guide, ask students on an occasional basis to assess what they've done and experienced in class that reflects how they are applying these principles. You might invite students to share experiences that show how individuals or the group as a whole has acted on these principles.

__% *Conflict Resolution Skill Assessment*

1. Students can form groups to choose a specific conflict resolution skill to demonstrate in a role-play or a dramatic skit and videotape it for the class.

2. Students can identify three skills that they want to improve and use successfully throughout the course. Students can write how they have experienced using the skill effectively and also write about situations in which using this skill would have made a positive difference in the outcome of a conflict. The teacher also notes situations in which he or she has observed the student using the skill successfully or situations in which using a particular skill might have made a positive difference.

3. Choose to write about a passage from a novel, short story, or play that illustrates how characters' use of conflict resolution skills helped them to resolve a conflict effectively or how their lack of skills escalated the conflict.

4. Choose a video clip from a comedy or drama on TV that illustrates how characters' use of conflict resolution skills helped them to resolve a conflict effectively or how their lack of skills escalated the conflict.

5. Select video clips from films or TV to write about, first analyzing the conflict and then making suggestions about how the conflicting parties might deal with the conflict constructively.

__% *Projects (A Sampling of Possible Projects)*

1. Peacemaking interview (see Lesson 34).

2. Investigating a community conflict (see "Taking Action on a Community Problem" in the Additional Activities section).

3. Students can create a project that illustrates the use, misuse, and nonuse of a particular concept or skill in the context of an interpersonal conflict. For example:

   - Take photographs that show peacemakers at work in your community or videotape an interview with a community peacemaker.

   - Observe how students and adults use or don't use one conflict resolution skill throughout the day, in classes, in public spaces, etc.

   - Write a story, script, or case study that shows an example of someone using a particular skill in a hard-to-handle conflict.

   - Create a public service announcement, advertisement, or video that communicates a message to young people that solving conflicts nonviolently is a cool thing to do.

   - Design a "Conflict Resolution Tool Kit" for peacemakers that includes the tools your group thinks people need to resolve conflict nonviolently. Try to use objects to represent the tools; if you can't locate the actual objects, make pictorial representations.

   - Design a peacemaker. In your group identify at least 10 qualities you think a peacemaker needs to have. Create a poster that illustrates what such a peacemaker would look like.

   - Create a TV ad to sell the "Conflict Resolution Tool Kit." This kit has the tools people need to solve conflicts nonviolently. Consider making it an infomercial.

   - Write a rap song that describes some skills people need for conflict resolution and that tries to convince them that conflict resolution is cool. Rehearse and perform your song for the class.

- Draw a cartoon or design a poster that would raise students' awareness of conflicts that arise from cultural misunderstandings, stereotyping, and misinformation with a message about what you can do prevent the conflict from occurring or escalating.
- Stage photographs with the title, "What's Going On Here?" that show common conflicts between adolescents or between adults and adolescents that could be used for discussion in class.

__% Journal Entries

You may want students to keep journals throughout the course to reflect on their experiences in the class, what they notice as a consequence of being in the class, and how they connect what they are learning in class to their own lives. Many of the questions suggested in the gatherings and closings can also be used for journal topics.

__% Final Written Assessment of the Class

See the Course Assessment Questionnaire in appendix E.

LESSON 1

Getting to Know Each Other*

OBJECTIVES

Students will:

- begin building positive relationships with peers;
- present opinions on key ideas to be explored in the unit or course;
- learn more about others in their class.

PEACEABLE CLASSROOM PRINCIPLES

- Affirmation and acceptance
- Personal connections
- Building community
- Democratic participation

AGENDA

1. **Gathering (optional)**

   Find Someone Who ...

2. **Review Agenda**

3. **Lesson Activities**

   - Paired Interviews
   - Opinion Continuum

4. **Checking Out What We've Learned**

   Students give feedback using one, two, or three words sharing how they felt about the class.

5. **Closing (optional)**

   Group Yes!

* Adapted with permission from *Resolving Conflict Creatively: A Draft Teaching Guide for Secondary Schools* © ESR Metropolitan Area, 1990.

Gathering (optional)

Find Someone Who ...: Give each student a copy of the Find Someone Who ... handout (p. 36). Ask students to circulate around the room and try to find classmates who match the descriptions listed on the handouts. When they find someone who matches one of the descriptions, ask them to write that person's name on the corresponding line. Allow about 10 minutes for this activity. After students sit back down, ask which descriptions were easiest to match and which were hardest.

Review Agenda

Write the agenda on the board and review it with the class.

Paired Interviews

Ask each student to find a partner, preferably someone he or she doesn't know very well. Students will take turns interviewing each other. Each interview will be about two minutes long. Interviewers can invent their own questions or use any of the following:

- What do you like to do on Saturdays?
- What place, city, or country would you like to visit?
- What do you like to do with your friends?
- If you had to eat the same meal every day for a month, what would it be?
- What's one thing you don't like about being your age?
- What's one thing you'd like to do before you are 25 years old?
- What's one thing you would change about your neighborhood that would make it a better place to live?
- What's one thing that every young person should have?
- What's your favorite holiday and why?
- What's one thing you would change about school that would make it a better place for you?
- What worries you most about the world today?
- What's one thing you could teach someone else how to make or how to do?

Begin the interviews. Signal when two minutes have passed and partners should switch roles. After the interviews are completed, have the group form a circle. Students introduce their partners and share one thing they learned about them with the group.

Opinion Continuum

Post signs at either end of the classroom, one that says "Strongly Agree" and one that says "Strongly Disagree."

Explain to the class that although people often think that things are either right or wrong, good or bad, usually there is a range of opinion in between these extremes. Because we all have different experiences and often have been given different information, opinions vary greatly.

Explain that you will be reading a series of statements about conflict. Students should arrange themselves along the continuum between the two signs depending on how strongly they agree or disagree with the statement. If students feel unsure about what they think, suggest that they place themselves near the middle. Remind students that there are no right or wrong responses to these statements.

Read one of the following statements. Give students time to find their places on the continuum, then ask one student, "What are some reasons that you chose that spot?" After that student has given her explanation, ask her to call on another student to explain his choice. Continue until several students have given their rationales, then go on to the next statement.

Sample statements:

- Conflicts usually lead to violence.
- People should never fight.
- If someone insults you, it's best to pretend you didn't hear what he or she said.
- People who have friends of different races know more about the world than people who don't.
- The world is divided into winners and losers.
- People who are prejudiced usually don't like themselves or have poor self-esteem.
- We should see each other only as individuals. We should basically ignore people's ethnic, religious, or racial identity.
- Everyone is prejudiced against some group.
- All conflicts are solvable.
- Put-downs and "fighting words" can be as violent and hurtful as physical fighting.

Remind students not to interrupt each other. Point out that listening to someone does not mean that you agree with him or her, but is a sign of respect and caring.

Checking Out What We've Learned

Form a circle. Let students know about the importance of doing things in a circle, where each person can see and hear everyone else. Go around the circle and ask students to say one, two, or three words that describe how they feel about the class today. If there is time, ask if there's anything they would like to be different next time.

Closing (optional)

Group Yes! (see appendix B)

FIND SOMEONE WHO ...

1. Is a morning person

2. Has seen a favorite movie at least three times

3. Plays a musical instrument

4. Speaks more than one language

5. Has the same middle name as you

6. Was born in the same month as you

7. Was born in another country

8. Plays a team sport

9. Likes to dance

10. Doesn't like chocolate

11. Has yelled at someone in the last week

12. Has been yelled at in the last week

13. Has ever won any kind of contest

14. Keeps more than one pet

15. Is a middle child

LESSON 2 Establishing a Positive Learning Environment*

OBJECTIVES

Students will:

- identify common expressions used to put down others;
- suggest expressions that are supportive of others.

PEACEABLE CLASSROOM PRINCIPLES

- Affirmation and acceptance
- Emotional literacy
- Caring and effective communication

AGENDA

1. **Gathering (optional)**

   Choose any Go-Round activity from appendix A.

2. **Review Agenda**

3. **Lesson Activity**

   - Getting to the Heart of It (Story and Discussion)

4. **Checking Out What We've Learned**

   Pair-Share: Name a put-down you've received that bothers you and a put-down that you want to stop using.

5. **Closing (optional)**

   Closing Connections

---

* Adapted with permission from *Resolving Conflict Creatively: A Draft Teaching Guide for Secondary Schools* © ESR Metropolitan Area, 1990.

Gathering (optional)

Choose any Go-Round activity from appendix A.

Review Agenda

Write the agenda on the board and review it with the class.

Getting to the Heart of It[*]

Materials: Two large hearts with the words "I am lovable and capable" written on them

Explain to the students that for open and honest communication to happen, it will be important to be as supportive of each other and as caring as possible. In order to talk freely, people need to feel that this is a place where we respect and trust one another.

Explain that, as a group, you are going to tell a story about a day in the life a student (about the age of the students in your class). This story will focus on the kinds of put-downs that a student might hear and the effect of those put-downs.

Copy and cut out the Line Cards (p. 41). Pass out cards #1 to #15 to various students. Make sure you've passed them out in numerical order so that it is easy for students to read their cards in sequence. At certain points in the story, students will read their cards.

Begin by holding up one of the hearts and explaining that every person starts out in life thinking that she is someone who is important—someone who thinks important thoughts, who has important feelings—someone who matters. This is called our "self-concept." Explore the idea of self-concept with the class. What do we mean by self-concept? Where do we get messages about ourselves that form our self-concept?

Begin telling the story outlined below. When it is time for a student to read from his or her card, pause and look in that student's direction. After you hear each comment, tear off a piece of the heart. By the end of the story, there will be only a shred of the heart left.

> Jamal's alarm clock rings. He turns his alarm off and sleeps another half an hour. He gets up, gets into the shower, and hears his sister banging on the door.
>
> She says, "*Line Card #1.*" ("Don't you know how to tell time? It's my turn in the bathroom.")
>
> Jamal finishes in a rush and faces his sister at the door, who says, "*Line Card #2.*" ("You're such a slug. You were supposed to be out of here 15 minutes ago.")
>
> He gets dressed and heads for the kitchen. He sees his mother and says, "Hi, what's for breakfast?"
>
> His mother says, "*Line Card #3.*" ("Don't you know what time it is? I can't get you breakfast now. I have to leave in 10 minutes. There might be some cereal left and a piece of fruit.")
>
> Jamal's mother looks at his wrinkled shirt and says, "*Line Card #4.*" ("That shirt looks awful. You're not going to wear that to school, are you?")

---

[*] Adapted with permission from *I am Lovable and Capable* by Sidney B. Simon (Chesterfield, MA: Values Press, 1991). Send for a catalog of other strategy books from Values Press, P.O. Box 556, Chesterfield, MA 01012.

Jamal grabs his backpack and a banana and runs to get the bus. As he sits down on the bus, he remembers the English essay that he left on his desk. He worked on it late last night so that he could turn it in on time.

When he gets to school Jamal tries to find his English teacher. He sees her in the copy room preoccupied with a stack of papers she's running through the copy machine. He starts to speak but she cuts him off, saying, "*Line Card #5.*" ("Not now, can't you see I'm busy?")

The bell rings and he's now late for homeroom. He scrambles for his seat and accidentally knocks some books off the desk next to him. The student at the desk says, "*Line Card #6.*" ("Is it so hard to walk and watch where you're going at the same time? You're such a jerk.")

His homeroom teacher looks up and says, "*Line Card #7.*" ("What is it this time? You're late again, you know.")

And so the day goes. In geometry class students are working in groups on proofs—not Jamal's favorite thing. He sits staring silently at the problem and one of his partners says, "*Line Card #8.*" ("So are you in this group or not? Don't you have anything to say?")

Between classes, Jamal sees his girlfriend. He calls out to her in the hall. He was so busy finishing his essay last night that didn't call her, even though he said he would. She sees him and says, "*Line Card #9.*" ("Don't even think about an excuse.")

He tries to apologize but she replies, "*Line Card #10.*" ("I don't want to hear it. Leave me alone.")

When he gets to English class there's no time to talk privately with his teacher. At the end of class it's time to turn in the essays. His teacher notices he doesn't turn anything in and she says, "*Line Card #11.*" ("So where's your essay, Jamal? Did the dog eat it this time?")

At lunch Jamal sees his girlfriend in the cafeteria. She's with a bunch of her friends. He says, "Can we talk a minute? It's been a bad day."

She looks up, still angry, and says, "*Line Card #12.*" ("So now you want to talk. Do you know how to pick up the phone?")

He walks away. A couple of friends he knows see the exchange with his girlfriend and give him a hard time. One of them says, "*Line Card #13.*" ("Guess you're not the big man anymore.")

Finally it's time for basketball practice. He's practicing free throws and nothing is going in. The coach notices and says, "*Line Card #14.*" ("You've lost your touch. Take a walk and let someone else shoot.")

Jamal gets home. It's his turn to cook dinner, but all he wants to do is sprawl on the couch, turn on some music, and turn off the day. He hears the door close as he opens his eyes. His mother walks in the living room and says, "*Line Card #15.*" ("Is this your idea of making dinner? I can't leave you in charge of anything.")

Discuss how put-downs make people feel. How can put-downs lead to conflicts or make conflicts worse? What's the opposite of a put-down? Contribute the idea that supportive comments show respect, acceptance, and encouragement.

Now take the other heart and hold it up. Tell the story over again, but this time have the students think of supportive, encouraging comments that could be said in place of the put-downs. This time the heart stays intact and you respond with pleasure, thanking people for their respectful comments.

For most students there are certain words, slurs, names, put-downs, and insults that immediately trigger anger or hurt feelings. Ask students to give examples (out loud or written anonymously) of some words and phrases that upset them. Invite students to explain to others why these words bother them. Ask students how they feel when they hear them. You may want to explore the historical and cultural reasons why some words trigger such intense feelings.

Discuss the specific words and phrases that are most upsetting to students—words that hurt people's feelings or "push people's buttons." Ask the group if they're willing to make an agreement not to use these words.

Ask students for ideas about how to respond to put-downs you hear in a way that doesn't put down the person saying it. You may want to agree on common language that you all use in the classroom to identify when someone has used a put-down. For example, "That's a foul," or "That's an ouch. Remember, we agreed not to use those words here."

Checking Out What We've Learned

Pair-Share: Name a put-down you've received that bothers you and a put-down that you've used toward an individual or group that you want to stop using.

Closing (optional)

Closing Connections (see appendix B)

LINE CARDS

1. "Don't you know how to tell time? It's my turn in the bathroom."

- -

2. "You're such a slug. You were supposed to be out of here 15 minutes ago."

- -

3. "Don't you know what time it is? I can't get you breakfast now. I have to leave in 10 minutes. There might be some cereal left and a piece of fruit."

- -

4. "That shirt looks awful. You're not going to wear that to school, are you?"

- -

5. "Not now, can't you see I'm busy?"

- -

6. "Is it so hard to walk and watch where you're going at the same time? You're such a jerk."

- -

7. "What is it this time? You're late again, you know."

- -

8. "So are you in this group or not? Don't you have anything to say?"

- -

9. "Don't even think about an excuse."

- -

10. "I don't want to hear it. Leave me alone."

- -

11. "So where's your essay, Jamal? Did the dog eat it this time?"

- -

12. "So now you want to talk. Do you know how to pick up the phone?"

- -

13. "Guess you're not the big man anymore."

- -

14. "You've lost your touch. Take a walk and let someone else shoot."

- -

15. "Is this your idea of making dinner? I can't leave you in charge of anything."

LESSON 3

Making Group Agreements

OBJECTIVES

Students will:

- develop agreements that will serve as guidelines for living and learning together in this class.

PEACEABLE CLASSROOM PRINCIPLES

- Mutual respect
- Democratic participation
- Shared decision-making

AGENDA

1. **Gathering (optional)**

   Go-Round: Identify one thing that someone can say or do that shows disrespect and one thing that shows respect.

2. **Review Agenda**

3. **Lesson Activity**

   - Group Agreements

4. **Checking Out What We've Learned**

   Students discuss the process of creating the agreement.

5. **Closing (optional)**

   Choose any closing activity from appendix B.

Gathering (optional)

Go-Round: Identify one thing that someone can say or do that shows disrespect and one thing that shows respect.

Review Agenda

Write the agenda on the board and review it with the class.

Group Agreements

Explain that the goal of this lesson is to develop a list of agreements that everyone can live with about working and learning together as a community.

Introduce brainstorming to the class. Explain that brainstorming is a process that fosters creative thinking. It is used in problem-solving to generate the maximum number of ideas for consideration. Here are some guidelines for brainstorming:*

- All ideas are accepted; every idea will be written down.
- There should be no comments, either positive or negative, on any of the ideas presented.
- Say anything that comes to mind, even if it sounds silly.
- Think about what others have suggested and use those ideas to get your brain moving along new lines.
- Push for quantity.

Ask students to brainstorm a list of ideas that will help make this class a positive learning experience. What guidelines will help the group to work together productively, communicate effectively, and treat each other respectfully? To help students get started, write down two or three agreements from the following sample list:

Sample List of Group Agreements

- Talk one at a time.
- Don't interrupt another student while he or she is speaking.
- Avoid being judgmental.
- Stay with suggested topics.
- Listen and discover, rather than give advice.
- Be open and honest.
- Look at people when you speak to them.
- Say "I" when speaking for yourself.
- Say "you" when speaking to another.
- When you disagree with someone, state your opinion without attacking the other person (for example, "I believe ..." or "The way I see it is ...").
- Share the talk space. Give everyone a chance to speak.
- Start on time.
- Don't make fun of what other people say or do.

---

* This list is reprinted with permission from *Resolving Conflict Creatively: A Draft Teaching Guide for Secondary Schools* © ESR Metropolitan Area, 1990.

- Keep what is said in the class confidential.
- Help each other out.

List the students' suggestions on newsprint. Discuss each of the items on the list one at a time. Clarify the meaning of each suggestion. Where it would be helpful, act out a violation of the suggestion with a student. Ask, "Have you ever been in situations where this suggestion was not observed? How would observing the suggestion make a difference in our class?"

After discussing the suggestions, explain that this is the basis for a class agreement about life together in the classroom. Ask for any revisions or objections to items on the list. When there are no more objections, have students sign or initial the agreement and post it.

Checking Out What We've Learned

Lead a discussion about the process of creating the agreement. Ask: "Looking at the process we used to create the agreements, what parts of the process were most helpful? What parts of the process could we use when making other group decisions?"

Closing (optional)

Choose any closing activity from appendix B.

LESSON 4

Working Together as a Group

OBJECTIVES

Students will:

- explore problems that can arise during group decision-making;
- identify attitudes, roles, and behaviors that can help groups make effective decisions and work cooperatively together.

PEACEABLE CLASSROOM PRINCIPLES

- Cooperation and collaborative problem-solving
- Building community
- Shared decision-making

AGENDA

1. **Gathering (optional)**

   Group Juggling

2. **Review Agenda**

3. **Lesson Activity**

   - Machine Building

4. **Checking Out What We've Learned**

   Share reflections and discuss skills, tools, and attitudes that help people make effective decisions and help groups work cooperatively.

5. **Closing (optional)**

   Go-Round: What quality do you possess that you would be willing to share freely with the group to help us work together more easily?

Gathering (optional)

Group Juggling (see appendix A)

Review Agenda

Write the agenda on the board and review it with the class.

Machine Building

Divide the class into groups of six to eight people. Tell them that the goal of each group is to act out the workings of a machine that represents a skill, attitude, or quality that is essential to peacemaking. Each group will perform for the rest of the class and ask them to guess what the machine is.

Rules for building the machines include:

- Everyone in the group must be part of the machine.
- Every machine must have some moving parts.
- Every machine must represent a skill, attitude, or quality that is essential for effective peacemaking and problem solving.

Give an example such as a toaster. One student could be the lever that you push down to start toasting. Two other students could be pieces of toast, squatting down when the lever is pushed and popping up when the toasting is finished. The toast popping up could represent the idea that in peacemaking and problem solving one person or party needs to take the initiative to bring the problem to the attention of others. Another group could pretend to be a clock, representing the importance of good timing—choosing the right time and place for people to work out a problem.

Each group will have about seven minutes to decide what their machine will be, what it will look like, and who will play each part, and to practice their performance.

Clear a space for center stage. When each group takes its turn, ask them to say "Curtain" when they are ready to perform. After the group has acted out its machine, have the audience guess what the machine is. Then have the students who performed explain what their machine represents.

Checking Out What We've Learned

Ask the class:

- How did your group decide what machine to build?
- What made this activity fun, challenging, or frustrating?
- What happened when some people had different ideas from other people? How did you come to agreement?
- What did you notice about yourself or your group that surprised you?
- What problems or challenges came up in your group that you needed to resolve?
- What tools, skills, and attitudes helped your group to be successful?

Closing (optional)

Go-Round: What quality do you possess that you would be willing to share freely with the group to help us work together more easily?

LESSON 5 Diversity in the Classroom

OBJECTIVES

Students will:

- explore their similarities and differences;
- explore how individuals bring different perceptions and meanings to the same idea;
- assess the positive and negative aspects of making assumptions.

PEACEABLE CLASSROOM PRINCIPLES

- Appreciation for diversity
- Affirmation and acceptance
- Personal connections

AGENDA

1. **Gathering (optional)**

   Concentric Circles

2. **Review Agenda**

3. **Lesson Activities**

   - Checking Out Perceptions
   - Checking Out Assumptions

4. **Checking Out What We've Learned**

   Pair-Share: Invite students to share a situation where they made an assumption that they later found out was wrong.

5. **Closing (optional)**

   Popcorn-Style Sharing: "In the future I want to be more curious/open-minded about ..."

Gathering (optional)

Concentric Circles (see appendix A)

Review Agenda

Write the agenda on the board and review it with the class.

Checking Out Perceptions

Write the word "ocean" on the board. Ask students to close their eyes for a moment and let their senses take over as they imagine the ocean—see it, hear it, feel it, smell it. Then ask students to describe what each of them saw, heard, and felt. Write down their words and phrases on the board. How are these images different? Some students probably have very detailed pictures of oceans, while other may have never seen an ocean except on a map. Some images may be dark and stormy while others may convey stillness and heat. Discuss how personal experiences affect what we imagine when we think of the word "ocean." Our experiences are like filters that affect how we see the world. All of us have slightly different filters that make meaning of the world. Our perceptions are never exactly like anyone else's.

You may want to share the following example with your students. Jamake Highwater, a Native American who is now an art historian and writer in New York City, recalls his confusion when he first encountered the English word "wilderness," meaning an untamed land, a wild and unpredictable place beyond the reach of civilization. As a Blackfeet Indian, he understood "wilderness" to be ordered and balanced, the natural state of the world with seasons moving predictably from one cycle of life to another. For Mr. Highwater's mother, her first visit to New York City seemed to match the English word "wilderness."

Divide students into groups of three. Each student will need a pencil and a sheet of scrap paper. Copy and cut out the Perception Cards (p. 52). Distribute three Perception Cards to each group. Explain that each group will select one card and students will write down what the word on the card means to them. Then each student in the group will read her definition in a go-round (no interruptions or questions during this phase). Remind students that the purpose here is to see how students' perceptions vary, not to determine a correct definition. (This is also an opportunity to notice the level of active listening skills in your class.) Each group repeats this activity three times, choosing a different card for each round. Each round should last about three minutes.

Checking Out Assumptions

Pass out a copy of Checking It Out (p. 53) to every student. Ask students to pair up with someone they don't know well. Explain to students that they will try to guess how their partners would answer the questions on the handout.

Tell students that they will have five minutes of complete silence to guess how their partners would respond to the questions on the handout. Ask them to write down what they think their partners would say.

After five minutes (or the time it takes students to finish) ask students to interview each other and check out the assumptions they made. Have them check the answers they wrote down against their partner's actual answers to the questions.

Bring the group back together. Ask students: "How did it feel to do this exercise?" (Many will say it was uncomfortable to make assumptions without knowing if they were right.)

Ask the class to define the word "assumption." One practical definition is: the quick predictions and automatic judgments we make based on what we believe to be true rather than what we actually know or have observed.

Ask the class, "If assumptions often lead to inaccuracies, why do we make them?" Draw this chart on the board:

ASSUMPTIONS

Pluses	Minuses

With the class, brainstorm a list of positive reasons for making assumptions, such as:

- They make life more predictable.
- If we didn't make them it would be as if we started each day knowing nothing.
- They can help us create goals and expectations for others.
- If we make positive assumptions, these can help people do their best.

Next, brainstorm a list of negative consequences of making assumptions. Ask, "How can assumptions hurt us and hurt our relationships with others?" Sample answers are:

- They can lead to misunderstandings.
- Assumptions can quickly lead to stereotypes, generalizations about a whole group based on one experience or encounter.
- They can prevent us from "doing our homework" and checking out the facts.
- They can diminish our sense of curiosity.

Conclude with the following questions:

- Are there some situations in which making assumptions is appropriate? (For example, it may be appropriate with friends you know well or in repeat situations.)
- Are there particular circumstances in which making assumptions is a lousy idea? (For example, making assumptions is a bad idea during interactions with people you've never met before or in a situation that is completely new.)

Checking Out What We've Learned

Pair-Share: Invite students to share a situation where they made an assumption that they later found out was wrong. It is helpful to begin by modeling this for the students using the formula, "I used to think ... but then I discovered ..."

Closing (optional)

Popcorn-Style Sharing: Invite students to share a situation in which they might be willing to let go of an assumption. "In the future I want to be more curious/open-minded about ..."

PERCEPTION CARDS

TOLERANCE	DISCRIMINATION	EQUAL OPPORTUNITY
COMMUNITY	VIOLENCE	JUSTICE
FRIEND	FAMILY	FREEDOM
DEMOCRACY	POLICE	HARASSMENT
SCHOOL	STRENGTH	HERO
PEACE	RESPECT	SUCCESS

S T U D E N T   H A N D O U T

CHECKING IT OUT

Question	Your Guess at Your Partner's Answer	Your Partner's Answer
Number of family members you live with		
Place where you were born		
Number of years you have lived in the same neighborhood		
Favorite subject in school		
Favorite color		
Favorite holiday		
Favorite type of music		
Favorite thing to do on a weekend		
A place you'd like to visit		
Is your room always clean, a mess, or in between?		
One thing that you'd like to own but don't		
Favorite hobby		

Communication: What's the Big Deal?*

OBJECTIVES

Students will:

- explore why and how we listen;
- identify characteristics of good and poor listening;
- identify things we do and say that block effective communication.

PEACEABLE CLASSROOM PRINCIPLES

- Caring and effective communication
- Managing and resolving conflict

AGENDA

1. **Gathering (optional)**

   Pair-Share: When is it hard for you to listen? When is it easy?

2. **Review Agenda**

3. **Lesson Activities**

   - Back-to-Back Drawings
   - Demonstration of Poor Listening in a Discussion

4. **Checking Out What We've Learned**

   Suggest guidelines for being an active listener.

5. **Closing (optional)**

   Encouragement Cards

---

* Adapted with permission from *Resolving Conflict Creatively: A Draft Teaching Guide for Secondary Schools* © ESR Metropolitan Area, 1990.

Gathering (optional)

Pair-Share: Identify situations in which it is easy to listen and others in which it is hard to listen. Each person responds to the following questions:

- When is it hard for you to listen? What makes it hard to listen?
- When is it easy for you to listen? What makes it easier to listen?
- Do you listen differently in different situations?
- Discuss with whole group, exploring the questions of why and how we listen.

Review Agenda

Write the agenda on the board and review it with the class.

Back-to-Back Drawings

Materials: pencils, paper, set of 3x5 cards. On each card, draw a different collection of geometric shapes (five or six shapes per card); make enough cards for half the class.

Sample cards:

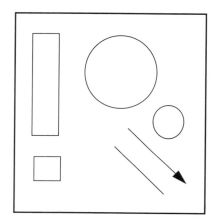 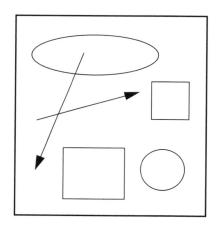

Explain that this is an activity that explores effective communication. Have students find partners. Have the partners sit in chairs, back to back. Explain that there are two roles in this activity: describers and drawers. The object of the activity is for the describer to accurately describe a series of shapes so that the drawer can reproduce the images.

Have students decide who will be the drawer and who will be the describer. Give each describer one of the cards, but tell the describer not to show the card to the drawer. Drawers will need pencil and paper. Once everyone is set up, remind everyone that the describer cannot show the card to the drawer. The describer must describe the card in words to the drawer. The drawer can ask questions.

When everyone understands the task, begin the activity. Allow 10 to 15 minutes for everyone to complete the task. If time allows, you may want to repeat the activity: redistribute the cards and have the partners switch roles. Before they start, add one more challenge. Divide the class in half with an imaginary line and explain that in one half of the class the drawers may ask questions of the describer. In the other half of the class, drawers may not ask questions of their describers.

Discuss this activity in the large group.

- What observations, comments, and reactions do you have?
- What was the effect of not being able to ask questions? For those of you who couldn't ask questions, did you figure out other ways to get information you needed?
- As a describer, how did you know if your drawer did or did not understand your directions?
- Did anyone have an experience using very specific language, or language you thought was specific? How did it help or hinder communication?
- As a drawer, what did your describer do that helped you draw?
- Looking back at the activity, what are some things that might have helped the communication process?

Write on the board "Things That Help Communication" and "Things That Hinder Communication." As the discussion proceeds, record student contributions in the appropriate categories.

Demonstration of Poor Listening in a Discussion

Before class, ask one student to lead a class discussion about violence. At the same time, ask nine other students to exhibit poor listening skills during the discussion. Copy and cut out the Blocker Cards (p. 59) and give one to each of them. Ask these students to wait two or three minutes into the student-led discussion before they begin saying their blocker statements.

Begin the activity by asking students to think about why we listen. Sample answers:

- to get instructions;
- to understand another person's feelings and point of view;
- to help others;
- to learn about others and the world around us;
- to be entertained.

Now have the volunteer lead the discussion on violence. He or she can choose one of the following questions to start off:

- How would you define a violent act?
- Is there any time when it's okay to hit children? If so, when? If not, why not?
- Why are people violent?
- Should violence be banned from children's television? Why or why not?

Ask the students to make note of how the discussion proceeds and how they communicate with each other.

After about 10 minutes, stop the discussion. Ask students to identify the communication blockers they heard and how those blockers affected the discussion. Write the communication blockers on the board.

Checking Out What We've Learned

Explain that good listening requires active participation. Ask students what good listening looks like and what it sounds like. Write their answers on the board in the form of a T-chart, listing the attending skills (nonverbal ways of showing a person is listening) and responding skills (verbal responses) that make up active listening:

ACTIVE LISTENING

What You See (Attending Skills)	What You Hear (Responding Skills)
Eye contact	Verbal encouragers like "Uh, huh," "Tell me more," and "Yeah"
Leaning forward a little or nodding	Agreeing with something the person has said
Sitting still, no fidgeting or playing with stuff	Restating what someone says
No interrupting	Reflecting what someone is feeling
Interested silence; giving a person time to respond	Asking open-ended questions like "What happened?" or "How did you feel about that?"

Have each student find a partner and practice active-listening skills. Each person gets two minutes to speak. While one partner is speaking, the other practices active-listening techniques. Speakers can speak on one of the following topics:

- an experience when they felt they were treated unfairly
- something a family member does that really bothers them
- a rule at school that they think is unfair
- a time they did something that they are proud of

Closing (optional)

Encouragement Cards (see appendix B)

BLOCKER CARDS

DISTRACTING/AVOIDING

Change the subject.

CRITICIZING

Criticize what the last person said.

INTERRUPTING

Interrupt the person who's talking

SARCASM

Make a sarcastic comment about what's been said: "Oh, please! Like that would ever work!"

"YES, BUT" STATEMENTS

Begin your point with "Yes, but" and always contradict what the other person just said.

LECTURING/MORALIZING

Lecture the group about what they SHOULD think or do.

BLAMING

Blame a type of individual for causing the problem.

ATTACKING QUESTIONS

Use an intimidating tone. Suggest that you doubt the previous speaker's sincerity.

HAVING ALL THE ANSWERS

Try to solve the problem for everyone else. Insist your solution in best.

LESSON 7
Active Listening

OBJECTIVES

Students will:

- learn attending skills (nonverbal ways of showing that your are listening;
- practice paraphrasing content and reflecting feelings.

PEACEABLE CLASSROOM PRINCIPLES

- Caring and effective communication
- Emotional literacy
- Mutual respect

AGENDA

1. **Gathering (optional)**

   Go-Round: Share a time when you really needed someone to listen and someone did, or a time when you wished someone had really listened and that didn't happen.

2. **Review Agenda**

3. **Lesson Activities**

   - Nonverbal Attending Skills
   - Paraphrasing
   - Reflecting Feelings
   - Extended Active-Listening Practice

4. **Checking Out What We've Learned**

   Debrief how students experienced these practices. Was it easier for you to listen or speak?

5. **Closing (optional)**

   Go-Round: "I'd like to try to listen differently the next time someone ..."

Gathering (optional)

Go-Round: Share a time when you really needed someone to listen and someone did, or a time when you wished someone had really listened and that didn't happen.

Review Agenda

Write the agenda on the board and review it with the class.

Nonverbal Attending Skills

Review the attending skills from the T-chart in Lesson 6. Write these skills on the board. Ask students to find a partner. Each person gets two minutes to talk about a specific topic. The listener's goal is to practice using nonverbal attending skills. Then partners switch roles. Here are some topics:

- an experience I had of being treated unfairly
- a family member that bothers me
- a rule at school that I think is unfair
- a time I did something that made me feel proud

After each partner has had a chance to speak and listen, bring the group back together for a discussion.

- How did you know that your partner was listening to you?
- What did it feel like to really be listened to without being interrupted?
- What made this a challenging exercise for you?
- Was it easier being the speaker or the listener?

Paraphrasing

Distribute the handout Conflict, Violence, and Peacemaking: What's Your Opinion? (p. 69). Give students a few minutes to fill out the opinion poll. When they have finished, ask students to star three statements that they have strong feelings about and that they want to discuss in a small group.

Explain to the group that they are going to practice paraphrasing. Paraphrasing is restating what someone has said in your own words. This helps the speaker feel understood.

Divide the class into groups of three. Have each group sit in a circle. One student in the triad will begin by giving her opinion on a particular statement from the handout. The student to her right will paraphrase what was said as accurately as possible, giving the first speaker a chance to correct, change, or add something to make the statement clearer. The second speaker will then make a statement, and the third student will paraphrase it. Finally the third student will make a statement and the first student will paraphrase it. Ask a student volunteer to do a demonstration with you. Ask him to respond to one of the statements on the handout. Paraphrase what the student has said and ask if this is accurate. You might want to write a list of "Paraphrase Starters" on the board such as, "I heard you say …," "You said that …," "I understand you to say …," "You're saying that …"

While the groups are in progress, observe how they are going so that you can point out and affirm examples of good listening and paraphrasing.

After the small groups have completed the activity, discuss the following questions with the whole class:

- Did you feel that the group members really heard you when you were speaking?
- How did you feel when you heard what you said being restated?
- How did you feel when you had to restate what someone else said?
- Do you think restating will help or hinder discussions? Why?
- Is it easier or harder to talk when the person listening uses the restating technique? Why?
- What makes it hard to restate?
- When is it useful to restate?

Reflecting Feelings

An important part of active listening is reflecting the feelings of the person who is speaking. This means trying to help the speaker identify his or her feelings. Sometimes people speak about a situation without identifying the feelings that are motivating them. Active listeners help the speaker uncover his or her feelings about the situation. This shows that you are listening and makes the speaker feel validated and understood. Reflecting feelings can also help people focus and describe more fully what they're experiencing. When reflecting feelings, the following starters are helpful:

- It sounds like you're feeling ...
- I'm sensing that you're feeling ...
- What I'm hearing is that you feel ...
- You sound ...

Example:

Speaker: "What a drag. There's nothing to do." (*thought statement*)

Listener: "It sounds like you're feeling bored." (*feeling statement*)

When you reflect what someone is feeling you give the speaker a way to clarify his or her feelings. You might say, "You really seem upset by what just happened." The speaker might respond, "No, not really upset, but I do feel annoyed that it's happened again."

Ask students to find a partner. Distribute the Thoughts and Feelings handout (p. 65) and the Feelings Vocabulary handout (p. 66). Do one or two examples with the whole group. Then have partners take turns, one person reading one of the thought statements and the other responding with the feeling statement. Encourage them to use the Feelings Vocabulary handout for a reference. After the first person has read three thought statements, switch roles.

Bring the class back together and discuss the following questions:

- What's challenging or awkward about reflecting feelings?
- In what situations would reflecting feelings be helpful?
- How might reflecting someone's feelings help a person who is upset?
- How might naming feelings help us understand ourselves better?

Extended Active-Listening Practice

Distribute and review the handout It's Easier For Others To Talk When I ... (p. 67). Divide the class into groups of three. Each person in the group will participate in two conversations and observe a third. Distribute and review the Listening Triads Feedback Sheet (p. 68) to each person. Brainstorm a list of five or six topics about which there is likely to be heated disagreement among students, or topics that bring up intense feelings and opinions. The speakers will pick the topics they want to talk about. Some topics might include:

- Capital punishment is wrong.
- Sex education should be available to all adolescents.
- If I'm old enough to vote and old enough to be drafted, I should be old enough to drink.
- Sometimes violence can be justified.
- Students should be allowed to make choices about what they learn in all their classes.

Give speakers two or three minutes in each round. When they have finished speaking, ask students:

- How did it feel to be listened to this way?
- What listening skills were the hardest to use consistently?
- What skills did you observe people using effectively?

Checking Out What We've Learned

Debrief how students experienced these listening practices. Ask: "Was it easier for you to listen or speak? Why?"

Closing (optional)

Go-Round: "I'd like to try to listen differently the next time someone ..."

THOUGHTS AND FEELINGS

Practice reflecting the feelings that are not stated in the thought statements:

1. *Thought statement:* "I am really dumb in math."
    Feeling statement: _____

2. *Thought statement:* "I hate that stupid teacher."
    Feeling statement: _____

3. *Thought statement:* "I can't believe it. I got an A on the test!"
    Feeling statement: _____

4. *Thought statement:* "Every time she does that I feel like knocking her out."
    Feeling statement: _____

5. *Thought statement:* "Leave me alone. Nobody cares about me anyway."
    Feeling statement: _____

6. *Thought statement:* "My brother is driving me crazy. He always picks up the phone when I'm talking to my boyfriend/girlfriend and then he pretends he needs to use it."
    Feeling statement: _____

7. *Thought statement:* "I hope I get accepted as a counselor at camp this summer. There are so many kids applying. I just don't know if I'll get the job."
    Feeling statement: _____

8. *Thought statement:* "Jeff asks to see my lab write-up every time before we have to hand them in. I'm sick and tired of Jeff depending on me to do his work."
    Feeling statement: _____

9. *Thought statement:* "When we have relatives over for dinner, my mother talks about all the stuff I've been doing at school. I really hate that."
    Feeling statement: _____

10. *Thought statement:* "My dad won't let me get a license until I can pay for car insurance myself. I'll be out of high school before I can save that much money!"
    Feeling statement: _____

S T U D E N T   H A N D O U T

FEELINGS VOCABULARY

afraid	devilish	helpless	negative	sorrowful
affectionate	disappointed	hopeful	nervous	sour
aggressive	disapproving	horrified	nice	spiteful
agonized	disdained	hurt		strange
amazed	disgusted	hysterical	obstinate	superior
angry	dumb		optimistic	surprised
annoyed		impatient		suspicious
anxious	ecstatic	independent	pained	sympathetic
apologetic	embarrassed	indifferent	paranoid	
argumentative	empty	inferior	peeved	tenacious
arrogant	enraged	insulted	perplexed	tense
ashamed	enthralled	intimidated	persecuted	terrific
at peace	enthusiastic	irritated	pleased	thrilled
	envious		proud	timid
bashful	exasperated	jealous	puzzled	
belligerent	excited	jolly		uneasy
blissful	exhausted	joyful	regretful	unworthy
bored	exuberant		relieved	
brave		kindly	remorseful	vengeful
	foolish		righteous	victimized
cautious	friendly	left out		victorious
cheerful	frightened	lonely	sad	vindictive
cold	frustrated	loving	safe	
comfortable	funny		satisfied	wary
conceited		mad	secure	wonderful
contemptuous	grateful	malicious	sedate	worried
crabby	greedy	mellow	self-conscious	
creative	grief-stricken	mischievous	self-pitying	
cruel	guilty	miserable	sheepish	
		mixed up	shocked	
delighted	happy	moved	shy	
depressed	hateful		silly	
determined	heartbroken		smart (cocky)	

S T U D E N T   H A N D O U T

IT'S EASIER FOR OTHERS TO TALK WHEN I ...

1. Make good eye contact.
2. Assume a nonthreatening distance (not too close, not too distant).
3. Am relaxed and show interest in the other person.
4. Listen attentively.
5. Don't interrupt.
6. Paraphrase or restate what the other person is saying to make sure I understand and to make the other person feel heard.
7. Ask clarifying questions: "When did this happen?" "Could you explain that?" "What do you mean by that?"
8. Encourage the other person to talk: "Can you say more about that?"
9. Affirm and reflect the other person's feelings.
10. Don't try to solve the problem for the other person.
11. Try to see the issue from the other person's perspective.
12. Show respect for the other person, even if I disagree.
13. Don't give advice, lecture, preach, judge, blame or criticize.

IT'S EASIER FOR OTHERS TO LISTEN WHEN I ...

1. Exchange facts and information freely.
2. Disclose my own feelings and thoughts.
3. Don't raise my voice or use an angry or hostile tone.
4. Don't use sarcastic language.

S T U D E N T   H A N D O U T

LISTENING TRIADS FEEDBACK SHEET

When You Are The Speaker:

Talk about something that you have strong feelings about. You have about three minutes. After your time is up, give feedback to the listener:

- What kind of "body language" did the listener use that showed good nonverbal listening skills?
- What did the listener say that showed that he or she was listening to you?
- How did you know the listener understood what you were thinking and feeling?
- How did it feel to be listened to in this way?

When You Are The Listener:

Your job is to listen in ways that let the speaker know that you are listening and understanding his or her thoughts, feelings, and ideas.

Try to use the following skills:

- Restate/paraphrase thoughts and ideas.
- Restate/paraphrase feelings.
- Give the speaker plenty of time to talk. Try displaying "interested silence."
- Encourage the speaker to say more about something, to be more specific, to give more detail or more information.
- Summarize what you've heard at the end.

When You Are The Observer:

Note the specific ways that the listener used and showed good listening skills:

- What kind of "body language" did the listener use that showed good attending?
- What did the listener specifically say that showed that he or she was listening?
- How do you know the listener was restating/paraphrasing the speaker's thoughts and ideas?
- How do you know the listener was restating/paraphrasing the speaker's feelings?
- How accurate was the listener's summary at the end?

S T U D E N T   H A N D O U T

CONFLICT, VIOLENCE, AND PEACEMAKING: WHAT'S YOUR OPINION?

		Agree	Disagree
1.	The world would be a better place without conflict.		
2.	Conflicts are never really resolved unless all parties involved get something they need.		
3.	The best way to avoid conflict is to be stronger and more powerful than all of your potential enemies.		
4.	A peaceful world can never really exist.		
5.	The world would be dull and boring without conflict.		
6.	People who have learned to respond to conflicts by using verbal or physical violence cannot change.		
7.	Peace is the absence of a conflict.		
8.	The first step towards violence is the refusal to listen.		
9.	People learn fighting and violence at home before they bring these behaviors to the world outside.		
10.	Telling racial jokes is okay as long as they don't offend the people who listen to them.		
11.	Violence on TV and in the movies should be restricted.		
12.	You can still be a strong person and choose not to fight.		

LESSON 8

How Do We Experience Conflict?*

OBJECTIVES

Students will:

- identify the messages they have received about conflict;
- listen to others share their experiences with conflict;
- connect their own perceptions of conflict to conflicts they observe in the larger society.

PEACEABLE CLASSROOM PRINCIPLES

- Caring and effective communication
- Personal connections
- Emotional literacy

AGENDA

1. **Gathering (optional)**

   Pair-Share: "When I get into a conflict, I usually ..."

2. **Review Agenda**

3. **Lesson Activity**

   - Conflict Microlab

4. **Checking Out What We've Learned**

   Ask students what they liked or didn't like about the microlab.

5. **Closing (optional)**

   Choose any closing activity from appendix B.

---

* Adapted with permission from *Resolving Conflict Creatively: A Draft Teaching Guide for Secondary Schools* © ESR Metropolitan Area, 1990.

Gathering (optional)

Pair-Share: Ask students to complete the statement, "When I get into a conflict, I usually …"

Review Agenda

Write the agenda on the board and review it with the class.

Conflict Microlab

Introduce a type of discussion called a "microlab." A microlab is a small-group discussion. Explain that, as the name suggests, a microlab is a kind of laboratory where participants can examine their own and others' experiences. It is designed to maximize personal sharing and active listening. The purpose of today's microlab is to get people thinking about messages they have received about conflict.

To divide the class into groups of three, ask students to count off. (For example, in a class of 21, the students would count off by sevens.) If the number of students in the class is not divisible by three, make groups of four with the extra students.

Explain that each person will have about one minute to talk to the other two people in the group, answering a question. When one person is speaking, the other two are only to listen, giving the person who is speaking their full attention.

Remind the group of the guidelines about speaking and listening:

- Talk one at a time.
- Don't interrupt someone who is speaking.
- Avoid being judgmental.
- Stay with suggested topics.
- Listen and discover, rather than give advice.
- Be open and honest.
- Look at people when you speak to them.
- Say "I" when speaking for yourself.
- Say "you" when speaking to another.

Emphasize that students should share only what they feel comfortable talking about. If students need time to think or if they would rather not respond, they are always free to pass.

Ask the first question listed below. Keep time for the class, letting students know when one minute has passed and it's time for the next person to answer the same question. When all the people in the group have had their turns, go through the same process with each subsequent question.

Questions:

- What messages do you get from your family about how to deal with conflict?
- Are these messages the same or different from the messages about conflict that you get from your friends? From the media (TV, movies, advertising, comic books)?
- What is your image of a strong and courageous person?

- What types of conflicts are most difficult for you to deal with? Physical violence? Emotional conflicts? Another type?
- What's something you like about the way you handle conflict? What's something you'd like to change about the way you handle conflict?

As you introduce each question, it is helpful to take a minute to give your own brief answer. This gives the students a model of how to participate and stimulates their thinking.

After the microlab is finished, ask for volunteers to share their answers with the whole group. Emphasize that the messages we receive from others often have a big effect on how we deal with conflict throughout our lives. It's important to become aware of those messages so that they don't rule our lives and limit our choices in the present.

Teacher's Note: Common Messages and Attitudes About Conflict

In some families conflict is ignored—it's not polite even to bring it up. In other families, conflict is ever-present and chaotic, with everyone fighting for him- or herself. In still other families, conflict is accepted as part of everyday experience and family members are encouraged to work things out openly and fairly.

Some people grow up thinking all conflict is bad, that conflict should be avoided at all costs. Others believe that conflicts provide the only way to "get your way" and that using power over someone else is the way to win respect and get what you want. Our beliefs about conflict will vary.

You might want to point out that not only do individuals have different beliefs about conflict but cultural groups have different beliefs about conflict. In some Asian cultures, conflict is rarely dealt with directly or quickly. This contrasts with an American conflict style that is often direct, confrontational, and immediate. Each style can be effective within a certain cultural context. However, if groups don't understand that different styles operate in different cultures, misperception and misunderstanding can make negotiations and problem solving difficult.

Checking Out What We've Learned

Ask students what they liked or didn't like about the microlab format. How was it different from other forms of discussion?

Closing (optional)

Choose any closing activity from appendix B.

LESSON 9

Exploring the Nature of Violence*

OBJECTIVES

Students will:

- develop a definition of violence;
- discuss violence.

PEACEABLE CLASSROOM PRINCIPLES

- Personal connections
- Social responsibility

AGENDA

1. **Gathering (optional)**

   Go-Round: What is one image that you think of when you hear the word "violence?"

2. **Review Agenda**

3. **Lesson Activities**

   - Microlab on Violence
   - Defining Violence

4. **Checking Out What We've Learned**

   Violence in Print Media

5. **Closing (optional)**

   Popcorn-Style Sharing: What is one important quality of someone you know who is a peacemaker?

---

* Adapted with permission from *Resolving Conflict Creatively: A Draft Teaching Guide for Secondary Schools* © ESR Metropolitan Area, 1990.

Gathering (optional)

Go-Round: Ask students, "What is one image that you think of when you hear the word "violence?"

Review Agenda

Write the agenda on the board and review it with the class.

Microlab on Violence

Divide the class into groups of three for a microlab. Explain that they will be exploring the nature of violence.

Begin by selecting one question from the list below. In the microlab, each person has about one minute to respond to this question. When the students have all answered the first question, repeat the process with another question. Have students respond to a total of three questions.

- Think about your first personal encounter with violence. What happened? How did it change your view of yourself, other people, the world?

- How would you define a violent act?

- What messages about violence did you get growing up? Did everyone who was important to you give you the same message?

- Do you think we live in a violent society? Why or why not?

- Do you think the United States is more violent now than it was 20 years ago? 50 years ago? 150 years ago?

- Is it ever okay to hurt another person physically? Where do you draw the line?

- Why are people violent? What makes some people more prone to commit acts of violence than others?

- How does violence affect how you live? How does it affect what you can and cannot do? How does it influence the choices you make?

Defining Violence

Ask students to stay in their microlab groups. Distribute a sheet of newsprint to each group. Ask each group to develop a definition of violence and then write their definition on the newsprint.

Next, ask each group to create a list of all the different types of violence. What are some categories for violent acts? Some examples are physical abuse, verbal abuse, and war. Have each group write their categories on the newsprint.

Post the newsprint and compare students' responses. Ask the class as a whole, "How do you know when you are seeing or experiencing an act of violence?"

Distribute the handout Defining Violence (p. 78) and read it together. Compare the handout with the lists made by the groups.

Checking Out What We've Learned

Divide students into groups of three or four. Distribute magazines and newspapers. Ask each group to find at least five articles, photographs, cartoons, or news clippings, each of which illustrates a type of violence described in the handout. You might want to collect some examples and prepare a poster to show students before they start working in groups.

Students may have difficulty identifying indirect and institutionalized violence. Encourage them to think of powerful institutions that support or tolerate mistreatment of individuals or groups. For example, ask them to consider the situation of children who have no access to health insurance and name some of the institutions involved in this form of institutionalized violence.

Have students share their clippings with the class. Did students find more representations of one kind of violence than another? Are some kinds of violence covered more often in the media?

Closing (optional)

Popcorn-Style Sharing: Ask students to describe one important quality of someone they know who is a peacemaker.

DEFINING VIOLENCE

Violence—force used to injure, hurt, threaten, or take advantage of someone.

> "Violence can be seen as destructive communication. Any adequate definition must include physical, verbal, symbolic, psychological, and spiritual displays of hostility and hatred. The definition must include both our acts and our inactions and that which is done directly to people or indirectly to them through what they esteem.

> "Violence should then include physical acts against another (a range of acts, from personal attack to war, that violate human autonomy and integrity); verbal attacks that demean and humiliate; symbolic acts that evoke fear and hostility; psychological attitudes that deny one's humanity and equality (legal, institutional, and moral); spiritual postures that communicate racism, inferiority, and worthlessness (beliefs and values that demean and categorize). Violence then becomes a dynamic rather than merely an act."*

Direct violence—war, batterings, assaults, murder, rape, child abuse.†

Indirect violence—economic and political structures that produce extreme inequalities resulting in unequal life chances and the repression of freedom of choice or the repression of human civil rights.

Interpersonal violence—violence that occurs between two or more people, including stranger violence between people who don't know each other, sexual violence where sex is forced on an unwilling person, or acquaintance violence between people who know each other.

Community violence—violence that takes place on a large scale within a particular community (rioting, police violence, gang warfare).‡

Institutionalized violence—institutionalized power used to deprive individuals and groups of basic needs and rights.

Individual aggression—a predisposition toward threatening behavior that can be verbally and physically violent.**

---

* Richard Bartlett Gregg, *The Power of Nonviolence* (New York: Schocken Books, 1966).

† Birgit Brock-Utne, "Feminist Perspectives on Peace," in Paul Smoker et al (ed.), *Reader in Peace Studies* (New York: Pergamon Press, 1990).

‡ Deborah Prothrow-Stith, *Violence Prevention Curriculum for Adolescents* (Newton, Mass.: Educational Development Center, Inc., 1987)

** Stanislav Andreski, *Military Organization and Society* (London: Routledge & K. Paul, 1968).

Exploring the Nature of Conflict

OBJECTIVES

Students will:

- construct definitions of conflict and violence;
- distinguish between conflict and violence;
- identify what's positive about conflict;
- analyze a conflict they have experienced.

PEACEABLE CLASSROOM PRINCIPLES

- Managing and resolving conflict
- Personal connections

AGENDA

1. **Gathering (optional)**

   What Color is Conflict?

2. **Review Agenda**

3. **Lesson Activities**

   - Webbing Conflict
   - Brainstorming What's Positive about Conflict
   - Pair-Share About a Conflict You've Experienced

4. **Checking Out What We've Learned**

   A Survey About Conflict and Me

5. **Closing (optional)**

   Choose any closing activity from appendix B.

Gathering (optional)

What Color is Conflict? (see appendix A)

Review Agenda

Write the agenda on the board and review it with the class.

Webbing Conflict

Ask students for their associations with the word "conflict." Record their ideas on the board using a web format. Write the word "conflict" in the center of the board or chart paper and circle it. The words students associate with conflict are written at the end of lines radiating from the circle. Related ideas can be grouped together. A completed conflict web might look like this:

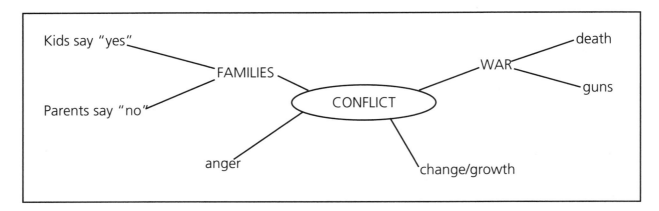

Discuss the web by asking:

- What do you notice about the web?
- Are there any generalizations we might make about our associations?
- Why are most of our associations negative?
- What are some examples of conflicts?

Brainstorming What's Positive About Conflict

Review the definition of violence from Lesson 9. Explain that many people equate conflict with violence. (You may want to write "Conflict = Violence" on the board to make this point.) Ask: "What is the difference between conflict and violence?" (When a distinction has been made, you can change the equation on the board to "Conflict ≠ Violence.") Point out that violence and conflict are not the same thing because most conflicts do not lead to violence.

Erase the words from the board. Ask students to brainstorm a list of things that are positive about conflict. Some examples of positive aspects of conflict are:

- it can be exciting;
- it can shape our thinking so that we have new ideas;
- sometimes it can bring us closer to another person once we've worked it out.

Explain that conflict is a part of life and that we all experience conflicts at home, at work, in school, and on the street. In fact, conflict is often beneficial. Having conflicts with other people may be uncomfortable, but trying to solve them can shake up our thinking and often leads to new ways of looking at things.

Pair-Share About a Conflict You've Experienced

Ask students to find partners. Explain that they will take turns talking and listening. Give each person two or three minutes to respond to the following question: "What was a recent conflict you experienced? Who was involved? What did he or she do? How did it turn out?"

After each partner has had a chance to speak, ask:

- What was that like?
- Did your partner really listen?
- What made you think so?
- What kind of body language shows that someone is listening (eye contact, facing the speaker, leaning forward)?
- What were the outcomes of some of the conflicts?

Checking Out What We've Learned

Give each student a copy of the Survey About Conflict and Me (p. 82). Have each student fill it out. Remind students to be as honest as possible. Assure them that other students will not see their responses. You may want to keep these so that you and your students can compare their attitudes before and after the unit. The survey also provides you with a good database for creating role-plays and conflict scenarios to use in conjunction with other exercises.

Closing (optional)

Choose any closing activity from appendix B.

S T U D E N T   H A N D O U T

SURVEY ABOUT CONFLICT AND ME

1.   Most people fight or argue when they ...

2.   Most people fight or argue over ...

3.   One good thing people get from arguing or fighting is ...

4.   One bad thing about arguing and fighting is ...

5.   People generally respond to conflicts by ... or ...

6.   I fight or argue when ...

7.   I get upset or angry when other students ...

8.   I make others angry when I ...

9.   When I'm talking to someone else who is really angry or upset, the most
        important thing to do is ...

10.   When I'm really angry or upset with someone, the most important thing for me to do is ...

11.   When I'm upset at, mad at, or bothered by another student I can ... *(list three)*

12.   When I have a disagreement or conflict with someone, we can agree to ...

LESSON 11 Responding to Conflict: What Do We Do?

OBJECTIVES

Students will:

- observe and analyze role-plays that reflect different approaches to conflict;
- identify the dominant style they use in responding to conflict.

PEACEABLE CLASSROOM PRINCIPLES

- Managing and resolving conflict
- Caring and effective communication

AGENDA

1. **Gathering (optional)**

   I Represent Conflict

2. **Review Agenda**

3. **Lesson Activities**

   - Conflict Styles Skits
   - Conflict Cards

4. **Checking Out What We've Learned**

   Telegram

5. **Closing (optional)**

   Choose any closing activity from appendix B.

Gathering (optional)

I Represent Conflict (see appendix A)

Review Agenda

Write the agenda on the board and review it with the class.

Conflict Styles Skits

At the beginning of class, explain that the purpose of this lesson is to introduce different styles of dealing with conflict. Distribute the handout Six Conflict Resolution Styles (p. 89) and review the definition of each style. Explain that one style is not necessarily better than the others. The point is to realize that there are different methods of dealing with conflict and to realize that we can choose the method that is right for the situation.

Distribute the Conflict Styles Skits (p. 86). Ask for volunteers to do a dramatic reading of each script. After each reading, ask students to identify the conflict style being demonstrated.

When students have finished their readings, discuss the following questions:

- Do people talk and listen differently depending on the conflict style they are using?
- In each style, who has the power and how does he or she use it?
- How can different conflict styles lead to different results?
- If you really want to resolve a problem—choosing not to just get mad or get even—what are the key points that will help you get there?

Ask students to brainstorm some of the advantages and disadvantages of each style. Which styles do they see most often in school? Why do they think students and teachers often choose these styles?

Divide the class into groups of three. Within each group, give each student two minutes to answer the following questions:

1. What conflict style do you use most often? How well does it work for you?
2. Are there one or two responses that you use all the time?
3. Are there any responses you never use?

Conflict Cards

Copy and cut out the Conflict Cards (p. 90). Keep the class in groups of three. Distribute one set of Conflict Cards to each group. Ask the three students in each group to take turns picking a card and reading it out loud. For each Conflict Card, ask the student to decide which conflict style would be most effective in dealing with this conflict, and which style would be least effective. Ask them to share the reasons for their choices.

After each student has had a turn, ask the group to choose one more example. For each example, ask them to discuss what outcomes might result from using each of the six different conflict styles. Ask the group to agree on the most effective and the least effective conflict style to use in each case. Give students about seven minutes for this discussion. Each group can report and justify their choices.

There are two other ways you may wish to use the cards. Groups can look through the whole set of cards and identify situations in which each style would be most effective. Alternatively, students can act out role-plays based on the cards to demonstrate different conflict styles.

Checking Out What We've Learned

Telegram (see appendix B)

Closing (optional)

Choose any closing activity from appendix B.

S T U D E N T   H A N D O U T

CONFLICT STYLES SKITS

Skit #1

Alex and Jamie are working on a presentation that is due tomorrow. Alex has his material ready but Jamie has arrived at their study date empty-handed.

Alex: I knew this would happen! You never get stuff in on time. I should have known I couldn't count on you.

Jamie: Look, there's still tonight.

Alex: Tonight? Tonight is too late! You can't just wait until the last minute. I told you that before. You're such an idiot!

Jamie: Alex, just listen. My mom says she can get some books for us—

Alex: You don't have any idea how to do a project like this. I'd rather do it myself!

Jamie: Oh, right—and then I'll get an F! You'd better think twice.

Alex: Oh, yeah? Why would I want to work with such a loser?

Jamie: I'm a loser? Look who can't even get a date!

Alex: You call that pimply-faced moron you're seeing a date? Get real!

Jamie: Shut up or you'll be sorry!

Alex: I'm sooo scared! Forget you.

Skit #2

Members of the Dance Committee are meeting to plan next month's dance.

Sondra: Look, we've just spent an hour arguing about a band. No one likes the same kind of music.

Aimee: I don't think we've looked hard enough.

Thomas: Sure we have. We've gotten at least ten suggestions.

Joanne: Well, it looks to me like we're not going to agree. Why don't we hire a DJ who will play different kinds of music?

Sondra: I guess that would work, but people really wanted a live band.

Thomas: We're running out of time and we've got other decisions to make. Let's just go with a DJ, okay?

Others: Okay, all right, etc.

S T U D E N T   H A N D O U T

CONFLICT STYLES SKITS (continued)

Skit #3

Carmen walks past Peter in the hallway.

Peter: Look at those legs! Hey, you all, clear the way so she can strut her stuff!

Carmen: Just because I have a short skirt on doesn't give you the right to make a public announcement.

Peter: Hey, you're doing the advertising, not me.

Carmen: Look, I've asked you before to stop hassling me, and you just keep at it. I want to go to a mediation about this.

Peter: Aw, give me a break. You make such a big deal about everything.

Carmen: I'm serious, it really bothers me. And I know for a fact I'm not the only one. I've talked to Sherrie and Kendra and ...

Peter: All right, all right. If you want to find a mediator, fine. I'll be happy to tell my side of the story.

Skit #4

Lee and Dana are talking at lunch.

Dana: So what do you want to do tonight? Some kids I know are going to the mall.

Lee: Let's do something different—how about going out dancing? Ken and Sandra had a great time at that new place last weekend.

Dana: That could get kind of expensive. I'm still paying back my mom the money I borrowed last Saturday night.

Lee: Oh, come on. Don't you know how to have a good time? You can always pay her back later—your mom's got plenty of money.

Dana: Well, I guess it's no big deal. I'll ask her to give me another week. But we'll have to do something less expensive next time.

Lee: Great. And your mom can drive us too, right?

S T U D E N T   H A N D O U T

CONFLICT STYLES SKITS (continued)

Skit #5

In the girls' bathroom:

Ayisha: Did you hear what Deena said about Kammie?

Sharon: Yeah, and Kammie found out. She said Deena better watch out—she's gonna get back at her for sure.

Ayisha: I heard she brought a knife. She wants to fight this afternoon. What do you think we should do? Deena's your friend.

Sharon: Hey, I'm not messing with this. It's her problem. I'm staying out of it.

Skit #6

After class:

Student: Do you have a minute?

Teacher: Sure.

Student: I want to talk about the books we're reading.

Teacher: What's on your mind?

Student: Well, the year's half over and we've never read anything by a Mexican American. Is there some way that we could have more choices about what we read?

Teacher: The problem is, this is an AP class and I'm required to teach certain texts. As far as I know, there aren't any Mexican-American authors on the list. I wish we could do more, but I don't have time to cover every single kind of author they leave out.

Student: I'm not talking about every single kind of author. But you know, about a third of the kids in the class are Mexican American and everyone might benefit from reading something that relates to that experience. There are a lot of good authors to choose from.

Teacher: If you think other kids might be interested, let's bring it up in class. Maybe we can figure out a way to include some other literature that's not on the list.

Student: So you'll bring it up tomorrow?

Teacher: It's a deal.

SIX CONFLICT RESOLUTION STYLES

1. Directing/Controlling:

"My way or the highway."

We do not, cannot, or will not bargain or give in. At times we are standing up for our rights and deeply held beliefs. It can also mean pursuing what we want at the expense of another person. We may also be caught in a power struggle and not see a way to negotiate to get what we want.

2. Collaborating

"Let's sit down and work this out."

We work with others to find mutually satisfying ways to get all of our needs met. We are interested in finding solutions and in maintaining or even improving the relationship. Other people involved are seen as partners rather than adversaries.

3. Compromising

"Let's both give a little" or "Something is better than nothing."

We seek the middle ground. Each party gives up something for a solution that may satisfy our needs only partially.

4. Accommodating

"Whatever you want is fine" or "It doesn't matter anyway."

We yield to another's point of view, meeting the other person's needs while denying our own. We may give in to smooth the relationship, or to get our way another time.

5. Avoiding/Denying

"Let's skip it" or "Problem? I don't see a problem."

We do not address the conflict and withdraw from the situation or behave as though the situation were not happening. We leave it to others to deal with.

6. Appealing to a Greater Authority or a Third Party

"Help me out here."

We turn to others whom we perceive as having more power, influence, authority, or wisdom to solve the conflict.

CONFLICT CARDS

Your mother insists that you go out with your family on Saturday night. You already have plans with a friend.

Your friend, whose birthday is today, wants you to skip school and celebrate.

Your best friend is always borrowing your tapes and never returns them.

You overhear a racial slur in the hallway and think the speaker is talking about the friend you are walking with.

Your friend is too drunk to drive you home from a party. This is the third time this has happened.

As you are talking to friends, someone passes by and stops. She thinks you just insulted her.

You think your teacher has been unfair in grading an essay. Your grades are always lower than you expect.

Your boss at the store where you work is always criticizing you. Your work never seems to be good enough.

The same kid wants to start an argument with you again! You know you will both end up screaming.

Your mother is really mad. You were supposed to put the laundry in this morning and you forgot.

You and two friends have spent 20 minutes arguing about what movie to see. You've had enough.

Someone is making fun of your girlfriend/ boyfriend. You're angry because this kid does this stuff all the time.

A friend wants to copy your math homework. It took you an hour and a half to do it.

(make up your own)

LESSON 12
How and Why Does Conflict Escalate?*

OBJECTIVES

Students will:

- participate in a role-play to experience and observe the escalation of conflict;
- explore the links between feelings and behavior, especially how anger influences what we do and say;
- identify common characteristics that all conflicts share.

PEACEABLE CLASSROOM PRINCIPLES

- Managing and resolving conflict
- Emotional literacy

AGENDA

1. **Gathering (optional)**

   Conflict Synectics (Making Metaphors)

2. **Review Agenda**

3. **Lesson Activities**

   - Exploring Conflict Escalation
   - Triad Role-Plays

4. **Checking Out What We've Learned**

   Brainstorm a list of characteristics common to all conflicts.

5. **Closing (optional)**

   Choose any closing activity from appendix B.

---

* Adapted with permission from *Resolving Conflict Creatively: A Draft Teaching Guide for Secondary Schools* © ESR Metropolitan Area, 1990.

Gathering (optional)

Conflict Synectics (Making Metaphors): Copy and cut out the Conflict Synectics Cards (p. 95). Students will create metaphors about conflict. "Conflict is like ..." Have students form pairs and have each pair choose one Conflict Synectics Card. Ask partners to work together to think up a metaphor about conflict that uses the object on their card. Example: "Conflict is like a ladder. You take steps up to the top where things become a lot more dangerous."

Review Agenda

Write the agenda on the board and review it with the class.

Exploring Conflict Escalation

Ask students how they know that what they're seeing or hearing is a conflict. You might want to make a T-chart on the blackboard or on newsprint and keep it visible while you're exploring escalation.

WHEN THERE'S A CONFLICT

What You Hear	What You See
Yelling	"In-your-face" confrontation
Name-calling	Rigid body language
Insults	Pointing fingers
Crying	Physical fighting
Abusive language	Angry facial expressions
Interrupting	

Explain that conflict between people can grow and intensify unless it is resolved or managed. Have students think back over the arguments and fights they've had at school, with friends, or at home. Explore the reasons why conflicts sometimes get out of hand.

Draw a staircase on the board or on newsprint like the one below.* Write the word "escalator" above the staircase and explore how that word is related to the word "escalate." (For example, on an escalator once you take the first step you automatically keep "escalating"—you can't go in the opposite direction without considerable effort.)

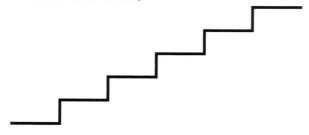

---

* The conflict escalator is adapted from William J. Kreidler's *Elementary Perspectives* (Cambridge, Mass.: Educators for Social Responsibility, 1990).

Triad Role-Plays

Explain that everyone is going to participate in triads—groups of three—to explore how conflicts escalate. In a triad, two people role-play conflict and one person observes. Ask students to form groups of three and choose a number: one, two, or three. In each group, numbers one and two will role-play the conflict; number three will be the observer. To set the scene, give the following instructions:

> **To number ones:** "It's lunchtime. The cafeteria is serving burgers and fries today. You are wearing a new white silk baseball jacket that your favorite aunt just gave you for your birthday. You know it was expensive, and your mother didn't really want you to wear it to school. As you go through the cafeteria line, you know you're looking good! You're heading for the catsup dispenser to put lots of catsup on your fries when ...

> **To number twos:** "You appear out of nowhere. You're in a big hurry because you have to take a make-up test in 10 minutes. Your teacher said this was the only time you could take your English test. You are racing to the catsup dispenser and step in front of another person standing there. That's you (point to the number ones). You slam down the handle and catsup goes all over the new white silk baseball jacket."

> **To number threes:** Your job is to observe the conflict and notice how each person's words and actions cause it to escalate.

Tell the triads to role-play what happens next. The first person to speak will be person number one, who now has catsup all over the front of his or her brand new jacket. The groups will have two minutes to interact. Tell them to remember the ground rule of no physical fighting. Say: "When I say 'Curtain,' begin. When I say 'Freeze,' stop talking and freeze where you are."

Say, "Curtain." This activity will become fairly loud, so make sure to close your door. Try to observe how different students respond to the situation. After about a minute and a half say, "Freeze." Ask students to sit down and focus their attention on the escalator you've drawn. Write the initial conflict on the bottom step of the escalator and the outcome on the top step. You may want to give the students in the conflict names in order to make the conflict easier to follow.

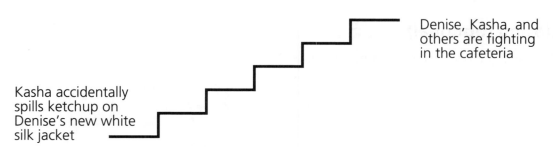

Ask observers what happened in the role-play. What kinds of responses and reactions made the conflict escalate? Record the observers' answers on the steps of the escalator. Be sure to discuss both spoken language and body language.

Some commonly identified steps on the escalator are:

- Kasha blames Denise.
- Denise blames Kasha.
- They trade insults and then begin shoving each other.
- Kasha ignores what happens and tries to walk away.
- Denise screams at Kasha and calls her names.
- Kasha freezes and doesn't say anything.

- Denise is upset and angry and Kasha ignores her feelings completely.
- Kasha tries to make a joke out of what happened.

Focus the next part of the discussion on feelings. What were students feeling in the beginning, in the middle, and at the end? Ask students who felt angry to share what their partners said and did that intensified their anger.

Ask a volunteer to do the same role-play with you two more times to demonstrate what happens when someone's feelings aren't acknowledged.

> First, the teacher takes the role of the "splatterer." Say things like, "So what? It's not my problem. Don't be such a baby! Forget you, I've got my own problems." Say anything that shows complete ignorance of the other person's feelings. After a minute of this, ask the student how he or she is feeling. Ask if the angry feelings intensified. Ask what the "splatterer" could have said that would have helped him or her feel calmer and less upset.

> Second, take the role of the "splattee" and ask the student to apologize immediately and offer lots of suggestions for what to do about the jacket. You say things like, "I don't want to hear it! I don't care what you can do, look at my jacket! You've ruined it! I don't want your solutions. My mother's going to kill me!"

Ask the class, "The student tried to apologize and offer suggestions. Both of these sound like good ideas. Why didn't it work?" Again, focus on the fact that the splattee's feelings were never acknowledged by the splatterer.

Summarize by saying that anger is the hardest emotion to control and manage within ourselves, and it's also the most challenging emotion to defuse in someone else. Let students know that the next lessons you do together will focus on anger.

Checking Out What We've Learned

Brainstorm a list of characteristics common to all conflicts.

Closing (optional)

Choose any closing activity from appendix B.

CONFLICT SYNECTICS CARDS

CONFLICT SYNECTICS CARDS

CONFLICT SYNECTICS CARDS

CONFLICT SYNECTICS CARDS

LESSON 13 "Reading" and Understanding Feelings

OBJECTIVES

Students will:

- connect feelings to personal experiences;
- use a story to identify feelings and assess their intensity;
- explore the relationship of feelings to motivation in school.

PEACEABLE CLASSROOM PRINCIPLES

- Emotional literacy
- Personal connections

AGENDA

1. **Gathering (optional)**

   Feelings Cards

2. **Review Agenda**

3. **Lesson Activities**

   - Feelings Charades
   - The Feelings Bull's-Eye
   - The Feelings-Motivation Connection

4. **Checking Out What We've Learned**

   Pair-Share: "I'd like to understand more about why I feel ... when I ..."

5. **Closing (optional)**

   Closing Cards

Gathering (optional)

Feelings Cards: Cut out and copy the Feelings Cards (p. 104). Each student chooses one card, then links up with one or more people whose card is either a synonym or an antonym of her own. When all the students have found groups, each person shares a personal experience that illustrates the feeling on his or her card.

Review Agenda

Write the agenda on the board and review it with the class.

Feelings Charades

Explain that being able to "read" feelings is helpful in a conflict. If we can pick up clues about how the other person is feeling, we may be better able to talk through the problem and find a solution. Also, when we are able to name how the other person seems to be feeling, the other person often feels validated and understood and therefore feels calmer.

Divide students into groups of five and distribute three Feelings Cards to each group. Tell each group to choose one of them to act out as a group without using words. Give each group two and a half minutes to work out their group mimes. Have each group perform their mime and ask the rest of the groups to guess the feeling. When all groups have finished, debrief by asking the class what kinds of feelings would be hardest or easiest to mime.

The Feelings Bull's-Eye

Read Gregory-Alan Williams' story "Pride and Prejudice" (p. 102) about his experience during the Los Angeles riots in 1992. After reading the story, take about five minutes to invite students to share their feelings and reactions to the story.

Next, draw a bull's-eye on the board or on newsprint, placing a heart in the center. Ask students to identify the feelings they imagine Williams experiences in the story.

When students identify a feeling, ask them where you should place it on the bull's-eye—near the heart for the strongest feelings or toward the outer circle for less intense feelings? Ask students to link the feeling to the action that produced the feeling. Students may link several feelings to the same action.

The Feelings–Motivation Connection

Pair-Share: Ask students the following questions. Give pairs two minutes each to share their responses.

1. Think about a negative learning experience you've had or a class you really disliked.
   - What made it negative?
   - What was the teacher doing?
   - How did you feel about this experience?
   - How did this experience influence what subjects you like or don't like today?
2. Think about a learning experience or class that was really positive for you.
   - What made it positive?
   - What was the teacher doing that made it positive?

- How did you feel about this experience?
- How do you feel about this subject or class today?

Bring the group back together and take four minutes for students to share their responses with the whole group. Point out how strong feelings from earlier experiences can influence the way we respond to new learning experiences.

Checking Out What We've Learned

Pair-Share: "I'd like to understand more about why I feel ... when I ..."

Closing (optional)

Closing Cards: Copy and cut out the Closing Cards (p. 108). Have students choose a Closing Card that reflects something they are thinking or feeling about themselves or the class.

S T U D E N T   H A N D O U T

PRIDE AND PREJUDICE*

By Greg-Alan Williams

On April 29, 1992, a jury acquitted a group of Los Angeles police officers accused of beating Rodney King, an African American. Many people were shocked by the verdict. After viewing a video of the beating that had been filmed by a bystander, many were convinced that the police had acted improperly. Within hours of the announcement, angry African Americans took to the streets to express their outrage. Gregory Alan-Williams, who is also an African American, witnessed the rioting. He later described how he felt as he saw the overturned cars, smashed windows, and smoldering fires:

> I understood clearly what was happening and why it was happening. A part of me wanted it to happen, spurred by the remaining shares of self-righteous indignation that scraped at my insides. But if I had raised my hand against another, when my rage was spent, and I could no longer recall with sufficient clarity the justifications that had driven me to such brutality and horror, what would I do? How would I survive the shame and self-hatred which would overtake me as the battered faces of my brothers bled and pleaded in my memory?

At an intersection, Alan-Williams saw a Japanese American try desperately to drive through the area only to be stopped by a barrage of bricks and bottles. Even after the man lost consciousness, the attacks continued. As Williams watched, he recalled an incident that took place when he was one of two black students in his junior high school:

> I was a few feet from the auditorium doors, engaging in some good-natured banter with another student, when some hard object—like a rock—slammed against my mouth: the flesh burst into bleeding pulp against my teeth. The strength of the blow, combined with the downward incline of the aisle, sent me reeling backward into the students behind me. They parted like the Red Sea. I fell over some seats, righted myself, and touched two trembling fingers to the pain in my mouth. I could feel the flesh hanging from where my bottom lip had been.

> Dazed and bleeding, I staggered back and forth across the aisle, unable to understand what had happened. I caught a blurry glimpse of someone standing laughing in the middle of the aisle. I couldn't make out his face but he was huge. Some kids were standing at the edges of the aisle, others had gathered up ahead and were watching from the double doors of the auditorium. A few joined my assailant in laughter. I was hoping desperately that someone upon this "enlightened landscape" would help me. Help me get away from this huge laughing figure, away from my shame and those who watched as I staggered about, bloody and afraid.

> A few days later, as I sat, stitched and swollen, in the vice principal's office, I came to understand what had happened, for the vice principal said that I had come to his school "walking too tall" and holding my head "a little too high and many of the students resented it. So," he said to my mother, of course, "what could you expect?"

> Now the vivid memory of that beating and abandonment, some twenty-five years ago, propelled me into the intersection. I remembered too well the feelings I had had, the hurtful words and images—I could not accept this attack, the suffering of this human being. It seemed that he and I had become one, that his suffering and mine had fused,

---

*Excerpted from *A Gathering of Heroes: Reflections on Rage and Responsibility* by Greg-Alan Williams © 1994. Reprinted by arrangement with Academy Chicago Publishers.

S T U D E N T   H A N D O U T

and with one loud and silent voice now cried for help within this single irretrievable moment.

My conscience heard our cry, and carried me forward to preserve justice for him and to reclaim justice for myself.

I moved neither slowly nor quickly, not in anger but in extreme sorrow. Sorrow for those who were seeing, but who could not see; sorrow for the ones who saw but who had lost the ability to feel. Sorrow for the hated and for those who nurtured hate with their silence. Although the man in the intersection was being robbed of his existence, my sorrow was not for death, but for the prevailing misery of life and grew from a remembrance of the ache that comes with knowing that one has been exiled from the human heart.

F E E L I N G S   C A R D S

HOPEFUL	FOCUSED	EXCITED
ALERT	CLEAR	STRETCHED
RELAXED	SHOCKED	PUZZLED
DISMAYED	UNCERTAIN	SKEPTICAL
SAD	DEFEATED	REJECTED
LONELY	DEPRESSED	AFRAID

FEELINGS CARDS

TENSE	UNSAFE	UPSET
THREATENED	STUCK	ANGRY
HOSTILE	SATISFIED	RELIEVED
AMUSED	PROUD	ENERGIZED
ACCEPTED	FRIENDLY	SECURE
INCLUDED	CALM	LOVED

C L O S I N G   C A R D S

DIFFERENCES	APPRECIATE	SURVIVAL
CONTRIBUTE	FUN!	EXCUSES
RESPECT	RESPONSIBILITY	ENCOURAGE
SCARED	LEARN	ACCEPT
OPPORTUNITY	BELIEVE	COURAGE
RISK	SUPPORT	POSITIVE

CLOSING CARDS

SURPRISE	INSPIRATION	CHANGE
GOAL	GROWTH	CHALLENGE
TRUST	CARING	LISTEN
PATIENCE	PROBLEM SOLVING	LOOSEN UP
REMEMBER	WHAT IF?	CHALLENGE
IMAGINE	AVOID	MISTAKE

C L O S I N G   C A R D S

LIGHTEN UP	LET GO	CONCERNED
WIN-WIN	SAFE	DREAM
CHECK OUT	RESIST	COMMIT
AWARE	FOCUS	TRY

OBJECTIVES

Students will:

- explore what makes them angry;
- become more aware of their own anger cues, triggers, and reducers;
- examine their responses to anger and explore alternative responses.

PEACEABLE CLASSROOM PRINCIPLES

- Emotional literacy
- Managing and resolving conflict

AGENDA

1. **Gathering (optional)**

   Anger Ball-Toss

2. **Review Agenda**

3. **Lesson Activities**

   - Anger Triggers
   - The Anger Mountain
   - Responses to Anger and Cooling Off
   - Responses to Anger Role-Play

4. **Checking Out What We've Learned**

   Share one thing you learned about yourself or about anger that you want to remember from today.

5. **Closing (optional)**

   Go-Round: "I used to think (feel) ... Now I think (feel) ..."

Gathering (optional)

Anger Ball-Toss (see appendix A)

Review Agenda

Write the agenda on the board and review it with the class.

Anger Triggers

Ask students to find a partner. Each partner has two minutes to describe a recent time when he or she became angry. Students should describe what happened to make them angry, how they responded, and what the outcome was.

Bring the group back together. Ask for volunteers to share their stories. As a class, create a list titled "What and Who Makes Me Angry." Ask students to be specific. Record their contributions on newsprint.

Ask students to identify the different causes of anger. Some common causes are:

- when someone hurts, criticizes, or embarrasses us;
- when we are denied what we want or need;
- when others have behaved in a way that we judge offensive and/or morally wrong;
- when we can't control a situation and feel powerless;
- when we witness or experience injustice, prejudice, or violence.

Ask students:

- Are there situations in which anger is a healthy response?
- Are there situations in which anger is counterproductive?

Remind students that anger is a normal emotion. There are different ways to express and deal with it. Some people fly off the handle, while other people just dismiss it. Make the distinction between feeling and behavior. Anger is a feeling; what we choose to do with the feeling is our behavior. A behavior may have positive or negative consequences.

Give each student a note card. Ask them to write "Anger Triggers" on the top and then list four or five behaviors, words, or phrases that make them angry.

Ask students to pair with a partner. Give each student about two minutes to share his or her triggers. Then give students about two minutes each to discuss the following questions with their partners:

- How do you know when you're angry? What are your physical cues that send you a signal that you're becoming angry?
- How do you usually react to being angry?
- Do you have a "long fuse" or a "short fuse"?

Invite students to do some sharing with the whole group. Point out to students that our physical cues that we are angry can give us warning signs to stop and think about what we want to do next.

The Anger Mountain

Ask students if they have ever experienced angry moments when they had trouble thinking about what to say and what to do—times when the anger seemed to blot out all the things they would have wanted to say or do. Ask students if they ever replayed the angry moment afterwards like a movie, deleting things they would like to take back and editing in all the things that would have helped them stay in control and prevent an outburst that left people feeling hurt and angrier. Ask for volunteers to share some experiences where runaway feelings of anger led them to behave in ways that had negative consequences. Be prepared to share a story yourself to start the discussion.

Distribute the Anger Mountain handout (p. 114). This graphic illustration is a useful tool to help students better understand what happens when they get angry. When your "hot button" gets pushed, you only have about eight seconds of mental and physical alertness before the built-in physiological responses to being angry take over. Once the eight seconds are up, you start going up the anger mountain. The rush of adrenaline makes it hard to go down the mountain until all your anger is spent.

This handout can be a starting point for discussing impulsive behavior—the things we say and do without thinking. The handout also provides an opportunity to discuss the feelings of regret and guilt that we often experience on our way down the mountain. This graphic helps students understand why it's important to learn techniques for managing and controlling anger.

Responses to Anger and Cooling Off

Remind students of the list "What and Who Makes Me Angry." Ask the class to brainstorm a list called "Ways People Deal With Their Anger." Let students know that the list can include all ways of dealing with anger, not just constructive ones. Record their ideas on newsprint. Some common responses are:

- Blow off steam: release angry energy by pounding a pillow, jogging, finding a place to scream where you won't bother anyone.
- Talk it out with the person you're angry with. Tell that person how you feel, and what you want to happen.
- Talk about it to a friend who's not involved.
- Chill out: take a few deep breaths, count to 10, listen to music, be alone for a few minutes.
- Stuff it in: pretend nothing's wrong.
- Get back at someone verbally through name-calling, sarcasm, putting someone down, intimidation and threats.
- Displacement: pick a fight or start an argument with someone else, destroy somebody else's stuff.
- Escape: read a book, watch TV, eat, play basketball, go out with friends.
- Lighten up: make a joke of the situation, laugh it off.
- Ignore the situation.
- Physical aggression: fighting, hitting, kicking.
- Stop, think, and ask questions: What just set me off? What do I really want to happen now? Am I willing to look for a solution?
- Tell myself, "I'm in charge of what I do." I can choose what to do right now. I don't want the other person to control what I do or say.
- Keep my voice quiet and calm.
- Say "I'm too angry to talk now, but I want to talk later."

Use any of the following discussion questions for further exploration:

- Which strategies might make the situation worse?
- Which strategies might be self-destructive?

- Which strategies would give you a chance to stand up for yourself without being abusive or physically aggressive?
- Which strategies are hardest for you to use? Easiest?
- Which strategies would help you to manage your anger so that you don't "lose it" and don't hurt others or yourself? Circle these strategies.

Distribute the Anger Reducers handout (p. 115). Ask them to fill out the top part of the handout looking to the items on the list for ideas. Then ask them to think about the kinds of things they can say to themselves in that eight seconds after the "hot button" is pushed so that they don't get on the escalator and lose control.

Responses to Anger Role-Play

Explain that the responses to anger can be put in three categories: suppression, aggression, and assertiveness.

> *Suppression*—Acting as if nothing happened. For example, if somebody insults us we can pretend we didn't hear it or change the subject.

> *Aggression*—Lashing out with words or physical attack. For example, if someone insults us, we think of a worse insult to throw back or punch that person in the face.

> *Assertiveness*—Letting the other person know that the insult is unacceptable without attempting to hurt the other person in return.

Ask two students to role-play a conflict. Provide the following background:

> In Melissa's English class, the teacher does not have very good control over the class and there is always a lot of fooling around going on. Nevertheless, Melissa needs a good grade in the class, and she has been trying to do the work the teacher has assigned.

> Michael never does any work in the class. He know he's going to fail anyway so he finds other things to do. He has been bugging Melissa all the time. He makes comments about her, pokes her when he goes past her desk, and brushes her papers off the desk and onto the floor. She's told him many times to leave her alone. She's told the teacher, but the teacher hasn't been able to stop Michael. Then one day when she is working hard on some writing the teacher had asked for, a paper wad smacks her in the back of the head. It's the last straw.

Ask the students to role-play what happens next. Freeze the action after about one minute. Ask the students who were performing the role-play to stay in character and say how they are feeling at this point. Then have them step out of character and describe how it felt to do this role-play.

Ask the class to think of some ways that Melissa could handle the situation assertively, that is, with firmness and directness, without avoidance or aggression. Brainstorm a list of assertive responses. Write the list on the board.

Once the list has been completed, ask two students to choose one of the suggestions and role-play the situation with that ending. When the role-play is finished, ask the players how their characters are feeling and how they themselves are feeling. How did the conflict work out? Repeat the process using other assertive solutions, as time allows.

Checking Out What We've Learned

Pair-Share: Share one thing you learned about yourself or about anger that you want to remember from today.

Closing (optional)

Go-Round: "I used to think (feel) ... Now I think (feel) ..."

S T U D E N T   H A N D O U T

ANGER MOUNTAIN*

YOU HAVE ABOUT 8 SECONDS—THINK FAST!

WHAT CAN YOU SAY AND DO
INSTEAD OF CLIMBING UP
ANGER MOUNTAIN?

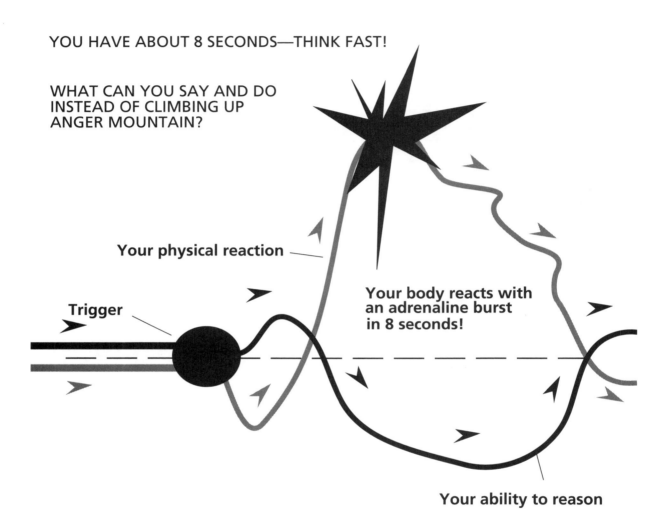

Your physical reaction

Trigger

Your body reacts with an adrenaline burst in 8 seconds!

Your ability to reason

*Adapted with permission from *Dealing With Differences* by Marion O'Malley and Tiffany Davis (Chapel Hill, NC: Center for Peace Education, 1995)

S T U D E N T   H A N D O U T

ANGER REDUCERS

What I can do to cool down my own anger:

I can_____

I can_____

I can_____

Here are things I can say to myself so that I don't do something stupid in the heat of an angry moment:

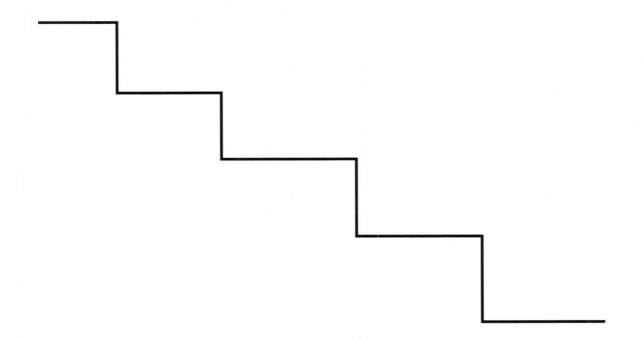

LESSON 15 — "You" Messages And "I" Messages

OBJECTIVES

Students will:

- observe two role-plays and discuss differences between "you" messages (aggressive responses) and "I" messages (assertive responses);
- practice identifying "I" messages and "you" messages;
- role-play sending "I" messages.

PEACEABLE CLASSROOM PRINCIPLES

- Caring and effective communication
- Emotional literacy
- Managing and resolving conflicts

AGENDA

1. **Gathering (optional)**

   Go-Round: Name something you experienced or tried in the last six months that was new or different.

2. **Review Agenda**

3. **Lesson Activities**

   - Assertion, Aggression, and "I" Messages
   - Turning "You" Messages into "I" Messages

4. **Checking Out What We've Learned**

   Do "back-to-back" role-plays to practice sending "I" messages; debrief the role-play.

5. **Closing (optional)**

   Pair-Share: When would you be willing to give someone an "I" message?

Gathering (optional)

Go-Round: Name something you experienced in the last six months that was new or different—something you had mixed feelings about or weren't sure how much you were going to like. At the end, explain that students will be trying something new today that might feel awkward at first.

Review Agenda

Write the agenda on the board and review it with the class.

Assertion, Aggression, and "I" Messages

Explain to your students that in this activity they are going to learn an assertive way of speaking. Review the difference between being assertive and being aggressive (see Lesson 14). Have any students used an assertive way of responding since we last met? Ask for volunteers to share examples.

Ask for two volunteers and ask them the read aloud the parts of Maria and Janet in Skit #1 on the "I" Message Skits handout (p. 121). After Skit #1 has been read, ask students to discuss the following questions:

- How do you think Maria felt about Janet in this skit?
- How do you think Janet felt about Maria in this skit?
- Do you think that Janet is going to stop spreading her things around the room?
- Why or why not?

List the feelings named by the class on the board or on paper under the heading "Skit #1."

Have the same students or two other students read Skit #2. Follow with a discussion:

- How do you think Maria felt about Janet in this skit?
- How do you think Janet felt about Maria in this skit?
- Do you think that Janet will make an effort to keep the room in order?
- Why or why not?

Ask students to compare the two skits:

- What were some of the comments made in the first skit?
- What were some of the comments made in the second skit?
- What were some of the nonverbal behaviors used in each skit?
- What was different about the way Maria communicated in the two skits?
- Which way was more effective?

Explain that the first skit contained "you" messages, and the second skit contained "I" messages. "You" messages tend to attack and blame another person. The receiver of the "you" message usually feels judged and blamed; he thinks primarily of defending himself. The likely reaction to a "you" message is to counterattack or withdraw from the relationship. The result of a "you" message is usually anger, defensiveness, resentment, and perhaps long-term damage to the relationship.

With an "I" message, the speaker communicates his or her own wants, needs, or concerns. The receiver of an "I" message learns that she has done something the speaker doesn't like. Although the receiver may still react defensively at first (nobody likes to feel wrong), the door is open for dialogue. "I" messages encourage focusing on solutions, not blame. With "I" messages, there is less likelihood that the relationship will be damaged. "I" messages are a relatively nonthreatening way to let others know what you want and how you feel.

Write the following "I" message formula on the board:

1. I feel ... *(state the feeling)*

2. when you ... *(state the behavior)*

3. because ... *(state the effect the behavior has on you)*.

Explain that these are the elements of an "I" message. It is helpful to use the formula when you are first learning to make "I" messages. However, when you are more comfortable with making them, you do not have to use this formula.

Turning "You" Messages into "I" Messages

Have each student find a partner. Distribute the handout Ingredients of an "I" Message (p. 122). Have students, in pairs, select five or six statements to work with and decide which of them are "I" messages and which are "you" messages. Then ask them to try changing the "you" messages to "I" messages. Review examples from the handout as a group and share suggestions for turning "you" messages into "I" messages.

Checking Out What We've Learned

"Back-to-Back" Role-Play: This is a way of setting up role-plays so that everyone in the class is involved. Ask students to find partners and stand back to back with them. One partner will play Person A, the other Person B.

Describe one of the following situations. When you have finished, have the students face their partners and enact the situation.

> Person A is standing in line in the cafeteria when Person B pushes right in front of her.

> Person B walks past Person A in the hall and calls Person A a name under his breath.

Call "freeze" after a minute or two. Now that they have a feeling for the situation, students can go on to creating "I" messages. Ask Person A to express his or her objection to Person B's behavior using an "I" message. When students have had a chance to give this a try, stop the role-play and discuss how it went.

- What feelings came up?
- What "I" messages did you think of?

Remind students that "I" messages express the speaker's feelings without blaming.

Do a new role-play with Person B as the person who must ultimately state his feelings using "I" messages. Sample scenarios:

> Person B lets Person A wear an expensive bracelet and Person A loses it.

> Person B trips over Person A's foot in the cafeteria and thinks Person A stuck her foot out on purpose.

As before, explain the situation, have the players enact it, freeze after one or two minutes, then have Person B think of an "I" message.

Closing (optional)

Pair-Share: When would you be willing to give someone an "I" message to let another person know what you feel and need? Make a commitment to try it before meeting again.

S T U D E N T   H A N D O U T

"I" MESSAGE SKITS

Maria and Janet share a room at home.

Skit #1:

Maria: I can't stand sharing a room with you. You're just a slob. Every time I try to straighten up in here so I can find my things when I want them, you mess it up again. Where do you get so much stuff? There's no room for me in here. I just can't live with you, and I hope you plan on living alone because nobody in the world is going to put up with this stuff.

Janet: Where do you get off calling other people slobs? You're really conceited. You think you're so perfect. Well, let me tell you not everybody thinks you're so great. You should know some of the things I've heard people saying about you. You can spend all your time housekeeping if you want to, but I don't see the necessity of fussing with stuff all the time. I clean up once in a while. It's not dirty in here, only a little messy.

Skit #2:

Maria: I'm really having trouble living in this room. It makes me really upset when I come in here looking for a little peace and there's stuff all over the place. I can't think when there's a mess all around me. Plus my things get lost, and I can't find them when I need them. Sometimes they're just buried. I need to have more order in here.

Janet: I'm sorry, Maria. I'll try to be neater. My mind's just on other things, and this doesn't bother me. Is there some way we can divide the room so my clutter doesn't get in your way? Maybe we can clear a space just for you.

INGREDIENTS OF AN "I" MESSAGE

An "I" message expresses what I feel, what's happened to make me feel that way, and what I need. We use "I" message to speak only for ourselves and not for or about others. "I" messages reduce tension and prevent the escalation of conflict because they allow the other person to save face and to understand what the speaker is feeling. Here are some examples of "I" messages:

- I feel pressured when you call me every 20 minutes on a school night. It's hard to get anything done. I'd rather have just one longer conversation.
- I feel mad that you told the whole school about us because I told you that in confidence. I want to be able to tell you stuff and know that what I say will not be shared with anyone else.
- I want some time to think about this. I feel uneasy about giving you an answer right now. Let's talk later.
- I want to go to the party with you. I feel embarrassed having to show up alone.

The following statements are false "I" messages. They sound like "I" messages but they contain demands, blame, judgments, and accusations.

- I won't invite him any more because he's a jerk.
- I think you're asking for big trouble.
- I feel like he should give me my tape back.

Read the statements below. Put an "I" next to all "I" messages and a "you" next to all "you" messages. Then change all "you" messages to "I" messages.

1. I hope things go better for me today.

2. You'd better get out of my chair.

3. Shut your mouth.

4. I need you to just leave me alone!

5. Don't tell me you understand. You don't know anything.

6. Sometimes I feel ignored when you don't call me.

7. Why don't you let someone else have a chance?

8. I want to make sure I understand. Could you repeat that?

9. I really don't like it when you touch my things without asking for my permission.

10. If you just would listen to me first, I wouldn't be so mad.

11. I think school should be a safe place.

12. I'm busy, so go bug someone else.

Getting What You Need Using "I" Statements

OBJECTIVES

Students will:

- formulate "I" messages;
- practice assertiveness in triads;
- explore other kinds of "I" speech that help people get what they need.

**PEACEABLE
CLASSROOM
PRINCIPLES**

- Caring and effective communication
- Emotional literacy
- Mutual respect
- Managing and resolving conflict

AGENDA

1. **Gathering (optional)**

   Go-Round: Think of a time when you felt you were being taken advantage of and stood up for yourself in a nonviolent way.

2. **Review Agenda**

3. **Lesson Activities**

   - Assertive "I" Statements
   - Assertiveness Triads

4. **Checking Out What We've Learned**

   Students reflect and pair-share about other "I" messages they would like to communicate to another person.

5. **Closing (optional)**

   Go-Round: Appreciation messages about the group, the class, the process.

Gathering (optional)

Go-Round: Think of a time when you felt you were being taken advantage of and stood up for yourself in a strong way without hurting the other person.

Review Agenda

Write the agenda on the board and review it with the class.

Assertive "I" Statements

At the end of the previous lesson, students were asked to think of a situation in their lives where an "I" message or statement might be helpful and committed themselves to trying it. Ask for volunteers to share their experiences in doing this. Ask the following questions:

- Was it hard to find the right time to deliver your "I" message?
- How did the receiver of your "I" message react?
- How are you feeling about doing this?

Have students pair up to discuss the benefits that result from using "I" messages. Ask each pair to identify two positive outcomes for the sender and two for the receiver. Share responses with the whole group.

Explain that by sending "I" statements accompanied by firm and confident body language, we can act in a strong, positive, and assertive way without attacking, accusing, or blaming other people. Expressing our wants and feelings in this way protects relationships and leaves the door open for dialogue. However, even though we have sent a careful "I" message, the receiver sometimes reacts with an attack or some other defensive response. You might want to distribute the handout Why Use "I" Statements? (p. 126) as a way to review appropriate situations for making "I" statements.

List on the board or distribute as a handout Five Steps for Sending Assertive Messages (p. 127). Explain that the body language and tone of voice we use when we send "I" messages affect how they are received. Demonstrate this by asking a student to do a role-play with you. The situation is that you are telling the student something and the student is not listening. Speaking in a soft tone while looking down at the floor, you deliver the following "I" message: "I feel frustrated when you don't listen because I won't be sure that you have the information that you need. I'd like you to listen now so that I won't have to repeat it." Ask the class:

- Was this effective?
- How is the other person likely to receive it?
- Is the person likely to comply with your request?
- How could you sent the message more effectively?

Replay the situation. This time deliver the same message in a firm tone of voice, looking directly at the student. Arrange with the student who is role-playing with you that he or she will argue with you at first, denying that he or she is not listening, but finally will hear what you're saying. When the student argues with you, model using the five steps, listening actively by paraphrasing, reflecting feelings, and asking questions to look for a solution. Ask the class:

- Was this more effective?
- Why?
- How did I respond when my partner acted defensively?

Assertiveness Triads

Explain that the purpose of this activity is to practice sending "I" messages in a firm tone of voice with assertive body language and to practice the Five Steps for Sending Assertive Messages.

Copy and cut out the Assertiveness Triad Scenario Cards (p. 128) or work with students to develop original role-play scenarios. Divide the class into triads (groups of three). Distribute three cards to each group. Two members of each group will role-play a situation while the third acts as an observer. After each role-play, group members will rotate roles.

In each role-play, the student playing the sender of the "I" message should choose a card and read it to the group before they begin. During the role-play, the person playing the receiver of the "I" message should resist, but not make the situation too difficult for the person sending the "I" message. When the receiver resists, the sender should use active listening to encourage the other person to look for a solution.

There will be two minutes for each role-play and one minute for observers to make comments about what they saw. (Keep track of time for the groups.) Make sure that each person has a chance to play all three roles.

After students have performed all three role-plays, bring the group back together and ask:

- What did you experience?
- Was it difficult? What was difficult about it?
- Was this easy for some people?
- Can you see yourself trying this in a real situation?

Checking Out What We've Learned

Have each student find a partner. Use a pair-share format to discuss other "I" messages students would like to communicate to someone.

Closing (optional)

Go-Round: Appreciation messages about the group, the class, the process.

STUDENT HANDOUT

WHY USE "I" STATEMENTS?*

"I" statements help the speaker move	
from this behavior or attitude ...	**... to this behavior or attitude**
From making the assumption that I understand and can speak for someone else's motivations, concerns or experiences ...	... to realizing that I need to clarify my own motivations, concerns and experiences.
From talking about another's experiences, what they think and feel ...	... to saying what I see, feel, think, and experience.
From denying or avoiding the problem or my role in the problem ...	... to admitting mistakes and taking responsibility.
From being silent or withdrawing ...	... to making requests and suggestions and stating preferences.
From making blaming, critical "you" statements ...	... to giving assertion messages that let someone know how I feel, what's bothering me, and what I need.
From assuming simplicity, being quick to pass judgment or place blame ...	... to assuming complexity and looking within.
From saying "Yes" to everything or saying "Yes" impulsively, just going along ...	... to saying "No" when I need to and identifying my limits and boundaries, as in, "I feel uncomfortable when ...; I need ..."
From giving general praise and sweeping judgments, even when those judgments are positive, as in, "You're such a good boy," ...	... to giving specific appreciation messages, as in, "I really appreciate it when you ...; it helps me a lot."

---

* Adapted with permission from Carol Miller Lieber and Rachel Poliner, Educators for Social Responsibility, 1996.

S T U D E N T   H A N D O U T

FIVE STEPS FOR SENDING ASSERTIVE MESSAGES†

1. Prepare the "I" message. Think about it ahead of time. Talk about it with another person. It may be a good idea to practice saying it.

2. Send the message. Use body language and a tone of voice that reinforces the message.

3. Wait a moment or two. The other person may not respond immediately. When the response comes, it may be defensive—the other person may offer excuses, attack, or withdraw.

4. Listen actively to the response, paraphrasing what the other person is saying and reflecting feelings. Ask questions that encourage the other person to look for a solution. Restate the problem and ask, "What do you think would be fair? What can we both do now?"

5. Look for a solution that meets both of your needs.

Note: Depending on how the other person responds, you may need to go through the steps above several times before reaching a solution.

---

† Reprinted from *Resolving Conflict Creatively: A Draft Teaching Guide for Secondary Schools* © 1990 ESR Metropolitan Area.

ASSERTIVENESS TRIAD SCENARIO CARDS

You have been grounded for a week and will miss a concert you really wanted to attend. Make an "I" statement to your mother or father.	You got a D on a paper you worked very hard on. You think the grade is unfair. Make an "I" statement to your teacher.
There is a group at school that is constantly making fun of the slower kids in class. Make an "I" statement to one of the group members.	A friend is spreading rumors about your boyfriend/girlfriend. Make an "I" statement to this friend.
A friend copied your homework without even asking and now you're both in trouble. Make an "I" statement to your friend.	Your parents refuse to change your curfew on weekends because they're afraid you won't be safe if you stay out too late. Make an "I" statement to your mother or father.
You think that your math teacher is picking on you because you dress sort of weird and your hair has a purple streak. Make an "I" statement to your math teacher.	Your friend is always borrowing your things without asking. Make an "I" statement to him or her.
You are constantly pressured by friends to drink when you don't want to. You hate the pressure. Make an "I" statement to one of the friends who is pressuring you.	A student in one of your classes makes fun of you because you're smart and like school. Make an "I" statement to this student.
Your parents are making you go on a family trip that you think will be very boring. Make an "I" statement to one of your parents.	In American Literature you are reading books written only by white males. You'd like to read books by other groups of Americans, too. Make an "I" statement to your teacher.

LESSON 17
Defusing Someone Else's Anger

OBJECTIVES

Students will:

- identify the difference between defusion and problem solving;
- review guidelines for defusing someone else's anger;
- practice defusing someone else's anger in group role-plays.

PEACEABLE CLASSROOM PRINCIPLES

- Caring and effective communication
- Emotional literacy
- Managing and resolving conflict

AGENDA

1. **Gathering (optional)**

   Go-Round: "When I'm angry, one thing someone can do or say to help me cool down is ..."

2. **Review Agenda**

3. **Lesson Activities**

   - Introduce Defusion
   - De-escalation Role-Plays

4. **Checking Out What We've Learned**

   Students identify behaviors and verbal responses that are most effective in defusing anger.

5. **Closing (optional)**

   Go-Round: "One thing I want to remember from today's class is ..."

Gathering (optional)

Go-Round: "When I'm angry, one thing someone can do or say to help me cool down is ..."

Review Agenda

Write the agenda on the board and review it with the class.

Introduce Defusion

Introduce the concept of anger defusion as the first, essential step necessary before problem solving can begin. Using one of the Role-Play Scenario Cards (p. 131), demonstrate the process with a student. Take the role of the defuser while the student plays the angry person. Ask the group what words or actions helped defuse the student's anger. Then distribute and review the handout De-escalating Conflict (p. 132).

De-escalation Role-Plays

Explain that the class will be doing group role-plays in which a student, parent, or teacher is angry. The goal is to use communication skills to help defuse the person's anger and move the situation to a point where people feel okay or are ready to solve the problem.

Copy and cut out the Role-Play Scenario Cards. Divide the class into groups of five students. Distribute three cards to each group. Let the group decide who will play Person A (the angry person) and Person B. Other group members will act as the audience.

Have the students playing Person A read the three scenarios to their own groups and let the group choose which scenario to act out first. Give groups five minutes to rehearse their role-plays. Encourage the students playing Person A to act dramatic: yell, blame, accuse! Explain to the students playing Person B that their goal will be to defuse Person A's anger so that he or she can cool down to the point of talking calmly and, possibly, begin to do some problem solving. The audience's role is to identify what behaviors and verbal responses help de-escalate the situation.

Begin the role-plays. When each role-play is finished, allow two minutes for the audience to give feedback. What did Person B say or do that helped defuse Person A's anger? Then ask the students playing Person A to name anything that Person B said or did that helped them cool down so they could begin to solve the problem.

Have group members switch roles for the each subsequent role-play.

Checking Out What We've Learned

After all the role-plays are finished, ask students to identify the behaviors and verbal responses that were most effective for defusing someone else's anger.

Closing (optional)

Go-Round: "One thing I want to remember from today's class is ..."

ROLE-PLAY SCENARIO CARDS

The essay you just wrote fell on the floor and Person B just stepped on it.	You accuse Person B of throwing your jacket on the floor. (Person B didn't do it. It slipped off the chair.)
Person B (your sibling) borrowed your favorite sweater without asking and stretched the neck way out of shape.	Person B keeps promising to get you a job at the restaurant where she works, but never follows through.
Person B accidentally knocked your books off your desk as she was rushing to the next class.	Person B did not invite you to a big party. You thought you were good friends.
You are Person B's parent and are upset about his report card. He had said that things were going fine at school but got a D in History.	Person B always seems to be whispering about you with friends when you walk past her in the hallway.
Person B (your parent) has not apologized for picking you up late at school twice this week.	You need to miss two classes this week for a rehearsal. Person B (the teacher) has just said that you can't get out of one class.
You studied hard for a big test and got an A on it. Now Person B (your teacher) says you must have cheated to get such a good grade.	You lent Person B your car and he returned it late so that you were late for work for the second time in two weeks. Now you've been fired.
You are Person B's parent. You are angry because he didn't do the laundry yesterday and now the clothes are really piled up.	You are Person B's parent. You are angry because she got home one hour after curfew and forgot to call.
Person B always wants to know what grade you got and makes a big fuss if your grade is better than hers. You're sick of it.	One of your friends left a really important message on the phone machine. Person B (your older sibling) forgot to tell you about it.
Person B has just returned your favorite videotape and it's broken.	Person B keeps calling you an old childhood name just to bug you.

DE-ESCALATING CONFLICT

Step 1: Defuse the Anger

If you're angry:

1. Cool off by using your anger reducers.
2. Share your feelings and give an "I" message.

If the other person is angry:

1. Listen attentively while the other person vents his or her anger.
2. Don't get defensive. Stay calm. Keep your focus on the other person. Encourage him or her to keep talking.
3. Restate and reflect the other person's feelings:

   "You feel ... because ..."

   "You sound ..."

   "I can see that you're upset with me because ..."

Sometimes active listening by itself will de-escalate the conflict. If the problem remains unsolved, decide whether or when you want to solve it.

Step 2: Solve the Problem

1. Agree to solve the problem. Choose a quiet time and place.
2. Share your points of view on the problem. Use "I" messages to express how you feel and what you need. Use active listening to hear what the other person is saying.
3. Brainstorm possible solutions or next steps.
4. Choose a solution that satisfies important needs for both of you.

LESSON 18 Giving and Receiving Feedback

OBJECTIVES

Students will:

- identify the differences between praise, criticism, and feedback;
- discuss their reactions to criticism and constructive feedback;
- practice giving and receiving feedback.

PEACEABLE CLASSROOM PRINCIPLES

- Caring and effective communication
- Managing and resolving conflict
- Emotional literacy
- Personal connections

AGENDA

1. **Gathering (optional)**

   Pair-Share: Ask students to think of a time when someone brought a problem to their attention in a way that helped them make a positive change.

2. **Review Agenda**

3. **Lesson Activities**

   - Criticism vs. Feedback Exercise
   - Giving and Receiving Feedback (Mini-Lecture)
   - Criticism, Praise, or Feedback?

4. **Checking Out What We've Learned**

   Brainstorm opportunities to give and receive feedback in class.

5. **Closing (optional)**

   Popcorn-Style Sharing: Name something you like and don't like about a specific learning activity.

Gathering (optional)

Pair-Share: Ask students to think of a time when a parent, a friend, or a teacher brought a problem to their attention in a way that helped them make a positive change. Share an example from your own life, then ask volunteers to share examples with the group.

Review Agenda

Write the agenda on the board and review it with the class.

Criticism vs. Feedback Exercise

Select 15 objects of any kind. Show the objects to the class for two minutes without letting students know the goal of the exercise. Remove or cover the objects and then tell students they have two minutes to write down all the objects they can remember.

Check what students wrote down and make comments in the form of praise and criticism.

Examples:

- "You all didn't do very well."
- "Most of you didn't even remember four items!"
- "You're the only person who ... " or "You did such a great job." (Note: if you plan to single out individuals, talk to them beforehand to get their permission)

Discuss how students feel after hearing your comments. Ask for feedback on the activity (what didn't work for them and concrete suggestions that would help everyone remember all 15 objects). Record the feedback. Try the activity again, incorporating student suggestions. After you checked out how students did the second time, ask students what kind of feedback helped them the most.

Giving and Receiving Feedback (Mini-Lecture)

Present the following mini-lecture. You are welcome to use the exact words used below or to present the key ideas in your own words.

Criticism shuts us down. Criticism usually makes us feel too hurt and defensive to listen, evaluate, and assess what we're hearing. Criticism makes us feel judged as people.

Empty praise is praise that is ultimately a judgment of the doer, not the deed, and is too general. Examples of empty praise are, "You're doing great," "Excellent," and "You're terrific." Empty praise often makes us feel uncomfortable and anxious because, although the feedback is positive, we still feel that we are being judged as people.

Try to give feedback on the deed, not the doer. Effective feedback will let you give your information and opinion to someone while keeping the lines of communication open. Feedback about the deed puts the focus on what a person did or said and how he or she did it, rather than on whether the person is good or bad. Think of feedback as playing back a videotape of what just happened. Feedback also lets the other person know that you're paying attention.

Distribute and review the Feedback Sandwich handout (p. 136). Explain that good feedback begins with a positive response to the event, task, activity, or behavior under discussion. The person giving feedback can then move on to make constructive suggestions. Continue the mini-lecture.

To give feedback effectively, use concrete, specific language that indicates what you saw, heard, felt, or experienced. If you use general words like okay, great, interesting, not good enough, the receiver won't get the specific information that he or she needs. Feedback statements can begin in different ways:

- *Naming what you witnessed a person say or do.* Examples: "You made everyone in the group feel welcome by inviting them all to say something in the beginning." "You spoke loudly enough so that we could all hear you." "You found three different solutions to the problem."

- *Giving reactions from your perspective.* When someone gives us feedback, he or she is letting is know how our words and behavior affected them. For example, "I liked it when you ..." "I noticed that ..." "I observed that you ..." "I appreciated it when you ..." "It would have helped me understand better if you had ..."

When feedback is given, the receiver is in control of the data. The receiver of the feedback can assess what aspects of the feedback ring true for him or her. The receiver also decides what to do with the feedback, how to use it, and what to do next time. One way to think of it is as a package you receive in the mail. You can choose to:

- Return it to the sender because it came to the wrong address.
- Keep the package and communicate that you received it.
- Keep the package, open it, and use what's in it right away.
- Keep it on the shelf for now. You might want to use it in the future.

Criticism, Praise, Or Feedback?

Ask each student to find a partner. Read aloud the statements on the Criticism, Praise, or Feedback? handout (p. 137). After each statement, give pairs one minute to decide whether the statement is criticism, praise, or feedback.

With the whole group, brainstorm five to ten situations where criticism bothers students the most. You might suggest that students complete the sentence "I hate being criticized when ..." Then ask the same pairs to write a statement in the form of constructive feedback that could be used to give specific information that might change a specific behavior.

Checking Out What We've Learned

Brainstorm opportunities for feedback in class (for example, after tests). Ask students to suggest times in class when feedback would be more helpful than either praise or criticism. Make a commitment to provide students an opportunity to give feedback out loud or in writing several times a week.

Closing (optional)

Popcorn-Style Sharing: Name something you like and don't like about a specific learning activity in this class or another class.

S T U D E N T   H A N D O U T

THE FEEDBACK SANDWICH*

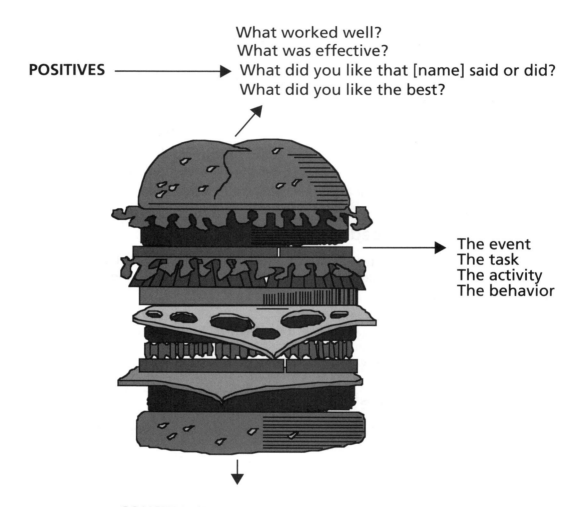

POSITIVES ⟶
What worked well?
What was effective?
What did you like that [name] said or did?
What did you like the best?

The event
The task
The activity
The behavior

CONSTRUCTIVE SUGGESTIONS

What could have made it even more effective?
What could you have done differently?
What could have made it work better?
What's one thing you would change for next time?

---

* Adapted with permission from *Dealing With Differences* by Marion O'Malley and Tiffany Davis (Chapel Hill, N.C.: Center for Peace Education, 1995).

CRITICISM, PRAISE, OR FEEDBACK?

1. Grandma told me how much she appreciated your card. She really liked the personal note you wrote on it.

2. You are such a slob. Are you sure nothing's growing in the closet?

3. I noticed that you weren't participating in discussions the last couple of days.

4. How many times do I have to tell you to put your dirty dishes in the dishwasher?

5. You really look terrific today.

6. It would work better for me if I could get my version of the story out before you asked a lot of questions.

7. I liked it much better when we got to choose our groups instead of being assigned one.

8. You need to do better next time.

9. I felt frustrated when this project took the whole week to finish instead of two periods. I'd like to check out what you're thinking about the amount of time it took.

10. You've improved a lot this week.

11. I found this project difficult to grade because it was messy.

12. I like the way you folded the laundry. It was so easy to put away.

13. No run-ons or fragments this time. It was a pleasure to read every paragraph.

LESSON
19 Point of View

OBJECTIVES

Students will:

- compare their perceptions of an ambiguous picture;
- discuss reasons behind their differing perceptions;
- read a short story and discuss each character's point of view.

PEACEABLE CLASSROOM PRINCIPLES

- Appreciation for diversity
- Managing and resolving conflict
- Emotional literacy

AGENDA

1. **Gathering (optional)**

   Mystery Package

2. **Review Agenda**

3. **Lesson Activities**
   - Old Woman/Young Woman
   - Introduction to P.O.V.
   - Soap and Water

4. **Checking Out What We've Learned**

   Share interpretations from paired discussions.

5. **Closing (optional)**

   Read parable of "The Blind Man and the Elephant."

Gathering (optional)

Mystery Package: Show a wrapped package to the class and ask students to guess what's inside. Reveal the object and ask students to share how they decided what they thought was in the package.

Review Agenda

Write the agenda on the board and review it with the class.

Old Woman/Young Woman*

Show the class the picture on p. 147 or another picture or photograph that can be interpreted in different ways depending on the feelings, perceptions, experiences, and knowledge that students bring to what they see.

Ask several students to describe what they see. Invite students who can see the picture from only one perspective to pair up with students who can see both perspectives and ask them to make suggestions that might help them see it. Then ask students what suggestions enabled them to see it. Is there a right or wrong view? Explore with students experiences they've had where two different perspectives were both right.

Introduction to P.O.V.

Explain to students that in every conflict there are different points of view (P.O.V.). Each person has a different view of the problem and has different needs and feelings.

Introduce the following scenario:

> A mother comes home from work and she is very tired. She had to work late twice this week. She wants to cook a real dinner for the family tonight and discovers that the kitchen is a mess. Her son Michael got really hungry after school and took out lots of food from the refrigerator to fix something to eat. He dropped a jar of mayonnaise on the floor and spilled some juice. He tried to clean up but the floor is still greasy and he left dirty dishes in the sink. He left all of his belongings strewn across the kitchen table and then went upstairs to work on his paper for English. He knows writing this paper will take him a long time. He's already eaten and has the rest of the night ahead of him to work.

Distribute the Points of View handout (p. 148). Ask students to identify the problem, feelings, wants, and needs of each person in the conflict. Ask students:

- What might be important to both people?
- Is there anything they can both agree on?
- When you don't understand or acknowledge the other person's point of view, what happens?
- How does this make it harder to resolve a conflict or maintain a good relationship?

---

* Reprinted with permission from *Resolving Conflict Creatively: A Draft Teaching Guide for Secondary Schools* © ESR Metropolitan Area, 1990.

Soap and Water

Distribute and read the short story "Soap and Water" by Anzia Yezierska (p. 142). After reading the story, take about five minutes to invite students to share their feelings and reactions to the story. Then ask students to form pairs in which one student takes on the perspective of Miss Whiteside and one student takes on the perspective of the narrator. For each character, students should identify:

- the problem;
- the feelings each experiences;
- the actions/behaviors that are linked to those feelings;
- the needs, wants, and concerns of the character;
- what experiences may have shaped or limited their point of view.

Checking Out What We've Learned

Come back together as a group and share interpretations from paired discussions. You might close the discussion by asking, "If Miss Whiteside had been open to listening to and understanding the narrator's point of view, what might she have said that would have encouraged the narrator to share her feelings and say more about her situation?"

Closing (optional)

Read this parable of The Wise Men and the Elephant:

Once upon a time, there were six wise men who lived together in a small town. One day, the six wise men decided to blindfold themselves for an entire day. On that day, an elephant was brought to the town. The six men wanted to see the elephant, but how could they?

"I know," said the first man. "We will feel him!"

"Good idea," said the others. "Then we will know what an elephant looks like." So the six men went to see the elephant. The first one touched the elephant's big, flat ear. He felt it move slowly back and forth. "The elephant is like a fan," the first man cried.

The second man felt the elephant's legs. "He is like a tree," he cried.

"You're both wrong," said the third man. "The elephant is like a rope." This man was feeling the elephant's tail.

Just then the fourth man pricked his hand on the elephant's sharp tusk. "The elephant is like a spear," he cried.

"No, no," cried the fifth man as he felt the elephant's side. "He's like a high wall."

The sixth man was holding the elephant's trunk. "You are all wrong," he said. "The elephant is like a snake."

"No, no, like a rope!"

"Snake!"

"Wall!"

"You're wrong!"

"I'm right!"

The six blindfolded men shouted at each other for an hour. And they never found out what an elephant is like.

S T U D E N T   H A N D O U T

SOAP AND WATER**

by Anzia Yezierska

What I so greatly feared happened! Miss Whiteside, the dean of our college, withheld my diploma. When I came to her office and asked her why she did not pass me, she said that she could not recommend me as a teacher because of my personal appearance.

She told me that my skin looked oily, my hair unkempt, and my fingernails sadly neglected. She told me that I was utterly unmindful of the little niceties of the well-groomed lady. She pointed out that my collar did not set evenly, my belt was awry, and there was a lack of freshness in my dress. And she ended with: "Soap and water are cheap. Anyone can be clean."

In those four years while I was under her supervision, I was always timid and diffident. I shrank and trembled when I had to come near her. When I had to say something to her, I mumbled and stuttered, and grew red and white in the face with fear.

Every time I had to come to the dean's office for a private conference, I prepared for the ordeal of her cold scrutiny as a patient prepares for a surgical operation. I watched her gimlet eyes searching for a stray pin, for a spot on my dress, for my unpolished shoes, for my uncared-for fingernails, as one strapped on the operating table watches the surgeon approaching with his tray of sterilized knives.

She never looked into my eyes. She never perceived that I had a soul. She did not see how I longed for beauty and cleanliness. How I strained and struggled to lift myself from the dead toil and exhaustion that weighed me down. She could see nothing in people like me, except the dirt and the stains on the outside.

But this last time when she threatened to withhold my diploma, because of my appearance, this last time when she reminded me that "Soap and water are cheap. Anyone can be clean," this last time, something burst within me.

I felt the suppressed wrath of all the unwashed of the earth break loose within me. My eyes blazed fire. I didn't care for myself, nor the dean, nor the whole laundered world. I had suffered the cruelty of their cleanliness and the tyranny of their culture to the breaking point. I was too frenzied to know what I said or did. But I saw clean, immaculate, spotless Miss Whiteside shrivel and tremble and cower before me, as I had shriveled and trembled and cowered before her for so many years.

Why did she give me my diploma? Was it pity? Or can it be that in my outburst of fury, at the climax of indignities that I had suffered, the barriers broke, and she saw into the world below from where I came?

Miss Whiteside had no particular reason for hounding and persecuting me. Personally, she didn't give a hang if I was clean or dirty. She was merely one of the agents of a clean society, delegated to judge who is fit and who is unfit to teach.

While they condemned me as unfit to be a teacher, because of my appearance, I was slaving to keep them clean. I was slaving in a laundry from five to eight in the morning, before going to college, and from six to eleven at night, after coming from college. Eight hours of work a day, outside my studies. Where was the time and the strength for the "little niceties of the well-groomed lady"?

** "Soap and Water" by Anzia Yezierska from *How I Found America: Collected Stories of Anzia Yezierska* © 1991 by Louise Levitas Henriksen. Reprinted by permission of Persea Books, Inc.

S T U D E N T   H A N D O U T

SOAP AND WATER (continued)

At the time when they rose and took their morning bath, and put on their fresh-laundered linen that somebody had made ready for them, when they were being served with their breakfast, I had already toiled for three hours in a laundry.

When the college hours were over, they went for a walk in the fresh air. They had time to rest, and bathe again, and put on fresh clothes for dinner. But I, after college hours, had only time to bolt a soggy meal, and rush back to the grind of the laundry till eleven at night.

At the hour when they came from the theater or musicale, I came from the laundry. But I was so bathed in the sweat of exhaustion that I could not think of a bath of soap and water. I had only strength to drag myself home, and fall down on the bed and sleep. Even if I had had the desire and the energy to take a bath, there were no such things as bathtubs in the house where I lived.

Often as I stood at my board at the laundry, I thought of Miss Whiteside, and her clean world, clothed in the snowy shirtwaists I had ironed. I was thinking—I, soaking in the foul vapors of the steaming laundry, I, with my dirty, tired hands, I am ironing the clean, immaculate shirtwaists of clean, immaculate society. I, the unclean one, am actually fashioning the pedestal of their cleanliness, from which they reach down, hoping to lift me to the height that I have created for them.

I look back at my sweatshop childhood. One day, when I was about sixteen, someone gave me Rosenfeld's poem "The Machine" to read. Like a spark thrown among oil rags, it set my whole being aflame with longing for self-expression. But I was dumb. I had nothing but blind, aching feeling. For days I went about with agonies of feeling, yet utterly at sea how to fathom and voice those feelings—birth-throes of infinite worlds, and yet dumb.

Suddenly, there came upon me this inspiration. I can go to college! There I shall learn to express myself, to voice my thoughts. But I was not prepared to go to college. The girl in the cigar factory, in the next block, had gone first to a preparatory school. Why shouldn't I find a way, too?

Going to college seemed as impossible for me, at that time, as for an ignorant Russian shop-girl to attempt to write poetry in English. But I was sixteen then, and the impossible was a magnet to draw the dreams that had no outlet. Besides, the actual was so barren, so narrow, so strangling, that the dream of the unattainable was the only air in which the soul could survive.

The ideal of going to college was like the birth of a new religion in my soul. It put new fire in my eyes, and new strength in my tired arms and fingers.

For six years I worked daytimes and went at night to preparatory school. For six years I went about nursing the illusion that college was a place where I should find self-expression, and vague, pent-up feelings could live as thoughts and grow as ideas.

At last I came to college. I rushed for it with the outstretched arms of youth's aching hunger to give and take of life's deepest and highest, and I came against the solid wall of the well-fed, well-dressed world—the frigid whitewashed wall of cleanliness.

Until I came to college I had been unconscious of my clothes. Suddenly I felt people looking at me at arm's length, as if I were crooked or crippled, as if I had come to a place where I didn't belong, and would never be taken in.

How I pinched, and scraped, and starved myself, to save enough to come to college! Every cent of the tuition fee I paid was drops of sweat and blood from underpaid laundry work. And what did I get for it? A crushed spirit, and broken heart, a stinging sense of poverty that I never felt before.

S T U D E N T   H A N D O U T

SOAP AND WATER (continued)

The courses of study I had to swallow to get my diploma were utterly barren of interest to me. I didn't come to college to get dull learning from dead books. I didn't come for that dry, inanimate stuff that can be hammered out in lectures. I came because I longed for the larger life, for the stimulus of intellectual associations. I came because my whole being clamored for more vision, more light. But everywhere I went I saw big fences put up against me, with the brutal signs: "No trespassing. Get off the grass."

I experienced at college the same feeling of years ago when I came to this country, when after months of shut-in-ness, in dark tenements and stifling sweatshops, I had come to Central Park for the first time. Like a bird just out from a cage, I stretched out my arms, and then flung myself in ecstatic abandon on the grass. Just as I began to breathe in the fresh-smelling earth, and lift up my eyes to the sky, a big, fat policeman, with a club in his hand, seized me, with: "Can't you read the sign? Get off the grass!" Miss Whiteside, the dean of the college, the representative of the clean, the educated world, for all her external refinement, was to me like that big, brutal policeman, with the club in his hand, that drove me off the grass.

The death-blows to all aspiration began when I graduated from college and tried to get a start at the work for which I had struggled so hard to fit myself. I soon found other agents of clean society, who had the power of giving or withholding the positions I sought, judging me as Miss Whiteside judged me. One glance at my shabby clothes, the desperate anguish that glazed and dulled my eyes and I felt myself condemned by them before I opened my lips to speak.

Starvation forced me to accept the lowest-paid substitute position. And because my wages were so low and so unsteady, I could never get the money for the clothes to make an appearance to secure a position with better pay. I was tricked and foiled. I was considered unfit to get decent pay for my work because of my appearance, and it was to the advantage of those who used me that my appearance should damn me, so as to get me to work for the low wages I was forced to accept. It seemed to me the whole vicious circle of society's injustices was thrust like a noose around my neck to strangle me.

The insults and injuries I had suffered at college had so eaten into my flesh that I could not bear to get near it. I shuddered with horror whenever I had to pass the place blocks away. The hate which I felt for Miss Whiteside spread like poison inside my soul, into hate for all clean society. The whole clean world was massed against me. Whenever I met a well-dressed person, I felt the secret stab of a hidden enemy.

I was so obsessed and consumed with my grievances that I could not get away from myself and think things out in the light. I was in the grip of that blinding, destructive, terrible thing—righteous indignation. I could not rest. I wanted the whole world to know that the college was against democracy in education, that clothes form the basis of class distinctions, that after graduation the opportunities for the best positions are passed out to those who are best-dressed, and the students too poor to put up a front are pigeon-holed and marked unfit and abandoned to the mercy of the wind.

A wild desire raged in the corner of my brain. I knew that the dean gave dinners to the faculty at regular intervals. I longed to burst in at one of those feasts, in the midst of their grand speech-making, and tear down the fine clothes from these well-groomed ladies and gentlemen, and trample them under my feet, and scream like a lunatic: "Soap and water are cheap! Soap and water are cheap! Look at me! See how cheap it is!"

S T U D E N T   H A N D O U T

SOAP AND WATER (continued)

There seemed but three avenues of escape to the torments of my wasted life: madness, suicide, or a heart-to-heart confession to someone who understood. I had not energy enough for suicide. Besides, in my darkest moments of despair, hope clamored loudest. Oh, I longed so to live, to dream my way up on the heights, above the unreal realities that ground me and dragged me down to earth.

Inside the ruin of my thwarted life, the unlived visionary immigrant hungered and thirsted for America. I had come a refugee from the Russian pogroms, aflame with dreams of America. I did not find America in the sweatshops, much less in the schools and colleges. But for hundreds of years the persecuted races all over the world were nurtured on hopes of America. When a little baby in my mother's arms, before I was old enough to speak, I saw all around me weary faces light up with thrilling tales of the far-off "golden country." And so, though my faith in this so-called America was shattered, yet underneath, in the sap and roots of my soul, burned the deathless faith that America is, must be, somehow, somewhere. In the midst of my bitterest hates and rebellions, visions of America rose over me, like songs of freedom of an oppressed people.

My body was worn to the bone from overwork, my footsteps dragged with exhaustion, but my eyes still sought the sky, praying, ceaselessly praying, the dumb, inarticulate prayer of the lost immigrant: "America! Ach, America! Where is America?"

It seemed to me if I could only find some human being to whom I could unburden my heart, I would have new strength to begin again my insatiable search for America.

But to whom could I speak? The people in the laundry? They never understood me. They had a grudge against me because I left them when I tried to work myself up. Could I speak to the college people? What did these icebergs of convention know about the vital things of the heart?

And yet, I remembered, in the freshman year, in one of those courses in chemistry, there was an instructor, a woman, who drew me strangely. I felt she was the only real teacher among all the teachers and professors I met. I didn't care for chemistry, but I liked to look at her. She gave me life, air, the unconscious emanation of her beautiful spirit. I had not spoken a word to her outside the experiments in chemistry, but I knew her more than the people around her who were of her own class. I felt in the throb of her voice, in the subtle shading around the corner of her eyes, the color and texture of her dreams.

Often in the midst of our work in chemistry I felt like crying out to her: "Oh, please be my friend. I'm so lonely." But something choked me. I couldn't speak. The very intensity of my longing for her friendship made me run away from her in confusion the minute she approached me. I was so conscious of my shabbiness that I was afraid maybe she was only trying to be kind. I couldn't bear kindness. I wanted from her love, understanding, or nothing.

About ten years after I left college, as I walked the streets bowed and beaten with the shame of having to go around begging for work, I met Miss Van Ness. She not only recognized me, but stopped to ask how I was and what I was doing.

I had begun to think that my only comrades in this world were the homeless and abandoned cats and dogs of the street, whom everybody gives another kick, as they slam the door on them. And here was one from the clean world human enough to be friendly. Here was one of the well-dressed, with a look in her eyes and a sound in her voice that was like healing oil over the bruises of my soul. The mere touch of that woman's hand in mine so overwhelmed me, that I burst out crying in the street.

S T U D E N T   H A N D O U T

SOAP AND WATER (continued)

The next morning I came to Miss Van Ness at her office. In those ten years she had risen to a professorship. But I was not in the least intimidated by her high office. I felt as natural in her presence as if she were my own sister. I heard myself telling her the whole story of my life, but I felt that even if I had not said a word she would have understood all I had to say as if I had spoken. It was all so unutterable, to find one from the other side of the world who was so simply and naturally that miraculous thing—a friend. Just as contact with Miss Whiteside had tied and bound all my thinking processes, so Miss Van Ness unbound and freed me and suffused me with light.

I felt the joy of one breathing on the mountain-tops for the first time. I looked down at the world below. I was changed and the world was changed. My past was the forgotten night. Sunrise was all around me.

I went out from Miss Van Ness's office, singing a song of new life: "America! I found America."

S T U D E N T H A N D O U T

WHAT DO YOU SEE?*

---

* Photo designed by the American psychologist E.G. Boring.

POINTS OF VIEW

LESSON 20 Positions and Underlying Needs

OBJECTIVES

Students will:

- distinguish between the positions held by people in conflict and their underlying interests;
- learn to uncover interests in order to move toward a solution.

PEACEABLE CLASSROOM PRINCIPLES

- Managing and resolving conflict
- Caring and effective communication

AGENDA

1. **Gathering (optional)**

   Putting Up a Fight

2. **Review Agenda**

3. **Lesson Activities**

   - Definitions of Positions and Interests
   - Positions and Interests Role-Play
   - Reframing

4. **Checking Out What We've Learned**

   Share a position that a friend, a teacher, or a parent has taken in a situation with you and explore the underlying interests.

5. **Closing (optional)**

   Feelings Check-In

Gathering (optional)

Putting Up a Fight (see appendix A)

Review Agenda

Write the agenda on the board and review it with the class.

Definitions of Positions and Interests

Begin the activity by writing these two statements on the board:

> "You can't go out this weekend until all your homework is done."

> "I know you've got a busy weekend. I'm concerned about whether you have scheduled enough time to do your homework."

Say, "I'm going to read these statements to you as if I were your parent." Then read the statements. Ask students, "How do you feel when you hear each statement? What's different about them? If you were the teenager involved, how would you react to each statement?"

Introduce the concepts of position and interest and present the following definitions to the class:

> A *position* is a statement of what a party demands or wants. Often it is a solution that is quick, short-term, and appears to be the easiest way to solve the problem (often at the other person's expense). A position represents one way, among many, to solve the problem and meet that person's needs. Positions are often framed as demands, "shoulds," or threats.

> An *interest* is usually the long-term need or concern underlying a position. Important needs do not go away and must be addressed in negotiated agreements. An interest is the "why" behind the position.

Divide students into pairs to do 60-second brainstorms. For each position statement you read, have pairs discuss possible interests underlying the statements.

Sample position statements:

- Parent: You've got to be home by midnight.
- Student: I deserve a passing grade. You can't fail me.
- Boy: I can't ask you to the prom.
- Parent: If he gets in your face, you get in his and fight back.
- Sibling: I don't want you around while I'm studying.
- Student: Don't ask me again about the party. I'm not going.
- Teacher: Three incomplete assignments and your grade drops five points.
- Community: Teens will be picked up by the police if they're on the streets after 11 p.m. on school nights.
- School: Students have to have a C or better in every course to play sports.
- Student: You've got to come with me to the interview tomorrow.
- Homeowner: No city is going to tell me what I can do on my property.
- School Board: We have no money to buy new text books.

Positions and Interests Role-Play

Ask two students to read the Sibling Dispute Script (p. 152). Discuss the positions and underlying interests of each character and explore what the goal might be if characters choose to solve the problem.

Getting to the Interests

Sometimes when we are in a conflict we say things in an accusatory or blaming way. To keep lines of communication open, the person on the receiving end of an accusation can choose to de-escalate the conflict by reframing confrontational remarks. Reframing is restating a remark or position by:

- uncovering underlying interests, needs, fears, and concerns
- laundering out accusations
- using neutral language
- changing negative language to positive language
- changing the orientation from past to future

Have the group practice reframing one or two examples from the handout Getting to the Interests (p. 153). Then ask students to pair up, selecting five or six examples to discuss and rewrite. Review examples from the handout with the whole group.

Checking Out What We've Learned

Share a position or demands that a friend, a teacher, or a parent has taken in a situation with you and explore what might be some of the underlying interests beneath that position.

Closing (optional)

Feelings Check-In (see appendix B)

SIBLING DISPUTE SCRIPT

Scenario: It's Saturday, early afternoon. Juan, age 17, and Clara, age 14, are siblings.

Clara: Juan, you've got to take me to my basketball practice and pick me up in two hours. I need to leave in 15 minutes.

Juan: Wait a minute! Why can't Mom take you?

Clara: She can't. I didn't tell her I needed a ride until yesterday and she'd already made plans to go to her mother's. Come on, get ready to go.

Juan: Find your own ride. Look, this is my only time to relax this weekend, and the NBA playoff is on this afternoon. I've waited all week to watch this.

Clara: Listen, Juan, you know the rules. You can drive and I can't. When you're not doing anything, and it's an emergency, Mom says you've got to help out and drive.

Juan: Look, this is your fault. You're the one who messed up by not telling Mom soon enough. Just forget the practice today.

Clara: I can't miss it or I'll get cut! This is a big deal to me. Give me a break, will you? I'm only asking this once. You've got the rest of the weekend to fool around.

Juan: Right! I have to work tonight and I've got to study for my biology exam tomorrow. And then there's your stupid play Mom is making me go see. I just want some time for myself!

Clara: You said you wanted to come see my play! I can't believe this! I'm always doing things for you. Remember the time I got you out of trouble when you missed your curfew? And the time I did your share of the housecleaning? Boy, are you a poor excuse for a human being! *(Sarcastically)* I'm sorry for living!

Juan: Oh, shut up and stop whining!

S T U D E N T   H A N D O U T

GETTING TO THE INTERESTS

For each statement, try to identify the underlying interests (needs, fears, or concerns). Make a list of possible interests that lie beneath the statement.

Write a reframed response in which you try to do one or more of the following:

- name an underlying interest
- launder out accusations
- use neutral language
- try to change negative language to positive language

Example: She can't give me that grade. It's totally unfair—and the witch won't even tell me why.

> *Interests:* Respect, fairness, understanding.

> *Reframe:* It sounds like you want a fair hearing.

1. She's such a slob. She's taken over the entire locker. I demand a new locker partner.
   Interests:
   Reframe:

2. Why do I always get stuck cleaning up? He always disappears when there's work to do. Well, I'm just not going to do it this time.
   Interests:
   Reframe:

3. I'm sick and tired of being told what to do. He can't boss me around just because he's my boyfriend.
   Interests:
   Reframe:

4. There's no way I'm going to have this paper done for that jerk by tomorrow.
   Interests:
   Reframe:

5. Right! Only one more assignment. He keeps piling it on.
   Interests:
   Reframe:

GETTING TO THE INTERESTS (continued)

6. He's such a nerd. He thinks he's so smart. He makes me sick.

    Interests:

    Reframe:

7. My mom is so stupid. She promised I could spend the weekend with Kim and now she says I can't.

    Interests:

    Reframe:

8. He's always late. I'm never going to ask him for a ride again.

    Interests:

    Reframe:

9. She is bad news. Don't trust her. She tells lies about you to everyone she knows.

    Interests:

    Reframe:

10. I don't want to work with her. She never does her share in a group and sponges off everyone else.

    Interests:

    Reframe:

Win-Win Problem-Solving

OBJECTIVES

Students will:

- explore differences between Win-Win and Win-Lose approaches to problem solving;
- identify essential features of Win-Win problem-solving;
- analyze a conflict by suggesting Win-Lose, Lose-Lose, and Win-Win solutions.

PEACEABLE CLASSROOM PRINCIPLES

- Managing and resolving conflict
- Shared decision-making

AGENDA

1. **Gathering (optional)**

   The Safety Zone Problem

2. **Review Agenda**

3. **Lesson Activities**

   - Kisses
   - Win-Win Problem-Solving and Role-Play
   - Case Studies

4. **Checking Out What We've Learned**

   Pair-Share: Share a situation that you have been thinking about in a Win-Lose way and tell your partner how you could think of it in a Win-Win way.

5. **Closing (optional)**

   Popcorn-Style Sharing: Name a problem you've had in the last six months and the steps you've taken that have helped work it out.

Gathering (optional)

The Safety Zone Problem: Set up the problem by saying there has been a catastrophe and the only way the whole class will be safe is if everyone has at least one foot inside the safety zone, a five-by-five-foot square marked off by masking tape. Let students know that no one is safe unless everyone is safe. Give students three minutes to make a plan and do it.

Review Agenda

Write the agenda on the board and review it with the class.

Kisses

Materials: Chocolate kisses

Explain that students will be playing a game called "Kisses" to explore competition and cooperation. Have two students of approximately the same strength and size sit across each from each other at a desk. Explain that each student will represent half the class in this game. Position students so that their right or left elbows are on the desk and they are clasping each other's opposite hand. This is the arm wrestling position but don't use this term. If students call it arm wrestling, explain that this game is similar, but that the rules are different.

Explain that the object of the game is for both students to win as many chocolate kisses as possible for their teams in the time allowed. The rules are as follows:

- Once the game has begun, the two players may not talk.
- Every time the back of one player's hand touches the desk, the other player wins a kiss for his or her team.
- Someone from each team needs to keep track of the number of kisses the team wins.

Say, "Begin!" Allow 30 seconds for the students to play. Students will automatically compete against each other and will probably get only a few kisses. Discuss what happened:

- What did you see?
- How many kisses did each team win?
- What was the goal of the game? Did you succeed?

Ask students if they can think of another way to play the game so that each team can get enough kisses for everyone. Have students whisper their ideas to you. When you find a person who suggests that each person take turns allowing the other to push down his hand without resisting, have that person whisper the idea to a person on the other team.

Let this pair try the game again. Allow them 30 seconds. This time, each team will probably receive enough kisses for everyone. Discuss what happened.

- What was different this time?
- How many kisses did each team win?
- Did you achieve the goal of the game?

Ask students to compare the approaches that students used. Students will often interpret what they saw the first time as a struggle against each other. Explain that the first approach resulted in a Lose-Lose situation because neither side got many kisses. Students will use words such as cooperation and working together to describe the second approach. Explain that this was a cooperative, Win-Win approach.

Explain that when we face conflicts or problems we can use Win-Lose, Lose-Lose, or Win-Win approaches.

- Think of situations in which the result was Win-Lose. How did it feel if you were the winner? The loser? (If situations are framed as Win-Lose, are there usually more winners or losers?)

- Are there some situations that seem to be Win-Lose but turn out to be Lose-Lose? (Fights and screaming matches are the most common examples.)

- Win-Win outcomes are possible when both parties agree to work out the problem so that they both get something important that they need, both feel good about the solution, and they don't hurt themselves or others. Generate examples of Win-Win outcomes that students have experienced. How was this experience different than a Win-Lose or Lose-Lose experience? How did you and the other person feel afterwards?

Win-Win Problem-Solving and Role-Play

Distribute the Win-Win Problem-Solving handout (p. 159) and review the top half.

Select a male and a female to role-play the following scenario for the class:

Varun (va-ROON) is a high school student. He has been having trouble in math class, and tomorrow there is a big test. He's in the living room studying for this test and trying to work out some problems when his little sister, Priya, comes in from school. She's had a hard day and she feels she needs to have some fun and relax. She turns on the radio and finds some music to dance to. He wants quiet. They argue.

Assign the roles and have the students begin the role-play. Freeze the action when the argument gets very heated. Ask the class to describe what's going on.

- What are Varun and Priya feeling?
- What does each person need?

Introduce the Win-Win grid on the bottom half of the Win-Win Problem-Solving handout. Each box on the grid represents a different type of solution to the conflict. Discuss the possible outcomes of the situation.

- If Varun intimidates Priya and she turns the radio off, that is a Win-Lose solution because Varun get what he needs, but Priya doesn't.

- If Varun and Priya are having a big fight when their parents get home, they both might get in trouble. That would be a Lose-Lose solution.

Ask students to provide examples of each type of solution. Then spend time thinking up as many Win-Win solutions as possible. Select one Win-Win solution suggested by the class and have the actors replay the scene so that they arrive at that solution. When they are finished, discuss how that solution worked out.

Case Studies

Use new situations to explore Win-Win, Lose-Lose, and Win-Lose solutions. Divide the class into pairs. Ask each pair to generate examples of Lose-Lose, Win-Lose, and Win-Win solutions to conflicts, identifying likely consequences of implementing each solution.

Sample situations:

1. Tonya wants to use the phone. Her sister, Lisa, has been on the phone for over an hour.

2. Michael calls Cho Min a name in the hall. Cho Min is hurt and mad.

3. You don't know how to do a very important homework assignment. If you don't get it in on time your teacher will give you a zero.

4. A friend who drove you to a party is now drunk.

5. Hillel's mother wants him to unload the dishwasher. He'd rather do anything but that!

6. Your parents want you to go visit Grandma. You've already made plans to go to the movies with two of your friends.

7. Kim is mad at Santara for not inviting her to a party. Kim is giving Santara the silent treatment.

Checking Out What We've Learned

Pair-Share: Name a situation that you have been thinking about in a Win-Lose way and tell your partner how you could think of it in a Win-Win way. Share ideas with whole group.

Closing (optional)

Popcorn-Style Sharing: Name a problem you've had in the last six months and the steps you've taken that have helped work it out.

S T U D E N T   H A N D O U T

WIN-WIN PROBLEM-SOLVING

In Win-Win problem-solving, all parties agree to work out the problem so that:

1. Both people get something that they need.
2. Both people feel good about the solution they have chosen.
3. The people involved don't hurt themselves or others.

THE WIN-WIN GRID

	Priya doesn't get what she needs.	Priya gets what she needs.
Varun doesn't get what he needs.	Lose-Lose	Lose-Win
Varun gets what he needs.	Win-Lose	Win-Win

LESSON 22 Negotiation, Mediation, and Arbitration*

OBJECTIVES

Students will:

- define negotiation, mediation, and arbitration;
- list ways they negotiate in their daily lives;
- identify the skills of a negotiator.

PEACEABLE CLASSROOM PRINCIPLES

- Managing and resolving conflict
- Personal connections

AGENDA

1. **Gathering (optional)**

   Go-Round: "A time I got something I wanted was ..."

2. **Review Agenda**

3. **Lesson Activities**

   - Defining Negotiation, Mediation, and Arbitration
   - Negotiation Microlab
   - Negotiation Skills Web

4. **Checking Out What We've Learned**

   Ask students to write a sentence that describes a current situation for which they would like to negotiate a Win-Win solution.

5. **Closing (optional)**

   Popcorn-Style Sharing: Ask students to name one thing they liked about today's lesson and one thing they would have liked to be different.

---

* Adapted with permission from *Resolving Conflict Creatively: A Draft Teaching Guide for Secondary Schools* © ESR Metropolitan Area, 1990.

Gathering (optional)

Go-Round: "A time I got something I wanted was ..."

Review Agenda

Write the agenda on the board and review it with the class.

Defining Negotiation, Mediation, and Arbitration

Write the word "negotiation" on the board and ask students for a definition. Explain that in negotiation the disputants in a conflict "talk things out." Negotiation is a process in which two or more people talk with each other in order to reach an agreement.

It may be helpful to draw the following diagram on the board:

Negotiation

Write the word "mediation" on the board and ask students for a definition. Explain that mediation differs from negotiation in that the people involved in the dispute allow a neutral third person, a mediator, to help them resolve the conflict.

If you are using diagrams, draw the following mediation diagram:

Mediation

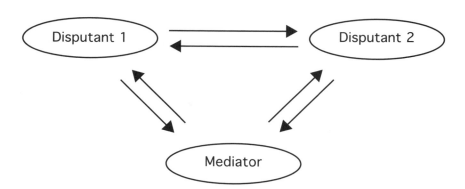

Explain that the mediator does not take sides or impose a solution on the disputants. A mediator helps the disputants reach a solution that both of them can accept.

Write the word "arbitration" on the board. Explain that this is a process in which a neutral third party imposes a binding decision. Arbitration is usually used when the disputants cannot reach an agreement themselves. Instead they agree to allow an arbitrator to impose a binding agreement on them.

Arbitration

In arbitration the disputants no longer speak to each other. Each one speaks to the arbitrator. In arbitration, disputants give up their decision-making power.

Pass out The "-Ate" Processes of Peacemaking (p. 166). Review the handout, soliciting examples of each process from the students.

Teacher's Note:

Examples of negotiation include:

Interpersonal: A teacher and student arrive a mutually acceptable schedule for the student to finish back assignments. Family members negotiate about who's going to do which chores and when.

Community: Neighborhood residents agree to let fast-food restaurants locate nearby if the restaurants build fences and plants trees and bushes to keep the neighborhood attractive. A school district agrees to develop a desegregation plan; teachers, administrators, students, and community members develop an action plan that is agreeable to all parties.

International:

> *Bilateral:* Negotiations between two parties, such as the START II (Strategic Arms Reduction) talks between the United States and the U.S.S.R.

> *Multilateral:* Negotiations involving more than two parties, such the Group of 7 talks among Canada, France, Germany, Italy, Japan, the U.K., and the United States about agricultural tariffs.

Examples of mediation include:

Interpersonal: Mediation is often used by parents and teachers in situations where siblings or students are fighting or quarreling and can't seem to work out the conflict by themselves. When parents or teachers mediate, they are ensuring that the children take responsibility for working out a solution.

Community: Mediation clinics in schools, neighborhoods, and public institutions are places where disputants can bring their differences and work out mutually agreeable solutions with the help of a neutral third party.

International: The 1978 Camp David Peace Accords between Israel and Egypt were mediated by President Jimmy Carter. Israel agreed to evacuate all its settlements in the Sinai in exchange for an Egyptian guarantee of demilitarization of the region. Both nations also agreed to full diplomatic recognition of the other.

Examples of arbitration include:

Interpersonal: Parents, principals, and teachers may be asked to play the role of arbitrator when siblings or students cannot work out their differences by themselves or with a mediator. Yet parents and teachers more often play the role of self-appointed arbitrator, rarely asking beforehand if the disputants have agreed to the idea of having a binding decision imposed on them.

Community: Referees at sports events are arbitrators, although we seldom think of them this way. Arbitration is most commonly used in settling labor and other business disputes.

International: Arbitration is uncommon in disputes among nations, however, many diplomats feel that arbitration has a promising future in settling international conflicts such as boundary disputes, fishing rights, and treaty violations (with neutral nations serving as arbitrators).

Negotiation Microlab

Divide the class into groups of three or four. Each group should choose one person to be the group's reporter.

In the small groups, each student has two minutes to address the following questions. Reporters should be prepared to report what people say to the class.

- When have you negotiated with a friend or family member?
- What was the solution? How did you feel about the solution?

Ask reporters for the types of negotiations that were mentioned and list them on the board or on chart paper.

Negotiation Skills Web

Explain that although all of us negotiate something every day, some of us are better at it than others. It's a skill, or, rather, a set of skills that can be improved by practice.

Using basketball as an analogy, ask students to think of elements of the game (for example, offense, defense, foul shooting, dribbling, passing, running, jumping, shooting). Make a web chart using the word "basketball." Ask students to think of skills, knowledge, or personal qualities a person needs to be a good basketball player. Move along quickly, spending no more than two minutes creating this web chart.

Using a musical instrument as an analogy, ask students to think of some of the skills, knowledge, or personal qualities you would have to have to be a good trombone player.

Now ask the class to think of the skills, knowledge, and personal qualities involved in being a good negotiator. Develop a web chart based on the students' answers. If students fail to mention important skills such as listening well, being aware of people's feelings, communicating clearly, being able to think of creative solutions, and being able to remain neutral, add them yourself.

Checking Out What We've Learned

Distribute one index card to each student. Ask students to write a sentence that describes a current situation for which they would like to negotiate a Win-Win solution.

Closing (optional)

Popcorn-Style Sharing: Ask students to name one thing they liked about today's lesson and one thing they would have liked to be different.

S T U D E N T   H A N D O U T

THE "-ATE" PROCESSES OF PEACEMAKING

	Who controls decisions?	Who controls the process?	What is the emphasis: the relationship or the problem?
Negotiate—Both parties agree to try to solve the problem by themselves. Disputants share their important needs and interests, identify common interests, and agree to explore solutions that are different from each party's original demands.	Disputants	Disputants	Relationship and problem
Mediate—Conflicting parties agree to work out a problem but request assistance from a neutral third party. Mediators do not judge who is right and who is wrong and do not tell parties what to do. Rather, mediators use a step-by-step process that enables parties to hear each others' concerns and interests so that they can discover possible solutions that are mutually agreeable. The disputants come up with their own solutions and decide how to make them work.	Disputants	Neutral third party	Relationship and problem
Arbitrate—Disputing parties agree to allow a neutral third party to hear both sides a make a decision that disputants must honor. Disputants can choose the arbitrator and set the framework and conditions of the arbitration.	Neutral third party	Neutral third party	The problem

LESSON 23 Group Negotiation Practice

OBJECTIVES

Students will:

- review features of effective negotiations;
- use the problem-solving process in a group negotiation to come to a shared decision that everyone agrees is a good solution.

PEACEABLE CLASSROOM PRINCIPLES

- Managing and resolving conflict
- Caring and effective communication
- Cooperation and collaborative problem-solving
- Shared decision-making

AGENDA

1. **Gathering (optional)**

   Go-Round: What's something you're good at that ends in "-ing"?

2. **Review Agenda**

3. **Lesson Activity**

   - Group Negotiation

4. **Checking Out What We've Learned**

   What do you want to remember about this process? What did you learn about yourself? In what situations might this process be helpful?

5. **Closing (optional)**

   Go-Round: Share a new idea or awareness from today's class.

Gathering (optional)

Go-Round: What's something you're good at that ends in "-ing"?

Review Agenda

Write the agenda on the board and review it with the class.

Group Negotiation

Explain to students that they will be working in groups of five, using a group negotiation process to reach agreement on a solution to a problem.

Divide the class into groups of five. Ask each group to choose one of the three negotiation problems listed in the chart on the following page. Review the roles listed below and give groups two minutes to decide who will be responsible for carrying out each responsibility.

Roles:

- A *recorder* who jots down relevant notes in each conversation round.
- A *facilitator* who makes sure that everyone gets his/her say without being interrupted.
- A *summarizer* who clarifies areas of agreement.
- A *reporter* who will share what you decided with other groups at the end of the exercise.
- A *process observer* who checks out how the group is practicing the process.

Explain that each group will participate in four rounds of conversation in order to reach final agreement. It's important to remind students of two things:

- Listen for specific instructions for each round.
- Stay with the specific task in each round rather than jumping ahead in the process.

Before groups begin the process, ask each student to write down her first-choice solution, the idea that appeals most to her, and to jot down a couple of reasons why she prefers this idea to any other.

Round #1: In a "go-round," each student shares her idea with the rest of the group and says something about why she prefers this solution to any other. Remind students that in a "go-round" each person gets a turn to share ideas. When they are not speaking their role is to listen. Ask them not to interrupt or engage in conversation. Remind the recorder to take notes!

Round #2: In another "go-round," each student shares his underlying positions (fundamental needs and concerns) and his "bottom lines" (the things that are nonnegotiable). Again, make sure the recorder takes notes.

> *Problem A:*
>
> - underlying positions: the things that would make the trip a real vacation for you (e.g., your preferences in climate, landscape, characteristics of the location, activities you want to do, special events you want to experience, food, etc.)
> - "bottom line": those things that would make a vacation unpleasant, unattractive, uncomfortable—your "no's" about climate, landscape, activities, food, etc.
>
> *Problem B:*
>
> - underlying positions: those things that would make this school gift count for something—what concerns or needs would you want this gift to meet?
> - "bottom line": any projects, resources, or equipment that are "no's" for you.

Problem C:

- underlying positions: the teen issues that matter most to you—in what way would you want this donation to improve the lives of teenagers?
- "bottom line": any projects or organizations that are "no's" for you.

THREE NEGOTIATION PROBLEMS

A. The Vacation Negotiation	B. School Gift Negotiation	C. Community Donation Negotiation
Your group has received a two-week all-expenses-paid vacation to any place in the world.	Your group is to make a recommendation to the school board for spending a $25,000 anonymous gift given to your school.	Your school has raised $5,000 to be used to better your local community. You need to decide what community project or organization will receive the donation.
Conditions: Your whole group must stay at the location you choose for the whole two weeks, although you may take day trips by yourselves or in smaller groups.	Conditions: The gift must benefit at least 10 percent of the student population in some significant way.	Conditions: The donation must benefit teens who are experiencing some difficulty growing up.
As a group you need to agree on: • the specific place you will go; • three ways in which this choice meets some important interests of everyone in your group; • the transportation you will take to travel there; • the transportation you will use to return home.	As a group you need to agree on: • one project, resource, or piece of equipment that the school will purchase or fund; • how this gift will benefit the student population; • three reasons why this is the best choice; • three ways in which this choice meets some of the interests of everyone in your group.	As a group you need to agree on: • the community project or organization that will receive the donation; • how this donation will benefit troubled teens; • three reasons why this is the best choice; • three ways in which this choice meets some interests of everyone in the group.

Round #3: Ask the summarizer and the recorder in each group to clarify areas of agreement. What are the common interests?

Round #4: Ask the facilitator to help the group to:

- Brainstorm solutions that meet the common interests of the group. Do this without arguing or discussing the ideas. Just make a quick list.
- Evaluate solutions assessing how each idea meets the interest of the group.
- Choose a Win-Win solution that works for everyone:
  - a solution that meets some important needs and interests of everyone in the group;
  - a solution that people feel good about;
  - a solution that meets the conditions identified at the beginning of the process.

Ask reporters to share their group's decision, responding to all the questions listed in the Three Negotiation Problems chart.

Ask the process observers to describe what happened in their groups.

- What did you notice about how your group used the process?
- What seemed challenging or easy for people as they practiced the process?

Invite anyone to respond to these questions:

- If your final decision was not one of the original ideas, how did you arrive at this final decision?
- How did this process work for your group? For you? What was hard for you to do? What was easy for you to do? What did your group do well?
- Any suggestions for what your group might do differently to be more effective next time?

Checking Out What We've Learned

What do you want to remember about this process? What did you learn about yourself? In what situations might this process be helpful?

Closing (optional)

Go-Round: Share a new idea or new awareness from today's class.

LESSON 24 Interpersonal Negotiation

OBJECTIVES

Students will:

- learn a problem-solving process;
- explore qualities and skills essential for effective negotiation;
- practice negotiating.

PEACEABLE CLASSROOM PRINCIPLES

- Managing and resolving conflict
- Caring and effective communication

AGENDA

1. **Gathering (optional)**

   Choose any gathering activity from appendix A.

2. **Review Agenda**

3. **Lesson Activities**

   - Demonstration of Interpersonal Negotiation
   - The Negotiation Process Step by Step
   - Negotiation Triads

4. **Checking Out What We've Learned**

   Debrief the role-play triads: What did students find easy, useful, or challenging?

5. **Closing (optional)**

   Ask students to write a sentence that begins, "In my own life, I could use this process to ..."

Gathering (optional)

Choose any gathering activity from appendix A.

Review Agenda

Write the agenda on the board and review it with the class.

Demonstration of Interpersonal Negotiation

Use the Sibling Dispute Script (Lesson 20) to demonstrate interpersonal negotiation. Have two students read the script again and then pose the following questions to the class:

1. How could Clara begin the conversation differently, in a way that will encourage her brother to do some problem solving with her?

2. What needs and interests of each person must be considered when choosing the best solution?

3. Are there any interests they both share in this situation?

Write students' suggestions on the board.

Ask two volunteers to role-play the situation again, using the group's suggestions and trying to develop a solution. After they have finished, ask the group to identify communication and negotiation skills that helped the role-players reach a mutually satisfactory solution.

The Negotiation Process Step by Step

Distribute and review carefully The Negotiation Process (p. 174).

Negotiation Triads

Ask the class to form triads (groups of three). Ask each triad to choose three role-plays from the Negotiation Triad Conflicts handout (p. 176), or have them create their own conflict situations. In each role-play, two people will play the two principal roles and try to negotiate a solution to the conflict. The third person will act as an observer. The observer will give feedback to the role-players on their use of communication skills.

They should also make suggestions about what each disputant could have said that would have helped in the negotiation process. Distribute the Feedback Checklist (p. 175) to each student for use when acting as an observer.

For each role-play, ask students to decide who will play each of the two principal roles and who will be the observer. Allow five minutes for each role-play. Allow three minutes after each role-play for the observers to give their feedback. After each group has done three role-plays, provide two minutes for students to share their feedback with the whole group. Ask the whole class, "What did you notice actors doing that helped them to negotiate effectively?"

Checking Out What We've Learned

Debrief the role-plays. In practicing negotiation skills, what did students find easy, useful, challenging, etc.?

Closing (optional)

Pass out index cards, and ask students to write a sentence that begins, "In my own life, I could use this process to ..."

THE NEGOTIATION PROCESS

1. **Acknowledge that there's a conflict and agree to solve it.**

   At least one disputant needs to start the process by acknowledging the conflict and initiating the first conversation. This calls for a certain amount of self-awareness and "tuning in." If you are already feeling too emotionally charged, acknowledge it and then try to use techniques to calm down. If this is impossible, postpone dealing with the conflict until your emotions are more settled. If you're both ready to talk it out, agree on the problem that you want to solve right now.

2. **Define the problem and share points of view.**

   a. Each disputant shares his or her perception of the problem and states feelings, wants, and needs openly and honestly.

   b. Each disputant restates what the other person has said (right after the other person says it).

   c. Try to get to the underlying issues and concerns that have caused the conflict.

   d. Identify common interests and goals that will help you work it out together.

3. **Brainstorm solutions.**

   List all ideas, practical and impractical, that might resolve the conflict. Do not evaluate ideas at this point. Criticism now will only stop the creative flow of ideas. Ask questions about how each of you could make some changes and meet some of the other person's needs. ("What about ...? Could we ...? What if I ... and you ...? What can we do to make sure that you can ... and I can ...?") Think about trade-offs and "my turn/your turn" options.

4. **Evaluate solutions.**

   Consider the consequences of each possible solution. Which ones are most realistic and responsible? What constraints or limitations make some solutions more impractical than others? Discard ideas that have little chance of success or those that are too costly in terms of time, resources, or personal energy.

5. **Choose a solution.**

   The question to keep asking is, "Does this solution satisfy both of us? Does it meet some important needs for both of us?" It is crucial that both parties agree on the solution and feel good about the process used to reach it.

6. **Implement your solution.**

   What is the plan for putting the solution into action? Specify who should do what, when, where, and how. How will you know if it's working? It can be helpful to write down your plan. Set a time later to evaluate how your plan worked.

CONGRATULATE YOURSELVES ON A JOB WELL DONE!

S T U D E N T   H A N D O U T

FEEDBACK CHECKLIST

As the observer, look for communication skills that help the negotiation process. Did the role-players:

_____ Restate what the other person said?

_____ Reflect the feelings of the other person?

_____ Ask creative questions that help disputants better understand the problem and the points of view?

_____ Use encouraging phrases that invite the other person to talk?

_____ Use attending behaviors that show that the listener is really listening?

_____ Use summarizing statements that help to clarify the problem and possible solutions?

_____ State specific details (what, where, when, and how) that will help disputants implement their chosen solution?

Observers should also make suggestions about what each disputant could have said that would have helped in the negotiation process.

S T U D E N T   H A N D O U T

NEGOTIATION TRIAD CONFLICTS

Time: Friday, around 5:30 pm

Teenager: You and three friends have made plans to go to the mall for pizza and a movie tonight at 6 p.m. You've helped make all the arrangements in advance. Your dad is driving you there and another mom is going to take you all home. You've had a good week at school, your room is spotless, and you've done the laundry. And you've stayed out of fights with your siblings.

Mother: You just got home from work to find a phone message that your aunt has fallen ill and is having emergency surgery. Your husband is going straight to the hospital from work and you need to go to your aunt's house to take care of your uncle. You want your teenager to stay home and baby-sit your two younger children and fix them dinner.

Time: One week before a planned party

16-year-old: You want to have a party but are embarrassed about having your mother around. The other kids will laugh at you for it. You especially want to feel equal to your new friend, Rachel. She recently had a party with no parents present and all went well.

Mother: You are a single parent of an only child. You are concerned that there might be alcohol and drug use at the party, and too much making out. You have a friend who was killed recently by a drunk driver who was leaving a party. Your 16-year-old has not been acting very responsible lately: in the last three weeks she has not done her chores as agreed and has stayed out past curfew twice. Can she be trusted?

Time: One week before the prom

Student: Last weekend you confided to your best friend that you were thinking about breaking up with your boy/girlfriend after the prom. When you went to lunch on Monday and saw your boy/girl friend, he or she refused to even look at you. When you got in line to get your lunch several other kids asked about your breakup. You hadn't told anyone else and you're really upset with your friend because you rarely share secrets and you don't have many close friends. You also want the prom not to be a disaster.

Best friend: You only told one person about the breakup, and only because this other person asked why your friend was looking so down lately. You only said that he or she was thinking about breaking up and the story just kept going. You feel upset, too.

S T U D E N T   H A N D O U T

NEGOTIATION TRIAD CONFLICTS (continued)

Time: Lunch period

Student: You have been on overload for the last month with play rehearsals and a family crisis, and now you've got a cold that won't go away. You're behind in your assignments and you haven't begun to do your research for a project due next week. You want to work out a schedule to complete your assignments and you want to turn in your project a week late so that you can do a good job on the research.

Teacher: You have a homework policy that all the students know. Late assignments are worth 5 points instead of 10, with no exceptions. On the other hand, students can do additional assignments to receive additional points. You're reluctant to agree on a later deadline for the project because you worry that the student will only procrastinate and put off doing the work. To change a deadline you need to know that steps are being taken to complete the project throughout the next two weeks. You want the student to be able to do a good job and you're worried how other students will feel about changing deadlines.

Time: Saturday afternoon

Older sibling: You like to keep things neat in your room, and you like to invite friends over to listen to music and hang out. You told your younger sibling last night that you were inviting a friend over tomorrow and expected the room to be cleaned up. Your friend is coming over in half an hour and the other side of the room is still a mess. Your sibling spent the whole morning watching TV and now you feel stuck. You want to work out a deal for right now and you want to make an agreement about how to keep the room neat and organized in the future.

Younger sibling: You hate it when your sibling nags you about the mess because it always ends up in a fight. You also hate cleaning up by yourself. It's just too boring. And you resent that your sibling has friends over and kicks you out of your room. You'd be willing to clean up more if there were some way you can do it together. You would also like it if sometimes you could stay in the room when your sibling's friends come over.

LESSON 25 Introduction to Mediation *

OBJECTIVES

Students will:

- review the definitions of mediation and arbitration;
- identify examples of mediation;
- observe and analyze the mediation process.

PEACEABLE CLASSROOM PRINCIPLES

- Managing and resolving conflict
- Caring and effective communication
- Cooperation and collaborative problem-solving
- Shared decision-making

AGENDA

1. **Gathering (optional)**

   Go-Round: What do you usually do when you see friends or family arguing or fighting?

2. **Review Agenda**

3. **Lesson Activities**

   - Review the Definitions of Mediation and Arbitration
   - Mediation: Discussion and Demonstration

4. **Checking Out What We've Learned**

   On index cards, ask students to list two or three things they think are most important for the mediator to say or do in the mediation process.

5. **Closing (optional)**

   Choose any closing activity in appendix B.

---

* Adapted with permission from *Resolving Conflict Creatively: A Draft Teaching Guide for Secondary Schools* © ESR Metropolitan Area, 1990

Gathering (optional)

Go-Round: What do you usually do when you see friends or family arguing or fighting?

Review Agenda

Write the agenda on the board and review it with the class.

Review the Definitions of Mediation and Arbitration

Ask students to define mediation and arbitration. (Students learned these terms in Lesson 22.)

> *Mediation*—a process in which the disputants allow a neutral third person, the mediator, to help them develop a solution to the conflict. The mediator does not take sides or impose a solution on the disputants. A mediator helps the disputants reach a solution that they both can accept.

> *Arbitration*—a process in which a neutral third party imposes a binding decision. Arbitration is usually used when the disputants cannot reach an agreement themselves. Instead they agree to allow an arbitrator to impose a binding agreement on them.

Mediation: Discussion and Demonstration

Ask students if they have seen a situation where someone helped others settle a conflict or if they have been in an argument where someone tried to help them. Generate a list of examples in which a mediator helps individuals or groups resolve a conflict (e.g., personal experiences, television, movies, politics, history, community conflicts, etc.).

Write the word "mediator" on the board. Ask students to suggest what qualities a person needs to be a good mediator (e.g., listens well, is fair, is creative).

Introduce the basic steps of mediation on The Mediation Process handout (Lesson 26). Ask two students to help you role-play the following situation (or use one you have invented based on common conflicts in your classroom) to demonstrate the process. You, the teacher, will play the role of the mediator.

Scenario:

> Carla is Tom's older sister. She is often left in charge of taking care of the house because their mother works long hours. Carla and Tom argue about household chores. Carla thinks Tom doesn't do his share of the work. Sometimes she does his chores. Tom thinks Carla is a nag. He says he would do more if she would stay off his back. Also, Carla doesn't approve of Tom's friends. Some of them were picked up for shoplifting and she's heard that some of them are into drugs. Tom's friends are important to him.

In the role-play, act out all the steps of mediation through the successful resolution of the conflict. Remember to instruct the actors to go along with your mediation efforts rather than resist them.

After the demonstration, ask the class:

- What was the conflict about?
- What did each person want? What feelings did each person bring to the mediation?
- How did the solution meet important needs of both parties?
- Who came up with the solution?
- What questions helped the disputants reach a good solution?

Ask students to find partners. Give the pairs three minutes to list the sequence of steps they saw and heard in the mediation demonstration, from beginning to end. Ask a few students to share their step-by-step sequences. Let students know that they will be learning more about the mediation process and practicing it in the next class.

Checking Out What We've Learned

On index cards, ask students to write what two or three things they think are most important for the mediator to say or do in the mediation process. Collect the cards and read them out loud.

Closing (optional)

Choose any closing activity from appendix B.

LESSON
26 Mediation Practice*

OBJECTIVES

Students will:

- review the mediation process;
- develop criteria for a good resolution of a conflict;
- practice creative questioning in a fish-bowl role-play;
- participate in a practice mediation.

PEACEABLE CLASSROOM PRINCIPLES

- Managing and resolving conflict
- Shared decision-making
- Caring and effective communication
- Mutual respect

AGENDA

1. **Gathering (optional)**

    Concentric Circles

2. **Review Agenda**

3. **Lesson Activities**

    - Review the Mediation Process
    - Fish-Bowl Role-Play (optional)
    - Mediation Practice

4. **Checking Out What We've Learned**

    On index cards, students answer two questions in writing: What's something you learned about the mediation process and about yourself as a mediator? What questions do you still have about the process?

5. **Closing (optional)**

    Students trade index cards with each other and read them to the group.

---

* Adapted with permission from *Resolving Conflict Creatively: A Draft Teaching Guide for Secondary Schools* © ESR Metropolitan Area, 1990.

Gathering (optional)

Concentric Circles: Divide students into two concentric circles. Have each student in the outer circle face a partner in the inner circle. Explain that you will call out a topic for the students in one circle to speak on and a listening skill for their partners in the other circle to practice. All pairs of partners will practice simultaneously. After about a minute the round will end and the outer circle will move one person to the right so that students have new partners. Below are sample topics, listening skills, and a pattern for the activity.

> Inside wheel: What do you do that makes your parents really upset?
>
> Outside wheel: Practice paraphrasing/restating.
>
> *Change partners*
>
> Outside wheel: What makes a good friend?
>
> Inside wheel: Practice attending skills (nonverbal ways of showing that you are listening).
>
> *Change partners*
>
> Inside wheel: What three things do you want to do before you are 25 years old?
>
> Outside wheel: Practice summarizing.

Review Agenda

Write the agenda on the board and review it with the class.

Review the Mediation Process

Distribute The Mediation Process handout (p. 187). Ask students to read aloud steps one through four. After each step is read, ensure that the students understand the step through a brief discussion as follows:

> Step 1: Discuss the issue of when to intervene (e.g., not in the middle of a physical fight). Some issues to consider are: Am I the right person? Do I know one party better than the other? Can I assist without taking sides? Will both parties let me assist? Is it the right time to intervene? Are the parties relatively calm? Do we have enough time? Is this the right place?
>
> Ask students for ideas about how they might present the idea of mediation to friends who are having a conflict.
>
> Remind students that it is always the disputants' choice whether or not to accept intervention. Ask how students would feel if they approached friends in a conflict, offered help, and the friends said, "No." What would they do?
>
> Step 2: Discuss the importance of privacy. Ask why it is important to move to a private area. What would be the effect of doing the intervention in a public place?
>
> Step 3: Inform students that neutrality, or not taking sides, is a cornerstone of the mediation process. Ask students how the mediation process would be affected if either disputant felt that a mediator was taking sides. What kinds of statements or questions would signal to disputants that the mediators were taking sides? If you were a disputant, what would let you know that a mediator was not taking sides?
>
> Step 4: Ask students what they think are the reasons for these rules. What would be the result of not having these rules? What would they do if the disputants didn't agree to

observe the rules? If a disputant agrees to the rule and subsequently breaks it, what should a mediator do?

Steps 5-16: Remind students that a mediator does not impose solutions. At Step 12 explain that any conflict can be solved in lots of ways but that some solutions are better than others. Help students develop some criteria for a good resolution. Ask, "What are the characteristics of a good agreement?"

Some guidelines for a good solution are:

- Are both disputants satisfied that this is a fair solution?
- Is the resolution complete? Does it tell who will do what, when, where, and how?
- Is the resolution balanced? Do both disputants share responsibility for making it work?

Fish-Bowl Role-Play (optional)

Ask two students to volunteer to role-play a dispute. You, the teacher, will be the mediator. Have the class form a circle around the students doing the role-play. (This is called a "fish bowl.") Choose one of the situations on the Mediation Role-Plays handout (p. 190) to role-play. Review the conflict, making it clear that both parties have agreed to accept the help of a third party. Since in the course of the role-play you will be involving the class in asking questions to help find a solution, privately tell the students that you don't want an easy settlement. In the role-play, when you ask them whether they have any ideas for what they could do right now to solve the problem, make sure they say, "No." You will then ask the class for questions to help the disputants. Tell the actors to stay in their roles and try to think about how their character would respond to the questions.

Role-play the situation with the students, beginning at Step 5 and continuing through Step 11. Then freeze the action and turn to the class. Tell them, "You are all now mediators of this conflict. What would you say to these disputants to help them find a solution?" Ask for volunteers to approach the disputants with questions one at a time. Record the questions asked.

Write the questions on a chart or on the board. Continue to have volunteers create questions until the large group of mediators has led the disputants to a solution. Review the list of questions and ask which questions seemed to be the most effective for this pair of disputants.

Ask the students in the role-play how their characters are feeling right now and how they themselves are feeling. Invite the class to give positive feedback to the role-players for the work they did.

Ask the class which solutions came closest to meeting the criteria for a good solution set up at the beginning of the class.

Mediation Practice

Divide the class into groups of four to practice mediation. Give each group a Mediation Role-Play and the A Skillful Mediator... handout (p. 189). In each group, two students will be the disputants, one person will be the mediator, and one will be the observer. Ask each group to choose who will play each role.

Read and review A Skillful Mediator ... Encourage the observers to write down their feedback, using the Feedback Sandwich (Lesson 18) as a way to name what they saw and heard that seemed effective and give any suggestions they might have for the mediator. Remind the disputants to act realistic but not to be completely unreasonable.

Let students know they have about 15 minutes for the mediation and about 3 minutes for the mediator and the disputants to discuss what they experienced.

From the mediator's perspective: What went well? What was challenging for me? Is there anything I might have done differently?

From the disputants' perspective: How did it feel to have a mediator help me? How was it helpful? What did the mediator say or do that helped us reach agreement? Were there any points in the mediation where it would have been helpful if the mediator had used different language, asked different questions, or shifted the process in a different direction?

The observer then has two minutes to give feedback.

If time allows, have group members switch roles and repeat the mediation practice using a new situation.

Checking Out What We've Learned

Give each person two index cards of different colors. Tell students not to write their names on their cards. On one, ask students to write their answer to the question, "What's something you learned about the mediation process or about yourself as a mediator?" On the second card, have them answer, "What questions do you still have about the process?"

Closing (optional)

Have the students trade index cards with each other and read them to the group.

S T U D E N T   H A N D O U T

THE MEDIATION PROCESS

Setting the stage:

1. Ask those involved in the conflict if they would like your help solving the problem. Get agreement on this.

2. Find a quiet place to do the mediation.

3. Explain that you will help them come up with their own solution. You won't take sides or give advice or tell them how to solve the problem.

4. Ask the disputants to agree that they will:

   - try to solve the problem;
   - not engage in name calling or personal attacks;
   - not interrupt when the other person is speaking;
   - be as honest as they can;
   - keep confidential everything that is said during this mediation.

Getting the stories out:

5. Ask disputant 1, "What happened?" After he or she has finished, restate what was said and ask clarifying questions, such as "How did you feel?" Show that you are listening by reflecting back.

6. Ask disputant 2, "What happened?" After he or she has finished, restate what was said and ask clarifying questions, such as "How did you feel?" Show that you are listening by reflecting back.

7. Ask each disputant to restate how the other person feels and why.

8. Ask each disputant what he or she needs to feel that the conflict is resolved.

9. Ask, "Is there anything else?" Then summarize the whole problem, including key facts and feelings that have been shared by both disputants. Identify common interests and concerns and anything that both disputants feel is important to remember as they work out a solution.

Brainstorming solutions:

10. Ask disputant 1, "What can you do here and now to help solve the problem?" Encourage him or her to be specific. Restate what disputant 1 says.

11. Ask disputant 2, "What can you do here and now to help solve the problem?" Encourage him or her to be specific. Restate what disputant 2 says.

    If they get stuck, ask, "What would you tell someone else to do who had a similar problem? How would this solution work? Can you think of something else you could do? Can you say more about your idea?"

THE MEDIATION PROCESS (continued)

Resolution:

12. Help the disputants reach a solution that works for both of them. Help them make the solution specific. Who does what, when, where, how?

13. Restate the solution and all of its parts to disputants 1 and 2.

14. Ask each person individually if he or she agrees to the solution they have chosen.

15. Ask both disputants, "What can you each do differently if this happens again?" Restate their ideas.

16. Congratulate them on a successful mediation.

S T U D E N T   H A N D O U T

A SKILLFUL MEDIATOR ...

Sets the stage for building trust by:

- not taking sides
- being respectful
- using language that avoids judgment, advice, and blame
- listening carefully
- showing understanding

Helps disputants get their stories out by exploring:

- how people know each other
- what happened
- why it happened
- how people feel
- what people need
- what is important to both people

Helps disputants brainstorm solutions by:

- encouraging flexibility and give-and-take
- restating important needs
- asking "what if" questions ("What if he agrees to ...? Would you be willing to ...?)
- looking for trade-offs

Helps disputants reach resolution by:

- restating positive things you hear from both disputants
- summarizing progress
- getting agreement on specifics (who does what, when, where, how?)
- using positive language to summarize agreement

S T U D E N T   H A N D O U T

MEDIATION ROLE-PLAY 1: "THE MONEY PROBLEM"

Colby: You borrow money from friends a lot. Your family expects you to pack something for lunch, which you don't do very often because you don't want to have to bring your lunch to school. Your family gives you snack money, but you're always short on cash if you want a real lunch. You owe money to several kids and it will take you a while to pay them all back. You have not told your parents that you don't bring a lunch to school because you're afraid it will just cause another fight over money. You did borrow $3.00 from Ricky, but now you insist it was only one dollar. You thought you could convince him that this was the right amount, and you didn't expect Ricky to keep bugging you about the money and blow up in first period today.

Ricky: You lent $3.00 to Colby for lunch three days ago. You don't see yourself as being too popular and you have more money than a lot of other kids, so you sometimes lend money as a way to make friends. You thought Colby was a real friend. So when she swore you'd only given her $1.00, you were angry and hurt. You felt she'd taken advantage of you. You complained to another friend, who told you that Colby borrows money from other kids too and doesn't always pay it back. You want to think that Colby is your friend and would pay back the money willingly. Then you wouldn't feel so stupid.

MEDIATION ROLE-PLAY 2: "FLIRTING FABLE"

Lisa: A boy that you kind of like has been hanging around you in classes. You didn't say anything to your friend, Quiana, but you know she noticed that he was paying attention to you. You had hoped that he would ask you to go to the movies with him. Instead, Quiana moved in and started flirting with this boy and invited him to a video party this past weekend. You made a big scene in front of other girls in the bathroom and accused Quiana of being desperate and a "wanna-be," moving in on this boy just because he was paying attention to you. You were very upset and also said, "I bet you did more than make out with him, too!" which the other girls heard loud and clear. You knew you went too far after you said it, but there was no way to take it back. You're also hurt that you weren't invited to the video party. You're willing to talk this through because you want to remain friends.

Quiana: You know this boy was paying attention to your friend, Lisa, but she never said anything to you about him. You've been friends for a really long time and tell each other most stuff, so you thought since she hadn't said anything that she wasn't really interested in him. You were jealous of the attention she was getting, too. You were invited to the video party last weekend and you were asked to invite Lisa. You asked if you could invite someone else instead. So you sat next to this boy in math class and worked on some homework together and then you invited him, and he said yes. You met him at the party, but didn't really hang out alone together. The party was fun, but nothing happened between the two of you. When Lisa accused you of being a "wanna-be," it was partially true. You did want the attention. But when she accused you of messing around with him, you felt hurt, betrayed and embarrassed in front of the other girls in the bathroom. You want a total apology before you will even consider being friends again.

S T U D E N T   H A N D O U T

MEDIATION ROLE-PLAY 3: "AFTER THE SUSPENSION"

Michael: Sondra and you have been rehearsing a dance piece together and she's been getting on your case for some time now. She's been really demanding of your time and you've had it. You and Sondra got into a fight at the lockers the other day. You were suspended. You are angry and not talking to Sondra. You want to forget about the dance piece altogether.

Sondra: Michael and you have been rehearsing for a dance contest for a few weeks now. You have been angry with him because he hasn't shown up to a couple of rehearsals. The other day you yelled at him and threw your books at him by the lockers. He pushed you, was seen by a teacher and was suspended. You're angry about his attitude and that he pushed you but wish he'd talk to you again. You still want to rehearse together and present the dance piece at the assembly.

MEDIATION ROLE-PLAY 4: "STUDY PARTNER PROBLEMS"

Marianna: Carrie and you are friends and study together. Yesterday you made up a set of note cards to study for the history test today. Carrie had asked to keep them overnight so she could study more. You agreed, as long as you could get the cards in the morning so you could use them during your study period. When you met in the morning, Carrie didn't have the study cards. Carrie had given them to another friend to use, who promised to return them during study period. You never got the cards. Now you are so angry you find it hard to concentrate on anything and feel unprepared for the test. This is one class where you really worked hard for an A and you don't want to mess up your grade. You are upset that Carrie didn't give you the cards and that she gave the cards to someone else without asking. When you see Carrie at the beginning of history class, you blow up.

Carrie: You like studying with Marianna. You think Marianna is a history whiz and assume that her good grades in history come easily. When you arrive at school, you talk to a friend who feels totally unprepared for the history test. You offer her the cards with the promise that the girl will return the cards to Marianna during study period. When you see Marianna at the beginning of history class, you're surprised that Marianna is upset. You blow off Marianna's anger by saying, "What's the big deal? You always get A's anyway." The argument continues to escalate.

S T U D E N T   H A N D O U T

MEDIATION ROLE-PLAY 5: "MAKING TROUBLE BY MAKING FUN"

Jeffrey: You are new at school and feel unsure of your status. During P.E., when a group of about 10 kids is running laps around the field, you point to a group of special ed kids and make fun of the way they are playing soccer. You hope that making the other kids in your group laugh will make them like you, and that making fun of "out" kids is a way to be accepted. The rest of the kids laugh, but Chris grabs you and says, "Knock it off!" You're surprised. You'd like to be Chris's friend. You say, "What's it to you? I'm not calling you retarded."

Chris: You have a younger brother who is mentally retarded. You usually just ignore the way people talk about special ed students but today Jeffrey went too far. First you tell him, "Knock it off!" Then, when Jeffrey says, "What's it to you?" you get really mad and shove him hard.

LESSON 27 Cultural Sharing*

OBJECTIVES

Students will:

- affirm their cultural backgrounds by sharing information about their ethnic/racial group and other groups they belong to;
- identify values important to their families;
- discover commonalities and differences between their own family's values and those of their classmates;
- draw cultural shields and share their cultural backgrounds in a microlab.

PEACEABLE CLASSROOM PRINCIPLES

- Appreciation for diversity
- Mutual respect
- Affirmation and acceptance
- Personal connections

AGENDA

1. **Gathering (optional)**

   I Like My Neighbors Who ...

2. **Review Agenda**

3. **Lesson Activities**

   - Identity Shields
   - Cultural Sharing Microlab

4. **Checking Out What We've Learned**

   Popcorn-Style Sharing: What did you like about class today? What might you change?

5. **Closing (optional)**

   Go-Round: What is a traditional food or meal someone in your immediate or extended family prepares that you especially enjoy?

* Adapted with permission from *Resolving Conflict Creatively: A Draft Teaching Guide for Secondary Schools* © ESR Metropolitan Area, 1990

Gathering (optional)

I Like My Neighbors Who ... (see appendix A)

Review Agenda

Write the agenda on the board and review it with the class.

Identity Shields

Materials: Colored construction paper, markers

Cut colored construction paper into the shapes of shields or lay out an assortment of colored construction paper so that students can draw the shape of a shield on them. Distribute markers.

Ask the students to write their full names on their shields and any symbols (words or pictures) that show who they are, what's important to them, and groups to which they belong. After you've allowed them time to make their shields, ask students to show their shields and say something about their designs. What were the symbols they chose? What do their designs say about who they are and what is important to them?

Cultural Sharing Microlab

Divide the class into groups of three. Each person in the group will have two minutes to answer questions about his or her background. Keep time and notify the group when each two-minute period is over. First give your own answers as a model for the students. The questions for this microlab are:

- Where were your grandparents and/or parents born? Where did they grow up?
- What is your racial/ethnic background?
- What are two values or beliefs that are very important to your family and are also very important to you?

After all students have spoken, ask for volunteers to share descriptions of their cultural background—for instance, their racial/ethnic background, family traditions and affiliations, and values that are important to them. Write key words in their answers on the board or on chart paper. When an answer is repeated, place a check mark next to it to indicate how often it is said.

Ask the following questions related to values:

- How can we account for some of the differences in the family values listed here?
- To what degree are there similarities in the values listed on the board?
- How do you suppose these family values came about?

Checking Out What We've Learned

Popcorn-style Sharing: What did you like about class today? What would you have liked to change?

Closing (optional)

Go-Round: What is a traditional food or meal someone in your immediate or extended family prepares that you especially enjoy?

OBJECTIVES

Students will:

- identify qualities and attributes of people they think are powerful;
- understand the effects of power imbalances and uneven distribution of resources on a group.

PEACEABLE CLASSROOM PRINCIPLES

- Appreciation for diversity
- Social responsibility

AGENDA

1. **Gathering (optional)**

   Go-Round: Ask each person to share his or her ideas about qualities and attributes that make someone powerful.

2. **Review Agenda**

3. **Lesson Activity**

   - Haves and Have-Nots

4. **Checking Out What We've Learned**

   Exploration of power in your community.

5. **Closing (optional)**

   Popcorn-Style Sharing: Name one thing you can do that makes you personally powerful.

Gathering (optional)

Go-Round: Ask each person to share his or her ideas about qualities and attributes that make someone powerful. Chart the list and post it.

Review Agenda

Write the agenda on the board and review it with the class.

Haves and Have-Nots[†]

Materials: A big bag of pretzels or candies

It is best if you communicate minimally to the students as you set up this activity. If students ask questions as you are explaining the rules, use phrases such as "Just trust me" or "I'll be with you in a minute." In doing so, you reinforce some of the unwritten rules that go with status and power: someone/some people hold the knowledge, no one really seems to know the rules or the reasons, etc.

Begin by choosing two participants to be observers. Then divide the rest of the group so that there is one smaller group (the "haves") and one larger group (the "have-nots") by giving "x's" on slips of paper to the "haves" and "o's" on slips of paper to the "have-nots." Do not tell the groups they are the "haves" and "have-nots." This will become apparent. Ask the "x's" to go to one end of the room and "o's" to another.

Go to the "x's" first and privately give them the bag of pretzels and say, "These are all the resources you have and you have worked very, very hard for these resources. What you know is that these other folks want some of your resources and you must decide what to do with them."

Go to the "o's" and say, privately, "Those folks at the other end of the room have all the resources you need. It's up to you to figure out how you're going to get some or all of the resources you need."

If participants ask for more detailed instructions, you may repeat what you've said, but do not elaborate. Tell the participants they may begin. Privately ask each of the observers to observe one of the groups and take notes on what they hear said and see happening. Allow the activity to go on for about 10 minutes.

Note: Normally the teacher steps back after giving the initial instructions. If the "haves" decide to give away their resources too quickly (as there are usually some people who immediately want to defect to the have-not group), you may choose to caucus with them and say privately, "Remember, you have worked very, very hard all your life to get these resources."

Debrief the activity as a whole group, but ask the groups to sit together. Allow plenty of time and space for their responses to emerge, one person at a time. Ask the following questions to both groups. Start with the "haves," then the "have-nots":

- What happened?
- How did you feel?
- (To the observer of that group) What did you see happening?

Other questions you might ask are:

- What was your plan? Did you have one?

[†] Reprinted with permission from *Dealing With Differences* by Marion O'Malley and Tiffany Davis (Chapel Hill, NC: Center for Peace Education, 1995).

- What happened within the group?
- How did your discussion go?
- Who played what roles within the group?
- Was anyone tuned out or apathetic? Why?
- How do you get everyone involved? Is it necessary?
- If you were an "x," how would you describe the "o's"?
- If you were an "o," how would you describe the "x's"?
- How do you like being defined that way?
- Where were the pretzels at any given point in the game?
- What does this have to do with real life?
- How does this relate to your own situation?
- What is your definition of power?

Checking Out What We've Learned

Divide the class into pairs and pass out a 5x8 note card to each pair. Ask pairs to write "More Powerful Groups" on the left side of their card and "Less Powerful Groups" on the right side. Then ask them to make a list on the left side of the card of people, groups, and institutions that have power in their community, the United States, and the world. They can use their list of the qualities and attributes of power from the gathering activity as a reference. Allow pairs two minutes to brainstorm this list.

Then ask them to brainstorm a list of less powerful groups that are related in some way to the people, groups, and institutions on the left. Write these groups on the right side of the card. For example, a more powerful group might be doctors and a less powerful group related to doctors might be patients. Or a more powerful group might be white people and a less powerful group might be people of color.

Next, give pairs three minutes to answer the following questions:

- How would you describe the people and groups who have more power and those who have less?
- What differences do you notice when you compare the two lists? What's something that stands out for you when you compare the lists?
- Which list includes people and groups who "make the rules"? Why?

Ask students to share their observations with the whole group. Close the discussion by asking students to respond to the following questions:

1. How does power affect:
   - who has choices?
   - who gets resources?
   - what kinds of resources people get?
   - who's safe?

2. How does unequal power among different groups impact your neighborhood?

Closing (optional)

Popcorn-Style Sharing: Ask students to name one thing they can do that makes them personally powerful. Then ask each student to complete the sentences, "I can do it. I can ..." Model an answer first, then go around the room.

LESSON 29 More About Power[*]

OBJECTIVES

Students will:

- identify four "circles" of oppression: ideologies, institutions, interpersonal behavior, and internalized messages;
- explore how oppressive ideologies can influence institutional power, interpersonal behavior, and internalized messages;
- examine the links between oppression and violence;
- imagine how these circles of oppression might change in an egalitarian society.

PEACEABLE CLASSROOM PRINCIPLES

- Appreciation for diversity
- Social responsibility
- Personal connections
- Managing and resolving conflict

AGENDA

1. **Gathering (optional)**

   Go-Round: What images of teenagers do you see in the media? Who controls these images? What messages do they send?

2. **Review Agenda**

3. **Lesson Activities**

   - The Four I's of Oppression

4. **Checking Out What We've Learned**

   Groups post their diagrams showing circles of oppression and debrief the discussion.

5. **Closing (optional)**

   Students use sentence strips to make a display: "Breaking the Circles of Oppression."

---

[*] This lesson isadapted from the work of Jinnie Spiegler, RCCP National Center, New York, NY.

Gathering (optional)

Go-Round: Invite students to respond to this question: When you think about teenagers that you see on TV—in the news, commercials, comedies, and other programs—what images stick in your mind the most? After students have shared their responses, ask them to think about the general impression of young people that these images give. Who do they think controls the images that they see?

Explain that today's activity will explore how more powerful groups can use their power to control the images, treatment, and choices of less powerful groups.

Review Agenda

Write the agenda on the board and review it with the class.

The Four I's of Oppression

Introduce this activity by giving each student a copy of the handout The Four I's of Oppression (p. 202). Clarify the definitions on the handout by drawing a sample diagram on the board or newsprint. Draw four large, interconnected circles and label the top right circle "Ideologies." Inside the circle write the statement, "Young people are more likely to be violent and commit crimes than people of other ages."

Ask students, "How does this ideology about young people play out in institutions like schools, the media, work situations, laws, etc.?" Encourage them to generate examples, such as security guards roaming school hallways or community curfews for teenagers. Label the bottom right circle "Institutional Power" and list some of their answers inside.

Ask students how the same ideology affects interpersonal relationships in schools, the community, on the job, etc. (For instance, adults may walk away from young people out of fear; school officials may assume young people are responsible for minor crimes such as vandalism; police may routinely pull over young drivers or pick up teenagers who are walking alone in a residential neighborhood at night.) Write their answers in the bottom left circle and label it "Interpersonal Relationships."

Ask students what messages they might believe about themselves or each other if this ideology is a core belief in society. For instance, teenagers may withdraw from other teens they perceive as dangerous or may feel justified in breaking minor laws since that's what society expects from them.

Finally, write "Threat of Violence" in the area where the four circles intersect. Ask students how they think the threat of violence keeps these circles of oppression connected. How does each circle of oppression contribute to verbal, psychological, or physical violence? Point out that the assumption of inequality—that some groups are better or more deserving than others—can lead to members of the dominant group committing violent acts against oppressed groups. At the same time, it may encourage dominant groups to be fearful of violent acts committed by less powerful groups.

After exploring this example, divide students into groups of four or five and ask each group to draw the four interlocking circles on a sheet of chart paper. Hand each a card with one of the following statements on it:

- Men are stronger than women.
- African Americans and Latinos are dangerous.
- Immigrants are destroying job opportunities for other Americans.
- If you are poor or working-class, you don't have the same abilities as people who are middle-class or wealthy.

You may want to give two groups the same statement so that you can see differences and similarities in how people think about the same kind of oppression.

Ask each group to discuss together how the ideological statement on their card plays out in the other circles of oppression. Encourage them to write as many examples as they can in each circle. Give the groups about 10 minutes to work together.

Checking Out What We've Learned

When the time is up, post the charts and invite the whole class to respond to these questions:

- What do you notice about what's written on the charts? Are there any connections or similarities between one chart and another?
- How did you feel about this exercise? Was there anything you became aware of as you worked in your group? Did any strong feelings come up as you were doing this activity?

Closing (optional)

Divide students into pairs and give each pair a marker and a strip of paper or poster board measuring about 3 inches by 24 inches. Post a sign on the wall that says, "Breaking the Circles of Oppression." Write these questions below the title:

- What might be some ideologies or core beliefs that an egalitarian society would hold— e.g., that no group is inherently superior to any other group?
- What internalized messages would people believe about themselves in an egalitarian society?
- How might interpersonal relationships in an egalitarian society be different?
- How might institutions in an egalitarian society behave differently than in our society?

Ask each pair to choose one of these questions and write one response. Ask students to share their statements out loud. Then post the sentence strips under the title in question.

STUDENT HANDOUT

THE FOUR I'S OF OPPRESSION

In any society, the dominant group (one which uses its power to control less powerful groups) holds core beliefs or "ideologies" that are embedded in its institutions, including its government, economy, media, arts, education, and public policy. These ideologies are expressed through interpersonal relationships and through internalized messages about how people should view and treat themselves.

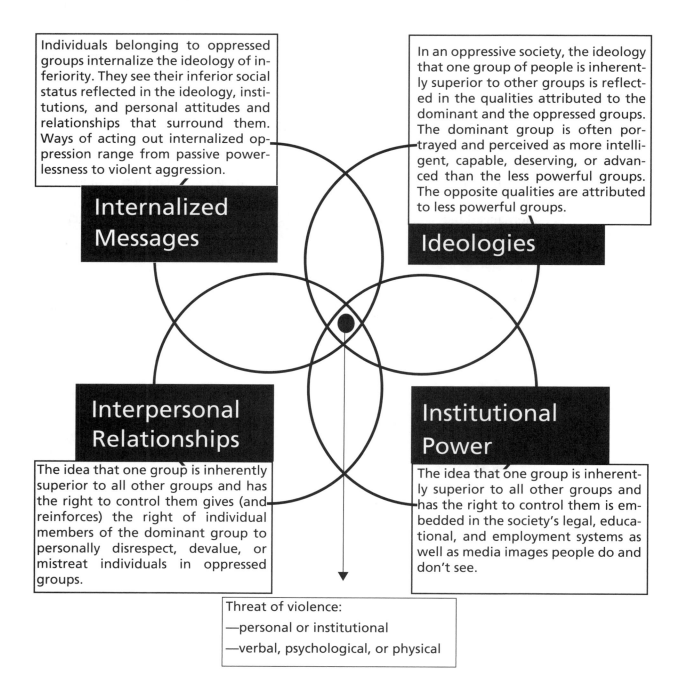

Individuals belonging to oppressed groups internalize the ideology of inferiority. They see their inferior social status reflected in the ideology, institutions, and personal attitudes and relationships that surround them. Ways of acting out internalized oppression range from passive powerlessness to violent aggression.

Internalized Messages

In an oppressive society, the ideology that one group of people is inherently superior to other groups is reflected in the qualities attributed to the dominant and the oppressed groups. The dominant group is often portrayed and perceived as more intelligent, capable, deserving, or advanced than the less powerful groups. The opposite qualities are attributed to less powerful groups.

Ideologies

Interpersonal Relationships

The idea that one group is inherently superior to all other groups and has the right to control them gives (and reinforces) the right of individual members of the dominant group to personally disrespect, devalue, or mistreat individuals in oppressed groups.

Institutional Power

The idea that one group is inherently superior to all other groups and has the right to control them is embedded in the society's legal, educational, and employment systems as well as media images people do and don't see.

Threat of violence:

—personal or institutional

—verbal, psychological, or physical

LESSON 30 Understanding Stereotypes, Prejudice, and Discrimination*

OBJECTIVES

Students will:

- examine the stereotypes they have about adults and identify stereotypes they think adults have about young people;
- define prejudice and discrimination and cite examples of both;
- explore how stereotyping and discrimination affect individuals.

PEACEABLE CLASSROOM PRINCIPLES

- Appreciation for diversity
- Emotional literacy
- Social responsibility

AGENDA

1. **Gathering (optional)**

   Go-Round: Describe a prized possession in your family that has a story.

2. **Review Agenda**

3. **Lesson Activities**

   - Stereotypes
   - Prejudice Web
   - Discrimination

4. **Checking Out What We've Learned**

   Students discuss prejudice and discrimination.

5. **Closing (optional)**

   Popcorn-Style Sharing: Tell something new that you learned about diversity or about yourself.

---

* Adapted with permission from *Resolving Conflict Creatively: A Draft Teaching Guide for Secondary Schools* © ESR Metropolitan Area, 1990

Gathering (optional)

Go-Round: Describe a prized possession in your family that has a story behind it.

Review Agenda

Write the agenda on the board and review it with the class.

Stereotypes

Ask students to find partners. In each pair, one person says, "Adults are ...," and the other person responds with whatever comes into his or her head. Repeat this 10 times, then switch roles.

Write "Adults are ..." on the board. Define "stereotype" (an oversimplified generalization about a particular group, race, or gender; usually derogatory). Ask students to volunteer some of the answers they and their partners came up with, and list them on the board. Go over the list to see which of the responses might be stereotypes. Ask, "Can you think of a real person or a story that counters this stereotype?"

Many people have stereotypes about young people. Ask the class to think of as many of these as they can. List students' responses on the board.

Discuss:

- How do these stereotypes make you feel?
- Does it matter if we stereotype people?
- What effects do such stereotypes have?
- Do they restrict people in some way? How?

Prejudice Web

Write the word "prejudice" on the board and ask students what comes to their minds when they think of that word. Chart their responses as a web.

Keep the following points in mind as you chart the web. These quotes come from *The Prejudice Book, Activities for the Classroom*, by David A. Shiman (New York, N.Y.: Anti-Defamation League of B'nai Brith, 1994):

- "Prejudice involves a feeling, favorable or unfavorable, toward a person, thing, or group without sufficient warrant."
- "Prejudice might be usefully described as a negative or hostile feeling/attitude toward a person who belongs to another group and is therefore presumed to have the objectionable qualities ascribed to that group."
- "Although these feelings may be positive or negative, most prejudices about people tend to be negative."
- "Even though a prejudicial judgment lacks a basis in fact ... a prejudiced person will often cling to his or her prejudice even when confronted by new and conflicting evidence."

After you have explored students' understanding of the word "prejudice," create a definition with the class. Include examples of prejudices that adults hold about young people.

Discrimination

Now write the word "discrimination" on the board and chart a web of students' associations with this word. As you chart the web, keep in mind the following points from *The Nature of Prejudice* by Gordon Allport (Reading, Mass.: Addison-Wesley Publishing Co., 1979).

- "We often separate ourselves from people whom we find uncongenial. It is not discrimination when we do so, so long as it is we who move away from them. Discrimination comes about only when we deny to individuals or groups of people equality of treatment which they may wish. It occurs when we take steps to exclude members of an out-group from our neighborhood, school, occupation, or country. Restrictive covenants, boycotts, neighborhood pressure, legal segregation in certain states, 'gentlemen's agreements' are all devices for discrimination."

- "... an official memorandum of the United Nations defines the issue: 'Discrimination includes any conduct based on a distinction made on grounds of natural or social categories, which have no relation either to individual capacities or merits or to the concrete behavior of the individual person.'"

Ask students:

- What is the difference between prejudice and discrimination? (Answer: Discrimination is an action based on prejudice.)
- What kinds of groups experience discrimination?

Explore examples of discrimination towards young people. Ask the group, "What kinds of things might adults do to discriminate against young people?"

Ask students to find a partner. Ask each partner to respond to the following question, "Think about a time, a specific event or experience, when you were discriminated against by an adult because you were a child or teenager. Who was involved? What happened? How were you feeling? What do you think the adult was feeling? Why do you think you thought of this experience? What does it have to teach you?" (You may want to write these questions on the board.)

Tell the partners that they will each have three minutes to share their experiences. Let students know when three minutes are up so that they can switch the role of listener and speaker.

Checking Out What We've Learned

Ask the following questions of the whole group:

- Should young people always be treated the same as adults? Why or why not?
- Are there times when young people should be treated differently than adults? If so, when?
- How might you respond to people who discriminate against young people? What would you say?
- How can young people protect and defend themselves against prejudice and discriminatory acts?

Closing (optional)

Popcorn-Style Sharing: Tell something new that you learned about diversity, about differences, or about yourself.

LESSON 31 Names Can Really Hurt Us*

OBJECTIVES

Students will:

- explore their early experiences with prejudice and discrimination;
- discuss the impact of prejudice and discrimination on our society;
- view the video "Names Can Really Hurt Us";
- share their reactions to the film.

PEACEABLE CLASSROOM PRINCIPLES

- Appreciation for diversity
- Emotional literacy
- Social responsibility

AGENDA

1. **Gathering (optional)**

    Pair-Share: Discuss the first time you became aware that prejudice existed.

2. **Review Agenda**

3. **Lesson Activities**

    - Microlab on Prejudice and Discrimination
    - Names Can Really Hurt Us

4. **Checking Out What We've Learned**

    What is one thing you would tell a friend about the video and discussion today?

5. **Closing (optional)**

    Feelings Check-In

---

* Adapted with permission from *Resolving Conflict Creatively: A Draft Teaching Guide for Secondary Schools* © ESR Metropolitan Area, 1990.

Gathering (optional)

Pair-Share: Give each partner three minutes to talk about the first time he or she became aware that prejudice existed. After each partner has taken a turn, ask volunteers to share some of the experiences they remembered.

Review Agenda

Write the agenda on the board and review it with the class.

Microlab on Prejudice and Discrimination

Ask each pair to join another pair to form groups of four. Designate one person in each group as the reporter (or ask the group to choose someone for that role). In the group, each person will take one minute to respond to each of the following questions. After all the people in the group have responded to a question, the group will go on to the next question. Write these questions on the board:

- What examples of prejudice and discrimination do you see in the world?
- Is it getting better or worse? What makes you think so?
- What would help reduce prejudice and increase tolerance?

Keep time and announce when each one-minute period is over. After each person has responded to each question, the group will choose three or four major ideas that came up in the microlab. The reporters will then summarize these for the class.

Names Can Really Hurt Us

Materials: The video "Names Can Really Hurt Us" (available from the NYC Public Schools, Office of Media and Telecommunications, 718-935-4359, or from the Anti-Defamation League, 1-800-343-5540); VCR and television

The focus of the video "Names Can Really Hurt Us" is the work of the Resolving Conflict Creatively Program (RCCP) in the area of prejudice reduction. The documentary follows Linda Lantieri, the director of the RCCP National Center, as she works intensively with a group of seventh to ninth graders from diverse ethnic and racial backgrounds who attend a middle school in New York City. During a two-week period, these young people move from an intellectual understanding of prejudice to a first-hand sharing of the pain of prejudice in their lives. They begin to feel empowered to help reduce prejudice, increase tolerance, and create harmony.

After viewing the tape, ask students to find partners and spend three minutes taking turns describing images in the film that stood out for them and explaining why they think these images struck them. When partners have finished, spend the remaining time listing on the chalkboard the images students cited from the film. After you have generated a list, try to determine why these images were so powerful.

Checking Out What We've Learned

Ask, "If you were going to describe this class to a friend who was not here today, what is one thing you would say about it?"

Closing (optional)

Feelings Check-In (see appendix B)

OBJECTIVES

Students will:

- explore how misunderstanding, prejudice, and the use of "ammunition" can contribute to the escalation of conflict;

- brainstorm ways to de-escalate conflicts based on difference;

- discuss diversity and conflict at school.

**PEACEABLE
CLASSROOM
PRINCIPLES**

- Appreciation for diversity
- Caring and effective communication
- Managing and resolving conflict

AGENDA

1. **Gathering (optional)**

   In pairs, students observe each other's faces and hands in silence, then share observations.

2. **Review Agenda**

3. **Lesson Activities**

   - How Do Differences Cause Conflict to Escalate?
   - De-escalating Conflicts Based on Difference
   - Diversity and Conflict at School

4. **Checking Out What We've Learned**

   Ask groups to report the two conflicts they think would be most important to talk about and resolve at school.

5. **Closing (optional)**

   Popcorn-Style Sharing: How do you imagine school would be different if these diversity conflicts were addressed?

Gathering (optional)

Ask students to find partners and sit face to face. Ask partners to look carefully at each other's hands and eyes for one minute in silence. Then ask students to describe the hands and eyes of their partners as fully and descriptively as they can. Give students three minutes to share with each other. Then as a whole group, take two or three minutes to do a popcorn-style sharing, inviting any students who wishes to share what they observed and learned.

Review Agenda

Write the agenda on the board and review it with the class.

How Do Differences Cause Conflict to Escalate?

Explain to students that difference can escalate—either intentionally or unintentionally—into conflict when there is misunderstanding, prejudice, and the use of "ammunition." Pass out the Diversity on the Conflict Escalator handout (p. 211). Read the handout aloud and generate other examples with the group.

Divide students into groups of four and distribute the Diversity and Conflict Scenarios (p. 212) to each group. Each person in the group reads one of the scenarios and then, as a group, students decide what caused the conflict: ammunition, misunderstanding, prejudice, or a combination of these. Encourage groups to discuss why they made the choices they did for each scenario.

De-escalating Conflicts Based on Difference

Ask each group to choose one of the scenarios and brainstorm what people could say and do that would help de-escalate the situation. Give students about 15 minutes to work together. As a whole class, ask each group to identify the conflict they chose to work with, what they think escalated the conflict, and what steps might help to resolve it.

Diversity and Conflict at School

Ask students to remain in their groups and think about and describe situations that they have witnessed at school where diversity issues have played a key role in a conflict. Ask each group to record its observations, and then answer the following question:

- If you were a member of a diversity team that included students, the principal, and several teachers, what two kinds of diversity conflicts would you most want to discuss and resolve?

Give students about 10 minutes for this activity.

Checking Out What We've Learned

Ask each group to report to the class the two conflicts that its members think would be most important to talk about and resolve at school.

Closing (optional)

Popcorn-Style Sharing: How do you imagine school would be different if these diversity conflicts were addressed? Give students three minutes to answer.

S T U D E N T   H A N D O U T

DIVERSITY ON THE CONFLICT ESCALATOR

There are three ways that diversity can escalate conflict:

1. **Ammunition**—The conflict begins to escalate, but not necessarily because of diversity. Then differences are dragged into the conflict as ammunition, usually in the form of name calling.

   Example:

   Roberto and Steven are two boys playing with a big squirt gun. Steven thinks it is his turn to shoot the gun, but Roberto won't give it up. They bicker for a while and as the conflict escalates, Steven says, "What are you, a homo?"

2. **Misunderstanding**—The conflict begins and escalates because of a misunderstanding that is rooted in cultural difference. The parties involved don't understand each other's actions because they don't understand each other's culture. As a result, each party misinterprets the behavior of the other.

   Example:

   Sondra, who is African-American, has just become friends with Sung Quat, a Cambodian classmate. As Sondra gets off the bus one morning, she sees Sung Quat across the school yard. She shouts and waves to her, but, to her surprise, Sung Quat folds her arms and turns her back. Sondra is hurt, thinking that she has been rejected by her new friend. What Sondra doesn't realize is that, according to Cambodian culture, she has just humiliated Sung Quat by causing everyone in the school yard to look at her.

3. **Prejudice**—The conflict begins and escalates because one or both parties have prejudices against the other. These prejudices lead them to make assumptions and to act based on their prejudices. These assumptions and actions contribute to the conflict escalating.

   Example:

   Jason and Marcus are using the computer, the only computer in the classroom. They are playing a math game. Alicia comes up and asks if she can play the game, too. "I'm really good at it," she says. "I play it at home with my Dad." Both boys wave her away. "This is for boys only," says Jason. "Yeah," says Marcus. "Girls are no good at computers."

Ammunition, misunderstanding, and prejudice may occur singly or in combination. For example, a conflict rooted in prejudice may involve ammunition as it escalates. Or one may lead to another: a conflict that begins as a misunderstanding can lead to the disputants developing real prejudices.

S T U D E N T   H A N D O U T

DIVERSITY AND CONFLICT SCENARIOS[*]

1. While watching the girl's basketball team practice, a friend says to you, "What a waste of money this is. Men want women who can cook, not shoot hoops."

2. Your neighbor says to you, "How come all black people are good dancers?"

3. Several classmates are talking. They are planning to tease a retarded man in the neighborhood by offering him money to tap-dance in the street.

4. Your friend tells you a joke that makes fun of Spanish-speaking people. You don't think your friend is a racist.

5. While you're waiting on line to get on the bus, one of your classmates calls out to someone across the street, "Hey, you! Are you queer?" The person across the street walks away quickly.

6. A student in your math class says to you, "Why are all Asian students so good at math?"

[*] ESR thanks Jeffrey Benson for these scenarios.

LESSON 33
Interrupting Prejudice and Stopping Verbal Abuse

OBJECTIVES

Students will:

- think about times when they interrupted prejudice or witnessed someone else interrupting prejudice;
- read a story about interrupting prejudice and verbal abuse;
- develop and review guidelines for interrupting prejudice and verbal abuse;
- role-play interrupting prejudice.

PEACEABLE CLASSROOM PRINCIPLES

- Managing and resolving conflict
- Appreciation of diversity
- Caring and effective communication

AGENDA

1. **Gathering (optional)**

   The Gift Box

2. **Review Agenda**

3. **Lesson Activities**

   - Pair-Share on Interrupting Prejudice
   - Guidelines for Interrupting Prejudice and Verbal Abuse
   - Interrupting Prejudice Role-Plays

4. **Checking Out What We've Learned**

   What new thoughts or insights emerged from this experience today? How might you use this experience in your daily life?

5. **Closing (optional)**

   Three-Minute Connections

Gathering (optional)

The Gift Box: Wrap two boxes. Put similar items in the two boxes, one wrapped neatly in gift paper and ribbons and another wrapped crudely with no ribbon. Have students vote for the box they wish to open and share. Open the box they selected. Then open the other box to show students that it contains the same thing. Discuss the following:

- Why did you choose the first box?
- What assumptions did you make about what was in each box?
- Was the decision based on outside appearance alone?
- When might we judge people in the same way?
- What can be missed by looking at the outside and not the inside?

Point out that we often make assumptions about people that are grounded in misinformation or prejudice.

Review Agenda

Write the agenda on the board and review it with the class.

Pair-Share on Interrupting Prejudice

In pairs, students respond to the following:

- Describe a time when you acted to stop prejudice or discrimination against another person.
- Describe a time when you acted in a prejudicial way towards someone or when you saw someone else do so and did not intervene.

Give pairs about five minutes to share and then provide three to five minutes for volunteers to describe the situations they remembered.

Guidelines for Interrupting Prejudice and Verbal Abuse

Begin by reading or telling a story about interrupting prejudice or verbal abuse. We recommend reading the story "The Most Mature Thing I've Ever Seen," by Susan Doenim, from *Chicken Soup for the Teenage Soul: 101 Stories of Life, Love and Learning,* by Jack Canfield, Mark Victor Hansen, and Kimberly Kirberger (Deerfield Beach, Fla.: Health Communications, Inc., 1997). The narrator is a high school student who tells a powerful story about a new student who comes to her school and doesn't know the unspoken rules that the other students live by. As a result she is ridiculed and humiliated, until one student steps forward.

Begin a discussion by asking students to share what makes it difficult to interrupt prejudice or verbal abuse. Reassure students that interrupting prejudice is not easy; it takes courage and carefully chosen words to respond in a way that's effective without hurting the other person.

Point out that there are three possible responses to a situation of prejudice:

1. *Avoidance:* Clamming up or ignoring;
2. *Aggression:* Attacking back;
3. *Assertion:* Confronting in a clear and open way by:
   - releasing the pain by expressing your feelings to a friend or ally (usually later and somewhere else);

- using your anger reducers so you can think about the words you want to say (you will not be listened to if you make the other person feel guilty or wrong);
- using strategies (active listening, clarifying questions, and "I" messages) to keep the other person's defensiveness to a minimum;
- maintaining a positive tone.

Introduce the following guidelines for interrupting prejudice. Post them on the board or newsprint. For each guideline, brainstorm a list of "starters" to help students interrupt prejudice and verbal abuse.

1. **Give an "I" message.**

    Sample starters:

    - "I don't feel comfortable when you say ..."
    - "If you had said that to me, I would feel ..."
    - "Do you think that's true for all people? In every situation?"
    - "I don't like it when ..."
    - "That's an ouch! I wouldn't want someone to say/do that to me. I don't think anyone deserves to be treated like that."

2. **Provide accurate information.**

    Sample starters:

    - "Here's what I think I know about the situation."
    - "I don't think ... really behaves that way."

3. **Ask clarifying questions.**

    Sample starters:

    - "Can you tell me why you think that about ...?"
    - "What exactly do you mean by ...?"
    - "Help me understand why this upsets you so much."

4. **Paraphrase and reflect.**

    Sample starter:

    - "This is what I heard you say: ... Is that the way you meant it?" (If the discriminator uses a slur, try not to repeat it. Use a letter to note the word or say "so and so"; this way you're making it especially clear how derogatory and hurtful you find the remark to be.)

5. **Sharing your perspective.**

    Sample starter:

    - "That sounds like an assumption to me. I don't think I know ... well enough to say that."

6. **Say what you need.**

    Sample starters:

    - "Even though I'm not ..., it hurts me to hear that word. Please don't use it again."
    - "I want to make a request. When I'm around, I'd rather you didn't use words like this. Can you agree to that?"

Interrupting Prejudice Role-Plays

Model a role-play in which you interrupt prejudice. Before class, arrange with a volunteer to play the discriminator. Use the Diversity and Conflict Scenarios from Lesson 32. After the role-play, debrief by asking these questions:

- What happened?
- How did the interrupter challenge the discriminator?
- What skills or behaviors do you think were effective?

Divide the group into triads and ask each triad to choose three situations from the Diversity and Conflict Scenarios. Have the groups role-play each of the three situations they chose, so that each person gets a turn to play the discriminator, the interrupter, and the feedbacker. Or you might want to divide students into larger groups of four or five, give each group one situation, and have them rehearse their role-play and present it to the whole class.

After the students have completed the role-plays, ask them:

- How did it feel to play the role of the discriminator? How did you feel when you were challenged by the interrupter? What helped you to listen to the interrupter?
- How did it feel to play the role of the interrupter? What was hard about interrupting prejudice in these scenarios? What helped you to focus your attention and say things the way you wanted to say them?

Checking Out What We've Learned

What new thoughts or insights emerged from this experience today? How might you use this experience in your daily life?

Closing (optional)

Three-Minute Connections: Set the timer and invite anyone who wants to share what he or she is feeling about the work today. Model this by speaking first.

From Being a Bystander to Taking a Stand

OBJECTIVES

Students will:

- identify what it means to be a target, bystander, or ally;
- read and discuss an article about high school students facing prejudice and discrimination;
- share ideas for how they can become allies to others in their school community in ways that prevent prejudice and promote diversity.

PEACEABLE CLASSROOM PRINCIPLES

- Appreciating diversity
- Social responsibility
- Personal connections

AGENDA

1. **Gathering (optional)**

   Go-Round: Share a time in recent memory when it was safe, fun, or cool to be in a group made up of individuals from different backgrounds.

2. **Review Agenda**

3. **Lesson Activities**

   - Targets, Bystanders, and Allies
   - Rotation Stations

4. **Checking Out What We've Learned**

   Students respond to the Rotation Stations.

5. **Closing (optional)**

   Students share responses to the Rotation Stations.

Gathering (optional)

Go-Round: Share a time in recent memory when it was safe, fun, or cool to be in a group made up of individuals from very different backgrounds (cultural and family background, ethnicity, religion, gender, groups in school, etc.)

Review Agenda

Write the agenda on the board and review it with the class.

Targets, Bystanders, and Allies

Before the class begins, create three signs using large letters that say "Target," "Bystander," and "Ally." Post the signs in three different places in your room.

Introduce this activity by saying that everyone is now, has been, or will be at some time a target of social oppression, in which a group or individual with more power or special advantages acts prejudicially toward you. For instance, adults may act prejudicially toward young people, whites toward people of color, the physically able toward the physically challenged, and so forth. At other times, each of us will also be a member of a group that acts prejudicially toward someone else: for instance, males toward females, Christians toward members of other religions, educationally advantaged toward less educated people, etc. Explain that all of us need allies and each one of us can be an ally to someone else.

When we witness a situation in which an individual or group is targeted, we can make a choice to be a bystander who doesn't say or do anything to change the situation. Or we can choose to be an ally, someone from the nontargeted group who works with and acts in support of a targeted person or group.

Pass out the *Boston Globe* article "Anti-Semitism at Sports Event Stirs Sharon" (p. 220) to each person as well as one of the Target, Bystander, and Ally Cards (p. 222). Each card explores the thoughts and feelings of one person who was a target, bystander, or ally in a series of anti-Semitic incidents involving several high schools. Ask students to read the article, then read their cards. After students have read their cards, ask them to place themselves under the sign that they think corresponds with the experience of the person described on their cards. When students have placed themselves by the signs, rotate from group to group, giving each student an opportunity to read his or her card.

After all students have read, take a few minutes to debrief this experience using any of these questions:

- What were you feeling? What did you become aware of as you listened to everyone?
- If you identified yourself as a member of the targeted group in this article, what would you want your allies to do to show their support? How could your school get the issue out in the open so people could talk about the situation in ways that are safe and constructive?
- If you identified yourself as an ally in this article, what would you want to say to students in the targeted group?
- If you identified yourself as a bystander in this article, what would you need to become an ally?

Rotation Stations

Write the questions below on sheets of newsprint, leaving plenty of space for students' answers. Post them around the room and provide a marker at each station. Divide the class into groups so that one group can stand by each question. Let students know that they will have about two minutes at each station to discuss and record their responses. Encourage them to try and record two or three responses at each station. After two minutes, ask each group to move to the right to the next station and address the next question. Remind students to take turns recording.

Station 1: Thinking about your school, identify groups that are targeted by individuals and groups with more status and influence. For each group you list, think of one way that you could act as an ally to students in a targeted group.

Station 2: Thinking about your school, what's already going on that helps make all groups feel included and welcomed?

Station 3: Thinking about your school, in what classes, activities, projects, and events do you notice the most positive interaction among students from different groups? What is it about these experiences that attracts a genuine mix of students?

Station 4: Thinking about your school, in what classes, activities, projects, and events do students tend to segregate by group? What is it about these experiences that leads to segregation?

Station 5: How can the school staff provide opportunities for students to "cross borders" in the classroom and in school activities, special projects and events?

Station 6: How can students "cross borders" during the school day, making an effort to get to know students from different groups, so that becoming an ally is a possibility?

Checking Out What We've Learned

After groups have finished responding to all the questions, give each student an index card and ask students to walk around in silence reading the responses. When they have finished reading, ask students to write down one thing they would like to change in their school that would promote diversity and one thing they can do to become a better ally to targeted groups.

Closing (optional)

Take three minutes to invite students to share what they wrote.

ANTI-SEMITISM AT SPORTS EVENT STIRS SHARON*

by Kate Zernike and Shirley Leung

SHARON, MASS.—This is a community that prides itself on confronting sensitive issues head-on, especially in its schools.

Diversity workshops were here before they became commonplace in other schools. And Sharon schools have a model community-service program, which encourages students to be more sensitive to people and situations outside this small wealthy suburb.

So school officials said yesterday that they were bewildered to discover that no student had come forward to report what was apparently a persistent barrage of anti-Semitic comments hurled at them by sports teams from other towns.

"It's upsetting that it's happening to the kids, but it's even more distressing that they wouldn't have said anything about it," Sharon High School principal Susan Dukess said. "The last thing you want is for kids to become complacent, because it allows this kind of intolerance to grow."

Dukess and other officials first heard of the incidents in an Anti-Defamation League report released last week, which said students from Sharon suffered a "pernicious pattern of anti-Semitic attacks...particularly when they travel to other towns for athletic events."

Despite a 36 percent drop in anti-Semitism in Massachusetts, the report singled out Sharon, a town of about 16,000 residents where about 60 percent to 80 percent of residents are Jewish, as an example of how many incidents go unreported.

According to the report, a swastika was drawn in the snow outside Foxborough High School while Sharon was playing a basketball game there in December. Foxborough athletes threw pennies onto the field during a field hockey game, and spat on football players and used anti-Semitic slurs. Anti-Semitic taunts were also heard by students in Canton.

Of 14 incidents the report alleged over the past year, school officials said they had heard about only three.

Yesterday, around town and at a Sharon High basketball game, residents said they were as surprised as school officials to hear the extent of the anti-Semitism.

But several alumni said the anti-Semitic comments are nothing new.

"It's something you dealt with," said David Greenfield, 20, who recalled pennies being thrown on the field when he played football for Sharon two years ago.

Henry Katz, chairman of the Board of Selectmen, said people of all ages had approached him and recalled similar memories in the days since the report was made public.

"They were talking about it as a fact of life," Katz said. "They never told the parents or the principals, either."

Katz said that just this week his sons, who are former high school athletes, told him about anti-Semitic comments they faced.

Greenfield, working at Stephen's Deli in town yesterday, said he used to laugh off the comments as "stupid."

"It just makes them out to be losers," he said. "Someone is always going to do something no matter what."

Other parents and alumni said students don't report anti-Semitic slurs because they don't feel anyone can do anything to stop it.

"There needs to be zero tolerance," said Stephen Gray, 37, who graduated from Sharon High in 1976.

But Dudley Davenport, who has been athletic director at the school for over 20 years, said he and other coaches had punished students who had been involved in anti-Semitic incidents that were reported.

"We've never backed off on any incident that's been brought to our attention," he said. "Maybe the kids think, 'If I complain there'll be retaliation.'"

STUDENT HANDOUT

Other parents said students often see the comments as just another sideline taunt—as much a part of the game as warming up. And students admitted that they dish out insults—though not racist ones—as heavily as they receive them.

Dukess said 15- and 16-year-old students struggling to fit in don't want to "rock the boat."

"There's a strong code of silence among adolescents," she said. "You don't rat on other kids, even kids who aren't from your town."

But students said the comments can sting.

"They treat us like we are lower than them," said Penny Walisever, 17, a Sharon High School senior who is Jewish. "It's sad when you see a swastika in the snow. It's something we're all aware about. It's about time something be done about it."

Among Foxborough students, some of whom were in Sharon yesterday, there was equal disgust.

Andrea Lutz, who graduated from Foxborough High School last year, said she never heard of any anti-Semitic slurs when she played basketball. The swastika drawn in the snow was the first time she encountered anti-Semitism, she said.

"I was really upset," said Lutz, 19. "In the car ride home, people were disgusted and embarrassed to be from Foxborough."

Other Foxborough students defended their school yesterday, saying a few troublemakers were giving their school a bad reputation.

"I don't think Foxborough is more anti-Semitic than any other school," said Sarah Biggieri, 17, a senior. But, she added, "I'm glad it got out. It needs to get out."

Dukess said she and other administrators will visit high school classrooms to urge students to report incidents.

Sally Greenberg, civil rights counsel for the Anti-Defamation League, said the League will meet with athletic directors, coaches and referees as well as review the Massachusetts Interscholastic Athletic Association's taunting policy to see if spectators can be thrown out of a game or force a forfeiture for anti-Semitic slurs.

* Reprinted, with permission, from the *Boston Globe*, February 19, 1996.

TARGET, BYSTANDER, AND ALLY CARDS*

My name is Susan Dukess and I am the principal of Sharon High School. Recently I found out some troubling news. Some athletes from other schools have been making anti-Semitic remarks to Sharon students at sporting events. An association called the Anti-Defamation League has put out a report about the situation. Since then, many students here at Sharon High School have been coming to me with complaints. They say they have also been targets of anti-Semitic behavior.

My name is Henry Katz. I am the chairman of the Sharon Board of Selectmen. Since the Anti-Defamation League report, many students have talked to me about the anti-Semitism they have been experiencing. I had no idea that the situation was so bad. But the students talk about it as though it's a fact of life. They never told their parents or the principal until now.

I'm Greta Lee and I play field hockey for Sharon High School. The last time we went to play Foxborough High School, some kids threw pennies on the field and spat at us. They also called us nasty names. Later, we saw a swastika drawn in the snow in front of the school. It's humiliating and I don't think we should have to deal with it.

My name is Doug Glass and I go to Sharon High School. I don't really understand what all this uproar is about. Sure, the kids from other high schools have been calling our athletes names and doing some pretty immature things. But kids everywhere do that kind of stuff. When sports teams come here to play us, or when we go away to play them, we insult them just as much as they insult us. It's part of the game.

---

* These cards are reprinted from *Creating a Peaceable School: Confronting Intolerance and Bullying*, a curriculum developed by Nancy Beardall. The cards were created by Nancy Beardall and Ravitte Gall.

TARGET, BYSTANDER, AND ALLY CARDS (continued)

I'm Lila Dinkins. I'm a student at Foxborough High School, and I'm on the soccer team. I think the kids at Sharon are a bunch of babies. It isn't as if they don't yell at us just as bad during sports game. I think they just want attention. They want to get us in trouble. They're just a bunch of spoiled, rich kids. They deserve to be put in their place anyhow.

My name is Greg Agnes and I go to Canton High School. I haven't personally made any of the comments that everyone is talking about, but I don't really see what the big deal is. I think the Sharon kids need to be taken down a couple of notches. Most of them are really rich and don't appreciate that most of us have to struggle in the world. I think that's why they've had to deal with all those comments.

My name is Penny Walisever and I'm a senior at Sharon High. I'm really upset about the way students from Foxborough and Canton have been treating us. They treat us like we are lower than them. It's sad when you see a swastika in the snow. It's something we're all aware of. It's about time we do something about it.

I go to Canton High and my name is Paul Cole. I play football. I'm ashamed at what some of my teammates have been getting into. The anti-Semitic remarks and actions are disgusting and I think they should stop. It's hard for me to do anything about it, though, because I don't want the other kids on the team to hate me. Team spirit and cooperation are really important. If I tell someone about what's going on and try to put a stop to it, my teammates will probably turn against me, and I can't afford that.

TARGET, BYSTANDER, AND ALLY CARDS (continued)

I'm Nina Winston, a student at Foxborough High. So what if we threw pennies on the field? It was just a joke. I can't understand why everyone is overreacting this way. They make fun of us, too. We were just getting back at them.

My name is Jeremy Katz. I'm one of Henry Katz's sons and I used to go to Sharon High School. The anti-Semitic harassment went on the whole time I was at Sharon High. I never told my father about it, though, or any other authorities. I guess I didn't think it was such a big deal, and also I didn't want to get people in trouble. Anyway, I didn't think anyone could really do anything about it.

My name is Carla Rhodes and I write for the local newspaper. I wrote an article about the anti-Semitic incidents directed against Sharon High School students. Susan Dukess, the principal of Sharon High, told me that there is a strong code of silence among adolescents. "You don't rat on other kids, even kids who aren't from your town," she said. "15- and 16-year-old students don't want to rock the boat."

My name is Jonathan Katz. Henry Katz is my father. I graduated from Sharon High two years ago, and while I was there I played on the football team. I vividly remember the kind of harassment my teammates and I were subjected to every time we would play teams from certain other schools. It bothered me a lot and made me feel humiliated. I was kind of relieved when this Anti-Defamation League report came out because then I felt like I could finally tell my father without having to bear the responsibility of getting a lot of people in trouble or feeling like I was a wimp or a baby.

TARGET, BYSTANDER, AND ALLY CARDS (continued)

My name is George Lowell. Two of my children go to Sharon High. Both of them are athletes, and I have been to a lot of their sports events. They insult the kids from the other schools just as much as the kids from other school insult them. I personally have never heard Sharon kids make racist comments. But, in general, Sharon kids dish it out as much as they get it.

My name is Stephen Gray. I graduated from Sharon High in 1976. I think that there needs to be zero tolerance for any form of racism. It really makes me sick to hear about what's been happening during sports games. Parents, teachers, and students should work together to protect against any of this kind of thing going on any longer. Why has it gone on for so long without authorities doing anything about it?

I'm Dudley Davenport, athletic director at Sharon High. I've been in this position for the past 20 years. During that time, the other coaches and myself have never backed off on any incident that's been brought to our attention. Maybe the kids think, "If I complain there'll be retaliation."

My name is Andrea Lutz and I go to Foxborough High School. I never heard any anti-Semitic slurs while I was playing basketball against Sharon High. The swastika drawn in the snow was my first encounter with what was going on. I was really upset. In the car ride home, people were disgusted and embarrassed to be from Foxborough.

TARGET, BYSTANDER, AND ALLY CARDS (continued)

I'm Sarah Biggieri. I'm 17 and I go to Foxborough High. I don't think our school is more anti-Semitic than any other school. But I'm glad the story got out. It needs to get out. I hope that other schools and communities will hear about it. Then they might be able to do what it takes to make sure that this kind of stuff doesn't go on where they live.

I'm a student at Foxborough High. My name is Jennifer Davis. I like my school and until now I have been really proud to be a student there. I think that we have a few troublemakers, though, and they're ruining the reputation of our whole school. Lately, whenever I tell people I go to Foxborough they give me a funny look. I don't think it's fair for other people to just assume that I'm racist because of the school I go to. I'm also mad at the kids who gave us this reputation.

My name is David Greenfield. I'm 20 and a former student at Sharon High. I have heard a lot of anti-Semitic comments on the playing field, but I never told anyone about them. The comments are stupid. It's just something you dealt with. It just makes those kids out to be losers.

I'm Sally Greenberg, civil rights counsel for the Anti-Defamation League. The League is scheduled to meet with athletic directors, coaches, and referees. We will review the rules of the Massachusetts Interscholastic Athletic Association to see if spectators can be thrown out of a game or if a game can be forfeited on account of racial slurs.

LESSON 35
How Can People Make a Difference?

OBJECTIVES

Students will:

- brainstorm a list of people in the community who are making a positive difference;
- interview one person who is making a difference in the community;
- write a report about the interview;
- do a presentation in class about the interview.

PEACEABLE CLASSROOM PRINCIPLES

- Social responsibility
- Personal connections

AGENDA

1. **Gathering (optional)**

   Go-Round: Ask students to describe a time that they helped out a friend or relative. Invite students to share how they felt after this experience.

2. **Review Agenda**

3. **Lesson Activities**

   - Introduce the "Making a Difference" Project

     Note: Introduce the project at least several weeks before having students present their projects.

   - "Making a Difference" Project Presentations

4. **Checking Out What We've Learned**

   Students make a poster, chart, or web titled "You Can Make a Difference."

5. **Closing (optional)**

   Popcorn-Style Sharing: Invite students to share one small thing they could do right now that would make a positive difference in the world.

Gathering (optional)

Go-Round: Ask students to describe a time that they helped out a friend or relative who needed some assistance. Invite students to share how they felt after this experience.

Review Agenda

Write the agenda on the board and review it with the class.

Introduce the "Making a Difference" Project

Explain to students that a final project for this class will involve interviewing a person whose efforts have made a positive difference in your community. Ask students to brainstorm a list of specific people to interview. The following suggestions might help them think of people to interview:

- A person whose job it is to make and/or keep the peace—a principal, a divorce or family mediator, a labor negotiator, a community police officer, a youth probation officer.

- A person who helps make life better for teens and families in difficult situations—a tutor, a mentor, a social worker, a suicide hotline staff person, a court-appointed family or child advocate, a person affiliated with a victim-offender reconciliation program.

- A person who participates in efforts to improve the quality of life in your community— a community activist, someone who helps to build housing for low-income families, medical professionals who volunteer at free clinics, a local employer who has reached out to the community.

- A person who deals with issues of prejudice, discrimination, and equal opportunity on a regular basis—a person who serves on the commission for equal opportunity and human rights in your town, a lawyer who tries discrimination cases, a diversity or human relations coordinator at a local school district, business, or college.

- A person who ensures that people live in a safe, sustainable environment—a pollution control monitor, a local environmentalist, a safety officer in a factory, a public health professional, a person who works for a recycling program.

After generating an initial list of people to interview, brainstorm a list of resources that could help students find other people to interview. (You may want to bring in resources for students to look through.)

Let students know that they can work individually or in pairs. They will need to document what they learned in a written narrative and share what they learned in a presentation to the class. Set up a timeline so that students are aware of dates for finalizing their choices, completing the interviews, finishing the written report, and presenting their projects in class.

Brainstorm a list of questions that will help students find out about the problems their interviewees are trying to address and how their work makes a difference for others.

Some sample interview questions are:

- How did you decide to do this kind of work?
- What kind of training and education is required to do this work?
- What are the best and worst parts of this job?
- What is one story you could tell that would help others understand the importance of your work?

You and your students may also want to create a list of suggestions for ways students should present what they have learned, including criteria for the written narratives, time limits for presentations, and focus questions for presentations.

"Making A Difference" Project Presentations

Divide students into groups of three and give each group some note cards so they can take notes on others' presentations. Have each student present his or her project within the triad.

In the same triads, have students share their perspectives on the following questions:

- Many people believe that each of us can make a difference. What do you think?
- If you were to give advice to a younger person who wanted to go out a make a difference, what would you say?

Give each student two minutes to respond.

Checking Out What We've Learned

Staying in their triads, students make a poster, chart, or web titled "You Can Make a Difference." The poster, chart, or web should reflect what students have shared today.

Closing (optional)

Popcorn-Style Sharing: Invite students to share one small thing that they could do right now that would make a positive difference in the world.

Pass out the Course Assessment Questionnaire (see appendix F). Ask students to complete it as homework.

LESSON 36 I Can Make a Difference*

OBJECTIVES

Students will:

- think about what they need to become effective peacemakers and opponents of prejudice and discrimination;
- affirm each other;
- reflect on this course.

PEACEABLE CLASSROOM PRINCIPLES

- Building community
- Social responsibility
- Affirmation and acceptance
- Personal connections

AGENDA

1. **Gathering (optional)**

   Go-round: What is one strength you possess?

2. **Review Agenda**

3. **Lesson Activities**

   - Affirmation Gifts
   - Appreciation Exercise

4. **Checking Out What We've Learned**

   Ask students to share their responses to the Course Assessment Questionnaire or have students complete this phrase: "Before this class I used to ... Now I ..."

5. **Closing (optional)**

   Closing Quotes

---

* Adapted with permission from *Resolving Conflict Creatively: A Draft Teaching Guide for Secondary Schools* © ESR Metropolitan Area, 1990.

Gathering (optional)

Go-Round: What is one strength you possess?

Review Agenda

Write the agenda on the board and review it with the class.

Affirmation Gifts

Ask each student to think about a quality he would like to have more of in order to really make a difference. This quality would be something that would help him be an effective peacemaker and/or help him resist prejudice and discrimination. Tell students to think of qualities they would like to receive all at once, like a gift.

Model a response. For example, say, "Sometimes I don't recognize prejudice. It goes by me, and I don't see it because I'm so used to it. I would like clear vision so I don't miss it." Once "clear vision" is identified as a quality you would like to possess, have the class repeat together, "Clear vision."

Go around the group and ask each student to describe the quality she has selected. After each student has spoken, ask the class to repeat together the name of the quality that was described.

Tell the students to pretend that the gifts they have described have been granted to them. Ask student to form pairs to answer the following questions:

- What will you do with this gift?
- How will your life be different as you use this gift?

Have each student write a slogan or a motto that represents how they would use that quality to make a difference in their own lives and the lives of others. List the slogans on the board or on newsprint.

Appreciation Exercise

Go around the room and stand behind each student for a few moments. Encourage two or three other students to say what they appreciate about this person (something she said in class, did for someone else, or that is true and positive about her). Have the student doing the appreciating use the formula for an "I" message: "I appreciate ... because ..."

After all students have been appreciated, ask the class:

- How did it feel to be appreciated?
- How did it feel to appreciate someone?
- Is there a way we can take this activity, in some form, into our daily lives?

Checking Out What We've Learned

Take five minutes for students to share their responses to the Course Assessment Questionnaire (assigned in the closing of Lesson 35, see appendix E) or ask students to complete the following statement: "Before this course I used to ... Now I ..."

Closing (optional)

Closing Quotes (see appendix B)

Infusing Conflict Resolution Into the Standard Curriculum

Because no two people are exactly the same, all human interaction involves dealing with differences. Thus, issues of conflict and cooperation are present in every classroom and subject area, influencing what students learn and how they learn it. This concept forms the foundation for infusing conflict resolution into the high school curriculum as well as integrating conflict resolution into the heart of the teaching and learning process.

Why infuse conflict resolution into the standard curriculum?

- Learning about the dynamics of conflict and the skills of conflict resolution gives students insight into the human interactions that make up the subject matter of many academic courses.
- Curriculum units themselves become more interesting and more personally relevant to students.
- Infusion offers students the opportunity to learn a systematic way of thinking about conflict and cooperation using historical, current, or fictional characters and events. For adolescents, examining the behaviors of others can serve as a bridge to building greater personal insight.
- Infusing conflict resolution into course content gives students a chance to practice and reinforce key conflict resolution concepts and skills.
- Integrating conflict resolution into standard subject matter challenges students to apply skills they have learned in other academic contexts.
- Infusing conflict resolution into the daily life of the classroom sends a message that conflict resolution is an integral part of the school culture, rather than just one course or unit for one grade level, or one program that impacts a small group of students.

Into which courses can I infuse conflict resolution?

Conflict resolution can be infused across the high school curriculum in any required or elective course. The goal of infusing conflict resolution is to deepen students' engagement with the subject matter, not water down the content. Your course content is likely to determine the infusion approaches you choose to use in the classroom.

What are effective approaches for infusing conflict resolution into the curriculum?

Effective infusion means choosing the approaches that are the best match for your course. The remainder of this chapter provides suggestions for using five infusion approaches in high schools. A full-length, sample infusion lesson that incorporates ideas presented below can be found in appendix E.

Infusing Conflict Resolution Concepts

In this approach the teacher explicitly integrates conflict resolution concepts into academic subject areas so that students are able to:

- gain a richer, more complex understanding of the people and problems they are studying;
- make meaningful connections between what they are studying and the world today;
- apply the concepts they explore in their course work to their personal lives.

For example, in a world history course, students can analyze the escalation of an international conflict and then look for parallel situations in the world today. In a literature class, students might discuss the internal and external conflicts that a character experiences in a particular situation and then reflect on the conflicts that they might experience in a similar situation.

You may discover that you already teach a unit that provides a natural match between the subject matter and conflict resolution. For example, a civil rights unit in a U.S. history course would provide an excellent opportunity to explore events and relationships through a conflict resolution lens, integrating activities that focus on prejudice and discrimination, positions and interests, conflict styles, and anger management.

Where do I begin?

1. Look through the list of core conflict resolution concepts below and identify three to five concepts that you want to emphasize in your course.

2. Next to each concept you've selected, jot down the teaching unit where you would like to infuse it.

3. Identify specific topics, events, issues, or literary or historical works within the unit where you want to have students work with the concept.

4. For each concept, decide whether you want to:

   First teach the concept (using core lessons from this book) and then apply it to your course content. Write down how you want to introduce the concept and two ways that students can apply the concept to deepen their understanding of the subject matter.

   Or:

   First teach the concept in the context of your course content, and then isolate the conflict resolution concept and relate it to students' own experiences. Write down how you want to introduce the concept using subject-matter content and two ways that students can apply the concept to their own lives and personal experiences.

   The decision you make will depend on your students' familiarity and comfort with the concept. For example, to study international responses to conflict, you might first exploring interpersonal conflict styles and then compare interpersonal conflict styles to global responses to conflict. On the other hand, you might want to explore processes of peacemaking that students see, hear, and read about on TV, on the radio, and in print before reflecting on the peacemaking skills they use in their own lives.

5. Write down how you want to assess students' understanding of the concept.

Core Conflict Resolution Concepts:

1) Conflict has a Positive Side

Students examine conflict by looking for the positive aspects of conflict, breaking down the myth that conflict is always bad and always produces negative results.

English/Social Studies
Use any historical or current event or conflict in a novel, story, or play to discuss how a conflict produced positive outcomes for individuals and groups involved. Look for insights, new learning, changes, and results that would not have occurred if the conflict had not occurred. Try having students use this formula:

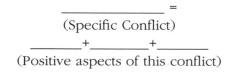

_____ =
(Specific Conflict)

_____ + _____ + _____
(Positive aspects of this conflict)

2) Conflict has Multiple Definitions

How we define a conflict often sets the stage for effective or ineffective problem-solving, especially because disputing parties can define the same conflict very differently. The more clearly and fully we can describe a conflict, the more information we have to manage and resolve it.

English/Social Studies

Use the "Five Dimensions of Conflict" pie chart (below) to define and describe a conflict in literature or social studies. One way to use the chart is to divide students into groups of five and have each person in the group work with one piece of the pie chart. Groups can focus on different aspects of a single conflict; alternatively, they can analyze different conflicts in the same piece of literature or various smaller conflicts that are part of a larger conflict within a specific geographical region or period of history.

FIVE DIMENSIONS OF CONFLICT

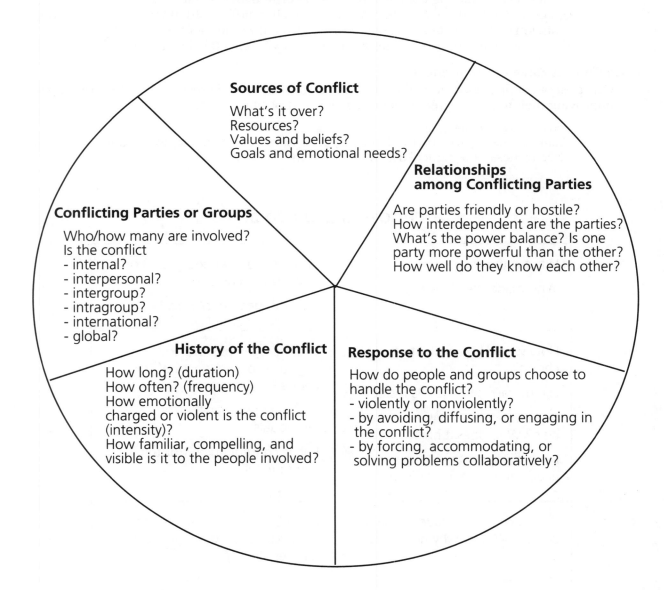

Sources of Conflict

What's it over?
Resources?
Values and beliefs?
Goals and emotional needs?

Relationships among Conflicting Parties

Are parties friendly or hostile?
How interdependent are the parties?
What's the power balance? Is one party more powerful than the other?
How well do they know each other?

Conflicting Parties or Groups

Who/how many are involved?
Is the conflict
- internal?
- interpersonal?
- intergroup?
- intragroup?
- international?
- global?

History of the Conflict

How long? (duration)
How often? (frequency)
How emotionally charged or violent is the conflict (intensity)?
How familiar, compelling, and visible is it to the people involved?

Response to the Conflict

How do people and groups choose to handle the conflict?
- violently or nonviolently?
- by avoiding, diffusing, or engaging in the conflict?
- by forcing, accommodating, or solving problems collaboratively?

3) Responses to Conflict Vary

People can respond to conflict in a variety of ways. Students examine the ways people respond to conflict under certain circumstances and assess the effectiveness of the responses used.

English
Students examine conflicts within a story or novel, describing how the characters respond, the supporting evidence from the text, and the effectiveness of the response used. Students can also explore alternative responses characters might have used and discuss how the outcome might have changed.

History
Using this chart, students can also examine conflicts between groups and nations, identifying violent and nonviolent responses to a specific conflict and the impact of those choices on every group involved. Students can also discuss how events might have been different if the groups had chosen alternative ways to respond to the conflict.

Science/Geography
Students can examine conflicts that arise over human activities that damage the environment (carbon dioxide emissions, which contribute to global warming; sulfur emissions, which cause acid rain; rapid industrialization; deforestation; habitat destruction) and ways societies respond to environmental change.

4) All Choices Have Consequences

One goal of conflict resolution education is to engage students in responsible decision-making, improving their ability to predict both negative and positive consequences.

English/Social Studies
Examine the choices that individuals, groups, or nations make, evaluating the effectiveness of a particular choice, using the frame below:

CHOOSING WHAT TO DO

What is the choice? Who made the choice?	What is the intended goal(s) of making this choice? Was this goal met? How?
How would you evaluate the choice? Is it moral? Is it legal? Is it safe? Does it seem fair? Who does it help? Who does it hurt? Does it respect the rights and needs of everyone involved?	What are the positive and negative consequences of this choice? Private consequences (for individuals)? Public consequences (for the community)?
Would you have made the same choice? Why or why not?	Describe a more effective choice. How would the consequences be different?

5) Win-Win Solutions

Students look at Win-Win, Win-Lose, and Lose-Lose solutions and their consequences. Students practice using a Win-Win problem-solving approach, exploring disputants' needs in order to reach a mutually agreeable solution to a conflict.

English
1. Students examine the underlying motives, wants, and needs of characters involved in fictional conflicts and propose possible Win-Win solutions.

2. Students select a conflict between two characters and use the Win-Win grid below to consider differences in solutions and outcomes for each character.

WIN-WIN GRID	**Character B doesn't get wants or needs met**	**Character B gets important wants and needs met**
Character A doesn't get wants or needs met	*Lose-Lose* A doesn't get_____ B doesn't get_____ What happens that produces this outcome?	*Lose-Win* A doesn't get_____ B gets_____ What happens that produces this outcome?
Character A gets important wants and needs met	*Win-Lose* A gets_____ B doesn't get_____ What happens that produces this outcome?	*Win-Win* A gets_____ B gets_____ What happens that produces this outcome?

Social Studies
Use the same grid (above) for exploring current or historical conflicts. In international conflicts, be mindful that national interests drive the decision-making process and that nations often believe that the only way they can secure their interests is by using a Win-Lose approach to resolving conflict. Discuss how a Win-Win approach that meets some national interests of both countries might actually result in greater security for both.

Science
Students can propose Win-Win solutions to environmental conflicts that meet the need for both environmental preservation and economic growth.

6) The Conflict Escalator

In a conflict situation, every response by the conflicting parties is either a step up or a step down in intensifying the conflict. Students use the concept of the Conflict Escalator to explore how conflict escalates or de-escalates.

English/Social Studies
Using a news article, video clip, text excerpt, or passage from a novel or story, graph the escalation of a conflict between two conflicting parties using an escalator with no more than seven steps. By placing a limit on the number of steps, students must select what they think are the most important actions that shaped the conflict. Let students

know that their steps can vary in size and that they may be headed up or down. For example, the escalator might look like this:

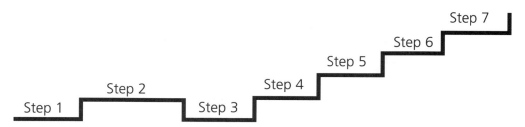

Students can use two different-colored markers to identify the actions of the two conflicting parties. After students have graphed the conflict, you may want them to identify the step where a de-escalating response could have changed the outcome dramatically. Then students can brainstorm responses that would have helped to de-escalate the conflict at this point and perhaps changed the climate so that problem solving could occur in the near future.

7) Communication Blockers and Encouragers (Put-Downs and Put-Ups)

Students explore the negative effects of communication blockers and put-downs (blaming, criticism, sarcasm, interrogation, interruption, etc.) and the positive effects of communication encouragers and put-ups (restating, reflection, open-ended questions, etc.). The emphasis is on looking at language and behavior that discounts or affirms the individual, fostering an atmosphere of either disrespect or respect. Students can pinpoint what language and behaviors keep the lines of communication open.

English
Students examine the ways that characters in literature use communication blockers (put-downs) and communication encouragers (put-ups) with one another.

History/Government/Global Studies
Students examine how the language and behavior of political leaders either blocks or encourages communication between conflicting nations or groups. Students can look specifically at how the language leaders use affects the political climate, making it more hostile and resistant to resolving differences or more conducive to negotiating a settlement.

8) Point of View

Students work on seeing things from a perspective other than their own. They attempt to "step into" another person's point of view and reflect on what the other person sees and feels.

Mathematics
Use statistical data to explore how point of view affects the questions researchers ask, how they construct a survey population or sample, what variables are chosen, and how the data are interpreted.

Geography
Present various maps of the world to students, examining the placement, location, size, position, orientation, and visual representation of countries and continents. Ask students: From whose point of view do you think this map was drawn? Why? How does the design of a map influence our thinking about different countries--their importance, size, or relationships among them?

History/Social Studies
1. Consider how texts define groups and governments. Ask students: When you

come across words like "enemy," "alien," "barbarian," "third world," "underdeveloped," "terrorist," "subversive," "outlaw," "economically disadvantaged," "minority," etc., who's doing the defining? Would the group defined in this way use the same term? Why or why not? How do words like these influence public attitudes and public policy toward this group?

2. Students can use role-plays to explore the points of view of nations or groups engaged in conflict. Give students role cards that represent the points of view of various parties involved in a conflict. Have students share their reactions to specific events, conditions, or policy choices from the point of view of each group.

3. It is rare that there are only two sides to a conflict. Use the chart below to consider the points of view that multiple constituencies bring to a conflict. This process can also help students appreciate how much harder it is to resolve conflicts that involve many different groups.

MULTIPLE POINTS OF VIEW

Groups immediately affected by the conflict	How does this group define the conflict?	What's the most important concern or need of this group?	What is the one thing that this group wants all other groups to understand about their experience?

English

Students can tell a story from the points of view of different characters through writing assignments or role-plays. You might want to ask pairs of students do this assignment together, using the Points of View handout (Lesson 19) to describe the points of view of two different characters.

Science

Students can use the Points of View handout (Lesson 19) to compare the perspectives of different groups involved in debates over environmental issues. Alternatively, students can compare the points of view of scientists responding to new theories or new evidence that challenges established theories.

9) Position and Interests

The ability to identify positions (demands) and interests (underlying needs) is essential for effective problem-solving. Until the different positions and interests of all conflicting parties are identified and understood, it is nearly impossible to explore mutual interests that might be part of an effective solution. Students in a range of disciplines can use the following grid to clarify individual positions, individual interests, and mutual goals and interests of disputing characters, groups, or nations.

GETTING TO THE INTERESTS		*Party B* Position (what you demand and want right now)
	Mutually Exclusive Goals	*Party B* Underlying Needs and Interests (reasons for the demand; the concerns that a good solution must address)
Party A Position (what you demand and want right now)	*Party A* Underlying Needs and Interests (reasons for the demand; the concerns that a good solution must address)	Mutual Goals and Interests

10) The "-Ate" Processes of Peacemaking

Students identify various peacemaking processes, assessing the strengths and limitations of each process, evaluating which process might be most effective at a specific stage in a conflict, and considering the conditions that must be present in order for this process to be effective.

Social Studies
When studying any historical or current conflict, students can use The "-Ate" Processes of Peacemaking handout (Lesson 22) to sketch out how each process might be used to resolve the conflict. They should then recommend the peacemaking process that they think would be the best next step for resolving the conflict.

11) The Dynamics of Power

People, groups, and institutions all use many different kinds of power. Analyzing the sources and forms of power, the balance of power among various parties, and the ways power is used is an essential part of understanding conflict.

English/Social Studies

To explore the nature, use, and distribution of power, students can use the questions in the Power Pie (below) to analyze conflicts in literary works or historical events. Discuss:

- whether power is used collaboratively (shared) or coercively;
- which parties have access to which kinds of power—for instance, personal or institutional
- positive and negative ways people exercise their power;
- how power is balanced among the various parties.

Ask students to write about an individual or character involved in a historical event or fictional conflict, reflecting on how different power perspectives influenced the behavior of the individual or character.

THE POWER PIE

Is power used *over* or *with* other parties?

Is power used positively or negatively?

Is power personal or institutional?

Is the balance of power even or uneven?

Social Studies

Students can use "power profiles" to analyze historical or contemporary conflicts. Ask the class to brainstorm a list of different forms of power. Examples could include: authority (formal decisionmaking power); power that derives from talent, skills or knowledge; charisma (personal charm and influence); privilege (power derived from belonging to a dominant group); the control of resources (such as wealth); or moral power (the ability to inspire and influence others through one's own convictions). Choose a conflict the class is studying and identify 10 different individuals, groups, or institutions involved. Assign each of these participants in the conflict a number from 1 to 10. Divide the class into groups and have each group create a "power profile" of one of the 10 participants, listing the types of power the participant does or does not have, but identifying their subject only by number. Then have the rest of the class guess which power profile matches which participant. To follow up, ask each group to rank the participants profiled from most powerful to least powerful. Compare and discuss the results.

12) Conflict-Management Grid

There are two things at issue in any conflict: 1) achieving our goals (what we want or need), and 2) maintaining our relationship with the other person. The choice we make in responding to a conflict reflects the relative importance we place on achieving the goal and/ or maintaining the relationship. We may place more value on one than the other, we may place great importance on both, or we may place little importance on either.

It is often difficult to define and sort out our goals. What we may want in the emotional charge of the moment may be different from what will meet our needs and interests. The conflict-management grid (see next page) invites students to discuss goals in detail and consider how our choices impact the relationships of those involved in the conflict.

Literature

Using fiction, look at characters in crisis and assess the decisions they make about how to handle an immediate conflict. Did their choices accomplish their goals? How did their choices affect their relationships with other characters involved in the situation? How might the outcome have been different if a character had used another conflict response?

History/Social Studies

1. You can use the conflict-management grid to examine the effectiveness of one nation's response to another nation's actions. You might also discuss how another decision might have resulted in a more effective means of achieving a nation's goals. Because nations generally use a directing/forcing response to another nation's aggression, it is particularly useful to assess how this response affects the relationship over time. Often, a directing response might appear effective in the short term, but may result in a further escalation of the conflict and worsen the relationship in the long run.

2. Another way to use the conflict-management grid is to look at presidential and majority-party recommendations for legislation and evaluate how Congress approaches pending legislation, especially if opinion about what to do is divided. Does Congress compromise meeting some interests of different groups (as often happens with tax-reform bills) or avoid legislation altogether (as in the health care reform debate in 1993)? When do members of Congress collaborate, meeting goals that are important to both parties? In what situations does Congress accommodate some groups and not others? Which relationships most influence legislative decisions?

CONFLICT-MANAGEMENT GRID

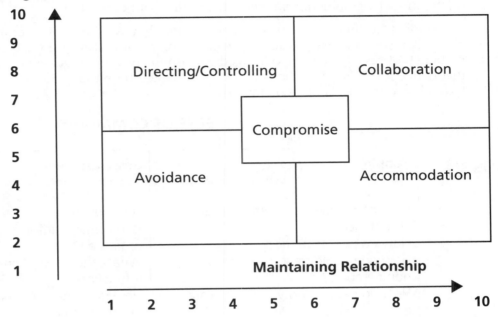

A **Directing/Controlling** response places more value on getting your goals met and less value on keeping or improving the relationship.

An **Accommodation** response places more value on the relationship and less value on meeting the goal.

Collaboration places a high value on both achieving your goal and keeping or improving the relationship.

Avoidance places a low value on both goals and the relationship— neither need is likely to get met.

Compromise is a middle-ground response that may only partially satisfy goals and attend to the needs of the relationship.

13) *Constructing Community*

People form communities of all kinds. Communities meet some of our most basic human needs. Communities can provide:

- a sense of belonging—loving, sharing, and cooperating with others;
- ways to achieve, feel powerful, and be respected;
- opportunities to make choices about our lives;
- times to play and have fun.

Every community creates its own culture. The more we know about a particular community, the more able we are to see the world from that community's perspective. Taking a closer look at communities can help us understand what makes communities successful, why people choose to belong to some communities and not others, how communities differ from each other, and why communities come into conflict with each other.

Ask students to think about time when they felt they were part of a community. What was it about that experience that made it feel like a community? How is this experience different than an bunch of people hanging out together? You might want to generate a list of characteristics that define a community. The chart below (adapted from the work of Terry Deal) is one way to think about aspects of a community.

ASPECTS OF COMMUNITY

People	Structure
Who belongs? How do people gain membership and acceptance? How do people participate? How do people treat members and nonmembers? How do people show that they care for each other?	What is the size and scale of the community? Is it formal or informal, loosely or tightly organized? What's the physical environment in which it functions? How does the community get the resources it needs?
Culture	**Politics**
What are the community's shared values and beliefs? What does the community stand for? What is its purpose? What experiences, rituals, celebrations does the group share in common? What are its rites of passage? Who are the heroes and role models? What stories, myths, tasks, and events are unique to this community?	How are power, status, and resources shared and distributed within the community? How are decisions made? Who makes the rules? What's right or wrong? Who gets to be a leader? What kind of power do leaders exercise? How are group norms established? How are conflicts resolved? What happens when people break the rules? How are people punished?

Literature
1. Explore the theme of "culture clashes" in novels, films, and stories—situations where communities are in tension, where the norms of a dominant community conflict with the norms of a nondominant community.

2. Explore the theme of the "outsider," a person who lives in a community where he or she doesn't feel accepted. What community values and norms make it difficult for the "outsider" to navigate in the community? How does the "outsider" deal with exclusion?

Social Studies
1. Interview people about their definitions of community. What communities exist within your school? Is a gang a community? What are other adolescent communities that give young people a sense of belonging? Why do some

communities function better than others? What's the civic community like where you live? Do students feel part of it? Why or why not? If they don't feel connected, what would need to change for students to feel like members of a civic community?

2. Investigate examples of nineteenth and twentieth century communities that were established intentionally, often in reaction against the norms of the dominant culture. In what way is the shelter and isolation of these communities restrictive and/or liberating? What do people gain by participating in these communities? What do they give up?

3. Find out more about communities that are home to different racial, religious, and ethnic groups. What makes some communities successful while others struggle? What happens when two groups living in the same city become polarized? (For example, students can examine Catholics and Protestants in Belfast; African-Americans and whites in Detroit; French- and English-speaking people in Quebec; Arabs and Jews in Jerusalem.) Find out about multicultural cities like Los Angeles, San Francisco, Miami, New York, San Antonio, Toronto, Vancouver, Jerusalem, and Sarajevo (before the break-up of Yugoslavia). In what ways do these cities turn differences into resources? How do they make people from diverse groups feel welcomed and connected to the larger civic community?

14) Bias Awareness

Students build an awareness of and insight into stereotypes, prejudice, and discrimination and explore their negative effects on individuals and groups.

History

Students can examine types of prejudice and discrimination as well as the roles that prejudice and discrimination play in historical events and conflicts. For example, students can examine the role that religious prejudice has played in European history; the history of racial discrimination in the United States; how the media portray different cultural and ethnic groups; or how the meaning of "All men are created equal" has evolved in the United States.

English

Students can examine literature and the media looking for assumptions, forms of stereotyping and prejudice, and acts of discrimination. Students can also discuss how different fictional characters cope with prejudice and discrimination. You might use the framework on the following page for analysis.

ANALYZING PREJUDICE AND DISCRIMINATION

Name of Character or Group:	How do these remarks or acts make the character or group feel?	How does the character or group cope with and respond to these remarks and acts?
Inaccurate assumptions made about this character: Evidence in the text:		
Stereotypical language used to describe this character or group: Evidence in the text:		
Prejudicial remarks spoken about this character or group: Evidence in the text:		
Discriminatory acts committed against this character or group: Evidence in the text:		

Infusing Conflict Resolution Skills

Infusing conflict resolution skills, such as active listening and problem solving, gives students a chance to practice their skills in new and varied contexts. For example, students might participate in a group negotiation that involves several constituencies affected by a local or global conflict. Or students might practice active listening in small groups while reviewing a step-by-step process for solving algebraic word problems. The emphasis here is on identifying places in your curriculum where students can use their conflict resolution skills to learn course content more effectively.

Where do I begin?

1. Look through the list of core conflict resolution skills in this chapter.

2. Identify three to five skills that you want to emphasize in your course.

3. Next to each skill you've selected, jot down a teaching unit into which you would like to infuse it.

4. Identify the specific topic, problem, event, or issue within the unit where you want students to practice using this skill.

5. For each skill, decide whether you want to:

   - First teach the skill (using core lessons from this book) and then apply the skill to your course content. Write down how you want to introduce the skill from an interpersonal perspective and two ways that students can apply the skill to deepen their understanding of the subject matter.

   Or:

   - First teach the skill in the context of your subject-matter content, and then apply the skill to students' own interpersonal experiences. Write down how you want to introduce the skill using subject-matter content and two ways that students can apply the skill in their own interpersonal relationships.

   The decision you make will depend on your students' familiarity and comfort with the skill. For example, negotiation may be an entirely new way of thinking about problem solving. Practicing an informal group negotiation first (see Lesson 24) can set the stage for participating in a mock multi-party negotiation involving representatives from several countries. On the other hand, sometimes it is more comfortable for students to practice skills like "reading" emotions by using fictional characters first, before identifying and discussing their own feelings.

6. Write down how you want to assess students' demonstration of the skill.

Core Conflict Resolution Skills:

1) Making Agreements and Reaching Consensus

It's helpful to examine how groups make agreements and reach consensus. You might want to explore four different decision-making processes with students, considering the strengths and limitations of each process in different situations (see chart on following page).

FOUR DECISION-MAKING PROCESSES

I Decide or You Decide (Autocratic Decision-Making)	Get Input (Participatory Decision-Making)	Vote On It (Democratic Decision-Making)	We All Agree (Consensus Decision-Making)
One person makes the decision alone. This happens when a person is responsible for making a choice by himself or herself. People make "I Decide" decisions when 1) one person is responsible for the safety and well-being of others; 2) one person is in charge of a situation; or 3) one person needs to act quickly and there is no time to talk to other people.	One person or a small group collects all ideas and suggestions, discusses the pros and cons of each idea with everyone, and then makes a decision that includes the best input from everyone.	Everyone generates ideas about what to do and then everyone votes on the best idea. Final choices can be made either by selecting the idea that receives the most votes or by voting until one idea receives a majority vote (more than half the votes) or a two-thirds vote.	Everyone participates and has a say before reaching agreement on a decision that everyone in the group can support. In consensus, the ideas that people don't like are thrown out or changed until the group can reach a final agreement. Consensus happens when each person in the group agrees with the decision.

Questions:

1. Which process do you think is fastest? Why?

2. Which process do you think is slowest? Why?

3. Which process would you use if a friend was hurt and might need medical care?

4. Which process would a group of friends use to decide which movie to see on Saturday night?

5. Which process would you use to decide which job offer to accept?

6. Which process would a teacher use to decide which math skills to teach?

7. Which process would a teacher and students use to decide on classroom rules?

8. Which process do we use most often in making public policy? Why?

English/Social Studies

Using literary, historical, or current case studies, examine how groups make decisions. Assess the effectiveness of the particular decision-making process used. You might want to pose some of these questions in exploring decision making:

- What decision process was used?
- Are people affected by the decision part of the decision-making process?
- Does the decision respect the rights and needs of people affected by the decision?
- Are people who are supposed to implement the decision involved in making the decision?
- Do the parties have what they need to make the decision work (people and resources)?
- Is it balanced? Does it seem fair to everyone involved?
- Does it help or hurt some groups more than others?
- How do people feel about the decision-making process?

2) Reading and Expressing Emotions

Students practice identifying and naming their own emotions and "reading" the emotions of others.

English

Use the Feelings Bull's-Eye (Lesson 13) to identify the emotions of characters in stories, plays, or novels. Then use the Find the Feelings chart (below) to list different emotions and describe their roles in the conflict. If you identify one emotion that is handled differently by different characters or by the same character under different circumstances, list it as many times as you like.

FIND THE FEELINGS

Feeling word	Who felt it?	What brought it on?	What action followed?

3) Active Listening

Students practice the skills of active listening (demonstrating their attentiveness through body language) and paraphrasing (repeating back what the speaker has said in their own words). Using these practices, students can help others clarify their thoughts and feelings. Students can also use these techniques to defuse anger and other strong emotions in others during conflict situations.

English

1. In pairs, students can role-play a dialogue that generated a conflict between two characters in a story or novel. However, this time the characters practice active listening in the conversation. How does this change the outcome?

2. Compare literary passages in stories, novels, or plays that show characters listening poorly to each other and characters engaged in active listening. Find passages that involve parents and kids, boyfriends and girlfriends, or best friends. Or look for situations where one character is trying to discover what happened to another character—for instance, a passage where a character "clams up" and another where a character opens up. What's the difference in communication?

3. Look for characters whose listening and communication techniques are integral to the story. What, if anything, happens between characters that sparks a change in how they communicate with each other?

Social Studies/Civics

1. Videotape Sunday morning news shows, "Nightline," Congressional debates, or other news programs where two people with opposing viewpoints speak about a controversial topic. Observe how they listen and respond to each other. Is there a dialogue that promotes greater understanding of the issue or a competition over who speaks the loudest and longest? Do facilitators encourage active listening? What impact do the media have on public conversation if responsive listening is not encouraged?

2. Select a bill or issue that was recently debated in the House or Senate that would be of interest to students or that is related to a topic you are studying in class. (For example, the 1996 crime bill involved a major debate about appropriating money for midnight basketball and other violence-prevention programs for young people. Another example is the question of creating and sustaining national service programs for young people.) Generate questions students would want to ask about the issue that would help them decide whether to support a particular recommendation. Then get transcripts from the Congressional Record of the debate. Have students take turns reading from the transcript. Did their questions get answered? Did the debate generate more heat or light? How did members of Congress respond to each other's comments and questions?

Mathematics

Divide students into pairs and give each a problem that has multiple solutions. One person says how she would solve the problem while the other person listens. Then her partner paraphrases, checking out if he understood her method of solving the problem.

4) "I" Messages

Students learn how using "I" messages to express one's feelings and needs can allow disputants to have a clearer picture of what the conflict is really about. Blaming is replaced by clear articulation of one's own feelings and needs.

English

1. Use the Why Use "I" Messages handout (Lesson 16) with a literature excerpt in which a character has a tough time saying what he or she feels, thinks, needs, etc. Find passages in the text in which a character uses an ineffective response from the left hand side of the handout. Then write an "I" message that the character might say instead.

2. Use video clips of TV shows to point out when characters are communicating with "you" messages. What's the consequence? Does the character get what he

or she needs? How do other characters respond? Then brainstorm "I" messages that the character might have said instead. How would the scene play out differently?

3. An "I" statement can be a turning point in a character's life or in the plot of a novel, play, or film. When a character finally speaks from his or her own experience and reveals what he or she is really feeling and really needs, other characters respond and listen differently. Find powerful passages where the use of an "I" statement by one character has a profound impact.

Social Studies

Find speeches and commentaries in which historical figures who are struggling for justice have spoken from their own experience in ways that express their feelings and reveal how specific conditions have impacted their lives, without blaming or attacking individuals (e.g., Chief Joseph; Martin Luther King, Jr.; Dorothy Day; Mahatma Gandhi; Daniel Berrigan; Cezar Chavez). You might want to compare these speeches to others where the speaker attacks and blames. What makes one kind of speech more powerful and compelling than the other? How do you listen to each kind of speech? Which one is more convincing?

5) Anger Management

How we deal with our anger and other highly charged emotions makes all the difference since anger is the emotion that often drives a conflict. Looking at the role that anger plays in the lives of literary characters and how anger can affect the outcome of historical and current events can help students become more familiar with anger and its effects. Examining anger more closely can also help students see the connection between our emotions and our behavior.

English

1. In plays, novels, or stories, have students track different characters' emotional states, noting how they deal with highly charged emotions, identifying the anger cues and triggers for that character. Also notice how the character manages his or her anger in constructive or destructive ways and how the character responds to another person's anger. Each character is likely to use different techniques to cool down. A useful point to make: There's no one right way to handle our emotions.

2. Look for incidents in stories where a character is very angry or upset but doesn't express it to anyone, whether to a friend or the person he or she is angry with. What is the result? Discuss the costs of keeping anger bottled up.

Social Studies

1. Identify situations in which leaders have transformed their anger into constructive action and others where anger has driven a leader to respond too quickly or act out of a need for revenge or retribution. In politics we are often reluctant to acknowledge that personal feelings can be the driving force in a decision, yet it happens all the time. Look at presidential biographies to find examples where personal slights, resentments, and anger at individuals have influenced policy decisions.

2. When nations are in conflict with each other, speeches by leaders on both sides are often laden with emotionally charged language. Compare the language in speeches and communiqués written in the heat of the conflict with those written when there is an attempt to work things out between the two parties.

6) Collaborative Problem-Solving

Collaborative problem-solving engages small groups of students in a five-step process:

1. Define the problem.
2. Gather information and assess the steps necessary to solve the problem.
3. Generate alternative solutions.
4. Select the means and resources to solve the problem in a way that factors in constraints and meets some interests of everyone in the group.
5. Implement the plan or solution.

One of the benefits of open-ended problem-solving is presenting students with a challenge to which there are a number of approaches and solutions. Debriefing problem-solving activities is an excellent opportunity for students to reflect on how they think through a problem and decide what to do.

Some guidelines for effective problem-solving:

1. Describe the problem in detail.
2. Set the challenge and the goal. Let students know that there are many ways to solve the problem.
3. Ensure that students have enough information to tackle the problem comfortably. Brainstorm possibilities and review the challenge to make sure that students know what they are doing.
4. Set constraints on what you can and cannot do.
5. Limit resources and materials.
6. Set criteria for assessment (teacher, students, or teacher and students).
7. Limit the number in a group; group students so that there is a balance of different skills among the students.
8. Give everyone a role and a responsibility.
9. Divide time between planning (research, brainstorming, and/or strategizing) and doing (actual design, solution, construction, etc.)
10. Give instructions in several ways and use examples, illustrations, and models to show what to do or how to do it.

7) Negotiation and Mediation

These two methods of solving disputes can be demonstrated in the classroom by inviting trained mediators or having students assume the roles of chief negotiator or mediator. These methods draw on the concepts of active listening, "I" messages, and getting to Win-Win solutions.

History
Students can reenact examples of mediations or negotiations that have been used to settle historical or current conflicts. Examples could include the Treaty of Versailles, the Camp David peace accords, or the North American Free Trade Agreement. Students can use the Negotiation Strategies chart (next page) to prepare for the negotiation.

English
Students can role-play characters in a conflict who are willing to settle their dispute through negotiation or mediation (e.g., what if Romeo's and Juliet's families went to mediation?)

NEGOTIATION STRATEGIES

Conflict Between Whom?	Conflict Over What?	Conditions That Reveal Conflict?

Positive Goal: To be able to	**Negative Goal:** To stop or prevent
Country or Group:	**Country or Group:**
Position/Wants	Position/Wants
Interests/Needs	Interests/Needs
Values	Values
Climate	Climate
Clarifying Questions	
Refocusing Questions	
Common Concerns and Interests	
Alternatives	**Obstacles**
Agreement in Principle	

Infusing Instructional Strategies for a Peaceable Classroom

The instructional strategies described in this curriculum can be used successfully in any required or elective course. They promote the principles of a Peaceable Classroom by:

- involving students in a cooperative process;

- creating opportunities for interaction among students;

- establishing an atmosphere where students are free to verbalize their feelings and ideas nonjudgmentally;

- demonstrating respect for different opinions and perspectives;

- linking personal stories and experiences to abstract concepts;

- using a multi-sensory approach or incorporating multiple intelligences in ways that encourage students to appreciate various learning strengths that different individuals bring to the group.

Where do I begin?

1. Choose a unit of study in which you want to use some of these strategies.

2. Look through the Teaching and Learning Strategies described in "Preparing to Teach This Curriculum" and select several strategies that you want to use to teach this unit.

3. Decide on the purpose for using each strategy and the subject-matter content that will be the focus of the activity you create. (See the table below.)

4. Create the activity, developing materials and questions that are content-specific.

5. Write down how you want students to give feedback on this strategy.

PURPOSE OF ACTIVITY

• to introduce _____ (new topic, skill, or concept)	• to make connections between students' own experience and _____ (topic, skill, subject matter)
• to review _____ (key topic, skill, or concept)	• to check out what students are thinking about _____ (key topic, concept, or issues)
• to practice _____in another way (skill)	• to gather more information about _____ (topic or concept)
• to explore in greater depth _____ (topic, issue, concept)	• to demonstrate competency _____ (skill)
• to apply in new situations _____ (topic, issue, skill, concept)	• to assess what students have learned about _____ (topic or concept)

Infusing Thematic Units on Conflict and Cooperation

Think about appropriate opportunities for developing thematic units and in-depth lessons that take a more comprehensive and complex look at how conflict has shaped the past as well as the world students live in right now. Creating a special two- or three-week unit of study can give you a chance to use the concepts and skills of interpersonal conflict resolution to examine the roles that conflict, violence, cooperation, and peacemaking play in the human experience.

Where do I begin?

- Brainstorm a list of content topics from throughout your course syllabus that could be synthesized into a coherent thematic unit focused on conflict and peacemaking.

- Brainstorm a specific list of case studies, books, readings, speakers, projects, and videos that you could use to explore this theme.

- Brainstorm a set of "big questions" that could help frame the unit you create. Here are some examples:

  - How do emotions drive behavior?

  - How does the quality of communication affect the behavior of conflicting individuals, groups, and nations?

  - How do attitudes about violence, aggression, and cooperation influence decisions that individuals and groups make?

  - What conditions and attitudes make negotiation between conflicting groups possible? What blocks effective negotiation?

  - How and when can peacemaking strategies be used to de-escalate local and global conflicts?

  - What understandings enable people with deep religious, cultural, and political differences to talk to one another and work toward effective change and resolution of differences?

Examples of Thematic Units for Extended Lessons:

Literature

1. Exploring Conflict Through Drama. Students form groups to read and perform selected scenes from different plays. Ask each group to focus on the use of conflict as a dramatic element and to use conflict resolution skills and concepts to analyze conflicts among or between characters. To follow up, ask each group to write and perform a brief one-act play.

2. Cross-Cultural Studies of American Literature. Students can explore cross-cultural differences among people in the United States through poetry, plays, short stories, essays, and memoirs. Ask each student to choose one writer and discuss how the author's work is informed by his or her personal experience and cultural background. Students can practice perspective-taking skills by choosing a situation or event and writing a response from the author's perspective or by forming pairs and enacting a dialogue between authors from different cultural backgrounds.

Literature/Social Studies

1. Visions of Utopia and Dystopia. Students can investigate the concept of community by investigating movements to establish intentional communities or by examining the portrayal of utopian or dystopian communities in novels and films. Students can form groups to create and describe their own visions of utopia.

2. War and Peace in Literature. Students can compare poetry, essays, plays, novels, or films that depict the experience of war or the struggle for peace. One approach is

to compare works drawn from two or more historical periods; another is to compare a variety of works set during a particular conflict. Students may also wish to discuss how different media shape the way the artist communicates his or her experience.

3. Impact of Immigration. Students can draw on films, memoirs, fictional writing, essays, speeches, and even folk music to explore the forces that have driven immigration and shaped how communities respond to immigrants under different historical circumstances. Examples could include the influx of Irish immigrants to America in the 1840s; waves of immigration to the United States in the 1920s and 1990s; or the recent influx of economic refugees to Europe from poor nations in Africa and the Middle East.

Social Studies

1. Institutionalized Discrimination. Students can prepare case studies of legalized discrimination against specific groups—for instance, the Nuremberg laws in Nazi Germany, the South African system of apartheid, or Jim Crow laws in the American South. Divide the class into groups to discover the origin and history of these laws, the historical context in which they were enacted, and their impact on society, groups, and individuals. After each group has conducted a case study, regroup the students so that they can compare and discuss their findings.

2. Growth of a Global Economy. Students can examine the costs and benefits of a global economy by breaking into groups focusing on specific issues. Examples could include free trade, international regulation of child labor, the internationalization of financial markets, and the role of the IMF. Ask each group to identify people affected by each issue, their interests, and potential conflicts or commonalities among them.

3. Peacekeeping. Explore the variety of ways that governments attempt to prevent conflict or to resolve disputes without resorting to armed conflict. Examples could include the negotiation of international treaties, the imposition of sanctions, the assertion of neutrality or noncooperation, or the effort to resolve conflicts through international agencies such as the United Nations. Ask them to examine the conditions that lead governments to choose a particular strategy. Students may also want to investigate and compare peacekeeping efforts by the United Nations and the League of Nations. Students can compare responses to different historical conflicts or different types of conflicts (regional rivalries, arms control, environmental conflicts) or can form groups to test different strategies for resolving a particular conflict.

4. Ethnicity and Nationalism in the Twentieth Century. Students can take a regional approach to exploring the relationship between ethnicity and nationalism. Ask them to identify countries or regions in which ethnic minorities are seeking or have achieved national independence—for instance, the nations of the former Soviet Union and East European communist-bloc countries, sub-Saharan Africa, northern Ireland, the Canadian province of Quebec, and the Middle East. Then divide them into groups to conduct case studies. In what ways do ethnic differences contribute to a sense of national identity? In what ways may ethnic and national identities conflict? What conditions may exacerbate this conflict? What conditions can help defuse it?

5. School Board Controversies. Take a look at controversial issues that have required your local school board or school boards elsewhere in your state to take action. How did the school board respond to the controversy? How did the board's actions affect various groups that had a stake in the decision? Did the decision meet the needs of some groups and not others? After studying the issue, students can take the roles of

individuals and groups involved and try to negotiate their own solution.

Social Studies/Science

Resolving Environmental Conflicts. Explore the causes and consequences of local, regional, or international environmental conflicts and compare the perspectives of different groups involved. Help students distinguish between the positions and interests of various groups and use the Conflict Escalator to map the progress these groups are making toward resolving the conflict in real life. Examples of environmental conflicts could include: global warming, destruction of the rain forest, acid rain, disputes over water rights, wetlands protection, and the protection of endangered species.

Infusing Peaceable Classroom Principles Into Daily and Weekly Routines

Modeling is the first and most important way we learn. Your personal commitment to practice conflict resolution skills in your interactions with students sends them a powerful message that these skills really matter. Think about how you can structure your classroom routines and lesson plans in ways that promote the principles of the Peaceable Classroom and nurture the spirit of creative conflict resolution everyday. The practices presented here can help you build a greater sense of community and mutual respect and can communicate to students that emotional and social learning are valued components of the teaching and learning process.

1. Discuss and create a vision of a caring, respectful, and responsible learning community.

2. Make agreements with your students about how to work, live, and learn together at the beginning of the school year. Keep revisiting agreements in order to identify problems and ways that students can help each other keep the agreements.

3. Provide community-building activities at the beginning of the year so that students can get to know each other.

4. Create lesson plans using the Workshop Approach, which includes a gathering, agenda review, main activity, assessment, and closing.

5. Include at least one gathering and one closing activity as part of your weekly schedule.

6. Identify both the academic goals and skills (what is to be learned) and social goals and skills (how students can work together to learn it and what they can do to support each other's learning).

7. Provide weekly opportunities for individual and group feedback, reflection, and assessment. How are students experiencing what's happening in the classroom?

8. For each lesson, highlight a Peaceable Classroom principle that underlies the teaching and learning process you use in the lesson.

9. Choose a different Peaceable Classroom principle to emphasize every month. Make it part of daily classroom life during that month.

10. Make it safe for students to acknowledge, express, and cope with feelings.

11. Provide classroom routines, activities, and "check-ins" that create a readiness to learn and that help students to settle in and focus.

12. Increase opportunities to affirm individuals and the group through positive attention and rituals/routines that celebrate successes.

13. Address personal, racial, ethnic, and gender put-downs in ways that help to interrupt and reduce put-downs and prejudice.

14. Use class meetings and Win-Win problem-solving to discuss and resolve problems

in ways that meet the needs of the teacher, the student, and the group.

15. Offer choices and involve students in creating and negotiating options for homework, review and study sessions, class assignments, projects, and tests.

16. Introduce clear processes for dealing with controversy constructively and addressing issues of concern that come up in the classroom.

17. Make participation a significant part of academic grading, asking students to assess and reflect on their own participation in specific activities, at the end of a unit, and near the end of a grading period.

18. Try to include 10 to 15 minutes of listening time every week in which you or students pose a question or problem to the group and you agree to listen to students without interrupting them for any reason. This is much harder to do than it sounds! However, your willingness to listen lets students know that respectful listening goes two ways in your classroom.

Additional Activities

This chapter consists of highly interactive, experiential activities that extend the concepts introduced in the core 36 lessons and further develop students' skills. This chapter contains some of the activities that students like and remember the most; however, these activities require one or more of the following:

- more than one class period to complete;
- a large space;
- advance preparation;
- special materials.

Here is a complete list of the additional activities, along with suggestions for when to use them.

Tinker Toys: A Communication Exercise—Use at the beginning of the school year to promote team building and group awareness or later in the year to strengthen team work.

Building Blocks of Cooperation—Use at the beginning of the school year to promote team building and group awareness or later in the year to strengthen teamwork.

We All Belong to Groups—Use after introducing the concept of diversity (Lesson 5).

Peacemaking and Peacemakers—Use after discussing violence and nonviolence (Lesson 9) or before or after exploring how people can make a difference (Lesson 35).

Security in Your Life—Use before or after exploring the issues of power, equity, and opportunity (Lessons 28 and 29).

Letting Go of Labels—Use before or after discussing stereotypes and prejudice (Lesson 30).

Crossing Cultures: A Simulation Game—Use after discussing the role of diversity in conflict (Lesson 32).

Taking Action on a Community Problem—Use after exploring how people can make a difference (Lesson 35).

Tinker Toys:
A Communication Exercise

OBJECTIVES

Students will:

- participate in a highly interactive team-building activity;
- consider how the quality, type, and style of communication affects a group's ability to accomplish a task effectively.

PEACEABLE CLASSROOM PRINCIPLES

- Cooperation and collaborative problem-solving
- Shared decision-making
- Caring and effective communication

AGENDA

1. **Gathering (optional)**

   Choose any gathering activity from appendix A.

2. **Review Agenda**

3. **Lesson Activity**

   - Tinker Toys

4. **Checking Out What We've Learned**

   Whole-Group Debriefing

5. **Closing (optional)**

   Choose any closing activity from appendix B.

Gathering (optional)

Choose any gathering activity from appendix A.

Review Agenda

Write the agenda on the board and review it with the class.

Tinker Toys

Materials: Multiple sets of Tinker Toys or other construction materials

In preparation for this activity you'll need to do the following ahead of time:

1. Decide where you will do this activity. You'll need the following spaces:

    *   a construction site for each team (in one large room or in separate rooms);
    *   a hallway or room that can serve as the message center (the only students allowed in this space are the messengers and they should not be able to see the construction sites or the original construction);
    *   an enclosed space where the original construction can be located. "Lookers" and "Feedbackers" need to be able to go in and out of this area.

2. Make copies of the Tinker Toys Roles handout (p. 264) and cut apart the strips so that each group of five to seven students can have a complete set of strips.

3. Make a construction out of Tinker Toys or other building materials. You can decide how complex the construction should be and whether it is abstract or looks like a vehicle, building, or person; but make sure it's something students will be able to build within the time limit. Divide the rest of the building materials so that you have four or five identical sets for each team to use to build a replica of your structure.

    One configuration could look like this:

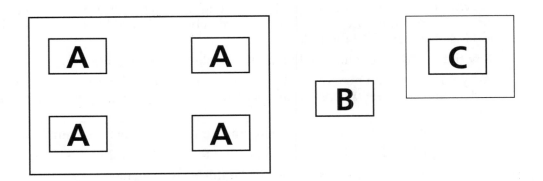

A=construction site   **B**=message center   **C**=location of original

Explain to students that they will be working in teams of five to seven students. Their goal will be to create an exact replica of a Tinker Toy construction that only a few team members will be able to see. Here are the rules and guidelines for the activity:

1. Group members will need to decide the roles that each of them will take. Each group will receive role reminders so that students can remember what they can do and to whom they can talk.

2. Each team will have about 5 minutes to organize themselves and about 20 minutes to build a replica of the original construction.

3. The teacher will serve as a monitor, making sure that students are where they are supposed to be and are doing what they're supposed to be doing.

Distribute one set of role descriptions to each group and go over them with the whole class. Ask the groups to begin assigning roles. Signal when 5 minutes have passed and tell the class that teams now have 20 minutes to complete their constructions.

Invite students to ask you questions during the activity. If team members aren't sure whether it's okay to do something they want to do, they can ask you. For example, a student might ask, "Can the Looker draw a picture of the original to give to the Messenger?" You can answer, "Yes." Or a student might ask, "Can a supplier bring pieces to the Messenger to see if they are the correct pieces to use?" You can again answer, "Yes." But if no one asks these questions, don't tell students about these loopholes in the rules. Be sure to congratulate any groups that think of asking a lot of questions about the rules. Good communication depends on not making assumptions about what's okay and what's not okay. Good communicators check things out.

Note: You can simplify the activity if needed by using fewer roles, creating more teams, and creating a smaller, simpler original construction. If you use fewer roles, we suggest using the Looker, the Messenger, and the Builder.

During the construction phase, give teams two or three reminders of how much time they have left. If some teams finish before others, they can observe other teams in silence. Call "Time" when 20 minutes are up.

After calling "Time," ask students to go back to their seats and respond in writing to some of the following questions. Allow students 10 or 15 minutes to write.

- What was difficult about this activity? What was fun?
- Did your team accomplish the goal of building an exact replica of the original construction? Write down what your team members did or did not do that made it easy or difficult to complete the task.
- How did you decide who would take what roles in your teams?
- Was your role what you expected it to be? What was fun about your role? What was hard about your role? What skills are particularly important for a person who takes your role?
- Do you think that some roles are more important than others? Explain your answer.
- Make a list of all the skills your team needed to be successful in this activity.
- How did communication restrictions make this activity challenging?
- How would you modify the rules to make the activity easier to accomplish?
- What did you learn about yourself as a team member and a problem solver? What do you need to work effectively in a group?

Checking Out What We've Learned

Discuss any of the questions above as a class. Be sure to allow plenty of time for discussion of this activity. The reflection and discussion period is what allows students to gain insight into communication and group work.

Closing (optional)

Choose any closing activity from appendix B.

S T U D E N T   H A N D O U T

TINKER TOY ROLES

Looker (only one person)	**What You Do:** You can see only the original construction. You cannot go to your team's building site.
	Who You Can Talk To: You can talk only to the Messenger.
Messenger (only one person)	**What You Do:** You must stay in the message center. You cannot see either the replica your team is building or the original construction.
	Who You Can Talk To: You can talk to the Looker and the Builder in the Message Center.
Supplier (only one person)	**What You Do:** You must stay at the construction site. You can distribute no more than six Tinker Toy pieces to the Builder at one time.
	Who You Can Talk To: You can talk to the Builder. You can ask "yes" or "no" questions to the Feedbacker.
Builder (one or two people)	**What You Do:** You can move between your construction site and the message center. You build the replica with the Tinker Toys supplied by the Supplier.
	Who You Can Talk To: You can talk to the Messenger and the Supplier. You can ask "yes" or "no" questions to the Feedbacker.
Feedbacker (only one person)	**What You Do:** You can go anywhere. You are the only one who can see both the original and the replica.
	Who You Can Talk To: You can listen to the Builder and the Supplier, but you can say only, "Yes, that's right," or "No, that's wrong."

Building Blocks of Cooperation

OBJECTIVES

Students will:

- think about how they work in groups;
- identify attitudes, roles, and behaviors that can help groups work effectively to solve problems.

PEACEABLE CLASSROOM PRINCIPLES

- Cooperation and collaborative problem-solving
- Shared decision-making
- Building community

AGENDA

1. **Gathering (optional)**

   Choose any gathering activity from appendix A.

2. **Review Agenda**

3. **Lesson Activity**

   - Building Blocks

4. **Checking Out What We've Learned**

   Whole-Group Debriefing

5. **Closing (optional)**

   Choose any closing activity from appendix B.

Gathering (optional)

Choose any gathering activity from appendix A.

Review Agenda

Write the agenda on the board and review it with the class.

Building Blocks

Materials: Each team of five to seven students needs a large number of construction blocks in four or five colors (foam or wooden blocks, Legos, etc.)

Divide the class into teams of five to seven students. Divide the blocks so that each team has more blocks of one color than of any other color.

Explain to the students that each team's challenge is to build as many towers as it can, using as many of its blocks as it can. Teams will have 15 minutes to complete the challenge. There are five rules for building towers:

1.   Each tower must be higher than the previous tower.

2.   The first tower must contain at least one block of each color.

3.   The color sequence you use in the first tower will determine your color sequence for the rest of your towers. Your color sequence starts from the bottom block of your first tower and should be read going upwards. You need to continue using the same color sequence as you build higher and higher towers. Note:

     •   You can represent a color using any number of blocks of that color.

     •   There are many ways to repeat the color sequence. Be creative.

4.   You can keep asking questions about the rules.

5.   Your negotiator can trade for blocks from other teams.

Emphasize that there are many ways to meet the rules. You may want to show students an example of a series of towers that meet the rules, such as the one illustrated below. This series meets the rules by ending the tower in the middle of the color sequence and continuing the color sequence in the next tower. The color sequence for this series of towers is blue, yellow, green, red.

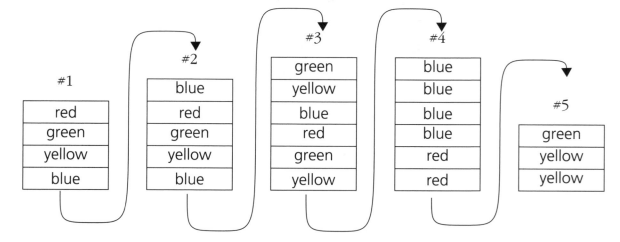

Pass out the Roles for Tower Building handout (p. 268) or write the roles on the board. Each team needs to decide who will play each role. Allow five minutes for choosing roles and making a plan for building the towers. During this time students may not touch the blocks.

Give each process observer a card with the following questions on it:

- How did the team decide who would take each role?
- Who made decisions?
- How did the team decide how to build the tower?
- What did people do or say that helped the group meet the challenge? Was there anything the team could have done differently to work more effectively together?

Ask the groups to begin building their towers. Signal the students to stop when 15 minutes have passed.

Checking Out What We've Learned

Lead a discussion about this activity. Ask the process observers from each team to speak first, answering some or all of the questions on their cards.

Then ask the class:

- Were you successful in meeting the goal of the activity? How would you assess your group's effort on a scale of 1 to 10?
- What was fun about this activity? What was hard or frustrating about it?
- How did it feel to play your role? How did you contribute to the success of your group?
- Was there any tension in the group? Did team members have to compromise or work out differences?
- Did you feel competitive with other groups? Why or why not?
- What skills and attitudes helped you work well together? Make a chart to record students' answers. (See the model below.) If you were not satisfied with how your team worked together, what could you do differently next time so that your team could be more successful?

A GOOD TEAM

What You Hear and Say	What You See or Do

Closing (optional)

Choose any closing activity from appendix B.

S T U D E N T   H A N D O U T

ROLES FOR TOWER BUILDING

Facilitator

Person who begins the discussion and ensures that all team members have their say.

Question-Asker and Summarizer

Person who asks questions and summarizes ideas and suggestions from the group.

Negotiator

Person who can negotiate with other groups to trade for blocks that you need.

Gatekeeper

Person who makes sure that the team stays focused on the goal (watches the time, color sequence, height of towers).

Encourager

Person who gives positive feedback and encourages students when they are making positive contributions to the group.

Compromiser

Person who can help the group sort out conflicting ideas and help the group reach decisions on what to do.

Process Observer

Person who watches, listens, and jots down notes about how the group accomplishes the task and works together. This person reports back to the whole class at the end.

We All Belong to Groups

OBJECTIVES

Students will:

- identify the groups to which they belong by birth, by culture, and by choice;
- share their thoughts and feelings about belonging to these groups

PEACEABLE CLASSROOM PRINCIPLES

- Affirmation and acceptance
- Appreciation for diversity
- Personal connections
- Building community

AGENDA

1. **Gathering (optional)**

   Choose any gathering activity from appendix A.

2. **Review Agenda**

3. **Lesson Activity**

   - Our Groups

4. **Checking Out What We've Learned**

   Discussion of Reflective Writing

5. **Closing (optional)**

   Group Wishes

Gathering (optional)

Choose any gathering activity from appendix A.

Review Agenda

Write the agenda on the board and review it with the class.

Our Groups

Present the following mini-lecture on cultural groups we are born into, grow up in, or choose:

> Everyone belongs to groups. We are born into some groups. For example, we may be born female, Chinese, or disabled. Other groups reflect the culture in which we grew up. For example, we may come from a family that goes to a Catholic church or that is Mexican-American. We also belong to other groups that we choose. We might join a soccer team, work at a job part-time, play in a band, write for the school newspaper, or volunteer at a local soup kitchen.

Pass out the two Groups I Belong To handouts (questionnaire and concentric circles diagram, pp. 272 and 273). Ahead of time, fill in the concentric circles diagram for yourself. Share this with the students as a model, then ask each of them to answer the Groups I Belong To questionnaire and fill in the concentric circles diagram. Point out to students that many of us have mixed feelings about some groups to which we belong. There are some things we really like that make us proud of our group affiliation; there are other things that may make us uncomfortable or angry about belonging to certain groups.

Divide students into diverse groups of three to share their responses with each other. Remind students that they can choose what they want to share and what they don't. Encourage students to ask open-ended questions to each other that help them learn more about groups with which they are unfamiliar. Allow groups 15 to 20 minutes for this discussion.

Checking Out What We've Learned

Use any of the following questions for discussion or reflective writing:

- How did this experience change your understanding of some groups? Complete the sentence "Before this conversation I didn't know that ..."
- Think about one of the groups to which you belong. When were you first aware that you were a member of that group?
- Think of a cultural group to which you don't belong, but one with which you have had some contact. When were you first aware of this group? What do you remember hearing others say about this group? What was your first personal experience with someone from this group? Did your thoughts about this group change after coming to know an individual from this group?
- Sometimes we're uncomfortable with the assumptions and stereotypes associated with a group to which we belong. What stereotypes and assumptions do you wish could disappear? Consider this example:

  "It is utterly exhausting being black in America ... While many minority groups and women feel similar stress, there is no respite or escape from your badge of color ... The constant burden to 'prove' that you are as smart, as honest, as interesting, as wide-gauging and motivated as any other individual tires you out ..."—Marian Wright Edelman, president of the Children's Defense Fund.

- Sometimes our loyalty to a group conflicts with the feelings, values, and desires we experience as individuals. Discuss or write about an experience when you had to make a choice between following the expected beliefs and attitudes of your group or following your own personal beliefs.

Closing (optional)

Group Wishes: Ask each student to think about a group that he or she belongs to such as:

- females or males
- teenagers
- families
- students at this school

Ask students to complete the following sentence, describing a wish about what members of a group they belong to might do differently: "I wish more ... would ..." To provide an example, you can use the following sentence about the group "adults": "I wish more adults would sit for 15 minutes each day and just listen to kids, without interrupting."

S T U D E N T   H A N D O U T

GROUPS I BELONG TO

1. Identify two groups that you belong to by birth (physical differences, gender, race, or ethnicity).

2. Identify four groups that reflect your cultural identity (cultural heritage, geographical region, religion, social and economic status, educational background).

3. Identify three groups that you belong to by choice (sports teams, clubs, youth groups, job, other interests).

4. Describe one thing about yourself that makes you feel different from everyone else.

5. Choose to focus on your **gender** or **racial/ethnic identity** for this question. Write down three things that make you proud to be a member of your group and three things that can make it difficult to belong to your group.

What Makes You Proud	What Makes It Difficult
1.	1.
2.	2.
3.	3.

GROUPS I BELONG TO

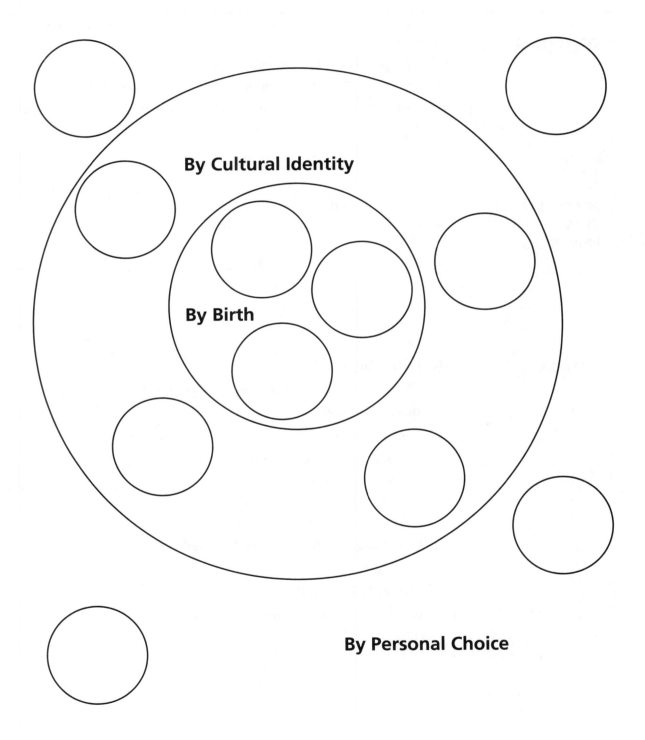

By Cultural Identity

By Birth

By Personal Choice

Peacemaking and Peacemakers

OBJECTIVES

Students will:

- brainstorm a list of peacemakers;
- create a collective definition of peace and peacemaking;
- identify the essential skills, qualities, and attitudes of an effective peacemaker.

PEACEABLE CLASSROOM PRINCIPLES

- Managing and resolving conflict
- Social responsibility

AGENDA

1. **Gathering (optional)**

   Choose any gathering activity in appendix A.

2. **Review Agenda**

3. **Lesson Activities**

   - Drawing Peace/Peacemaking
   - Anatomy of a Peacemaker
   - What is the Role of a Peacemaker?
   - Researching Peacemakers

4. **Checking Out What We've Learned**

   Writing About Peace

5. **Closing (optional)**

   Choose any closing activity from appendix B.

Gathering (optional)

Choose any gathering activity from appendix A.

Review Agenda

Write the agenda on the board and review it with the class.

Drawing Peace/Peacemaking

Begin by asking students to take a few minutes to create a definition of the word "peace" or "peacemaking." Ask students to share their definitions with the class. Write student responses on the board. Try to develop collective definitions of peace and peacemaking.

Divide students into groups of three or four. Give each group a large sheet of newsprint and markers. Ask students to cover their newsprint with images of peace by drawing pictures, symbols, or cartoons. Their murals should answer the question, "What does peace or peacemaking look like?"

Compare the murals with the collective definition of peace. Are they the same or different?

Anatomy of a Peacemaker

Ask students for a list of the skills, qualities, and attitudes that they think people need to have to be good peacemakers and problem solvers. Make a list of their responses.

Ask students if they can think of parts of the body that are associated with the different items on their list. For example, the quality of being a good listener is associated with the ears.

Divide the class into pairs or small groups and ask the groups to draw posters that will be titled "Anatomy of a Peacemaker." Each poster should contain a large drawing of a person. Have students draw their person in a way that highlights the qualities of a peacemaker. For example, a peacemaker might need to have big ears to help her listen well. Ask students to label and explain all the crucial anatomical parts of a peacemaker.

Ask students to share and explain their posters to the class.

Researching Peacemakers

Ask students to choose one peacemaker to research. Look for videos, correspondence, speeches, autobiographies, and bibliographies that will give students a picture of how these people have worked throughout their lives to make the world a more peaceful and just place. The Visionaries and Peacemakers handout (p. 277) presents a list of writers, philosophers, religious leaders, political leaders, community organizers, and others who have made contributions to peacemaking around the world. Students might choose one of these peacemakers to research. Students can also choose to interview a living peacemaker or can choose to report on organizations that work on peace and justice issues locally or globally.

Focus questions for student research might include:

- Identify this person's vision of peace.
- What did this person want to change?
- What obstacles made his or her work as a peacemaker challenging or difficult?
- How did this person change the lives of individuals in the communities in which he or she worked?

- What attitudes, personal characteristics, and commitments made this individual unusual? What qualities helped this peacemaker in his or her work?
- Find one quotation that reflects this individual's perspective on peace and peacemaking.
- How would you convince the class that this person deserves the title of peacemaker?
- How do you think this person would respond to a current problem that you are concerned about?

You and your students might want to plan a calendar of presentations throughout the year so that each student gets the opportunity to share his or her peacemaker's vision with the rest of the class.

What Is the Role of a Peacemaker?

Ask the class to brainstorm two lists: 1) What do peacemakers do? and 2) Name people whom you would describe as peacemakers (living or dead) from your community, across the country, and around the world. Record responses on the board or on newsprint.

Discuss the lists using the following questions:

- Is every person a peacemaker at some time in his or her life?
- Which students and adults play the role of peacemaker at school?
- What makes it hard to play the role of the peacemaker at school?
- Why is it worth playing the role of the peacemaker at school?
- Consider interpersonal, community, and global peacemaking. How are these similar or different?
- Do the peacemakers on our list share any common qualities? What are they?
- What kinds of challenges and struggles do peacemakers face?
- Do you think that a person who is not personally peaceful can make the world more peaceful? Why or why not?

Checking Out What We've Learned

Ask students to choose one of the following to write about:

- Describe a situation or scene that you think of as peaceful.
- What comes to mind when you hear the phrase "a world at peace?"
- What are the major obstacles to achieving peace?
- What kinds of changes would people have to make in their values and actions to make peace possible?
- What kind of changes can each of us make within ourselves to help us achieve peace in our personal lives?

Ask volunteers to share what they have written with the class.

Closing (optional)

Choose any closing activity from appendix B.

S T U D E N T   H A N D O U T

VISIONARIES AND PEACEMAKERS

Addams, Jane

Baez, Joan

Ball, George

Begin, Menachim

Ben-Gurion, David

Berrigan, Daniel

Biko, Steven

Bonhoeffer, Dietrich

Brandt, Willy

Brower, David

Buddha

Bunche, Ralph

Caldicott, Helen

Carter, Jimmy

Chavez, Cesar

Chief Joseph

Chief Seattle

Coffin, William Sloane

Corrigan, Mairead

Dalai Lama

Day, Dorothy

Debs, Eugene

Dellums, Ron

Deming, Barbara

Dewey, John

Douglass, Frederick

Dumas, Lloyd

Dunant, Jean-Henri

Edelman, Marian Wright

Einstein, Albert

Esquival, Adolfo Perez

Fisher, Roger

Forsberg, Randall

Gandhi, Mahatma

George, Susan

Gorbachev, Mikhail

Gruening, Ernest

Guthrie, Woody

Hamer, Fannie Lou

Hammarskjold, Dag

Hatfield, Mark

Havel, Vaclav

Henderson, Arthur

Heschel, Abraham

Kant, Immanuel

Kelly, Petra

King, Martin Luther

Lappé, Frances Moore

MacBride, Sean

Malcolm X

Mandela, Nelson

Marshall, Glen George

McGovern, George

Melman, Seymour

Milk, Harvey

Montessori, Maria

Morse, Wayne

Penn, William

Pope John XXIII

Reardon, Betty

Rankin, Jeannette

Robles, Alfonso Garcia

Romero, Archbishop Oscar

Roosevelt, Eleanor

Rustin, Bayard

Russell, Bertrand

Sadat, Anwar

Sagan, Carl

Sakharov, Andrei

Sato, Eisaku

Schell, Jonathan

Schumacher, E.F.

Schweickart, Rusty

Schweitzer, Albert

Sharp, Gene

Shriver, Sargent

Sivard, Ruth

Smith, Samantha

St. Francis of Assisi

Tolstoy, Leo

Thomas, Evan

Truth, Sojourner

Trumbo, Dalton

Tubman, Harriet

Tutu, Bishop Desmond

Vance, Cyrus

Walesa, Lech

Warnke, Paul

Young, Andrew

Wiesel, Elie

Security in Your Life

OBJECTIVES	Students will:
	• reflect on their own experience and concerns about personal security;
	• experience the differing degrees of security that U.S. citizens feel depending on family circumstances/socioeconomic status.
PEACEABLE CLASSROOM PRINCIPLES	• Personal connections
	• Social responsibility
AGENDA	**1. Gathering (optional)**
	Students write about and discuss personal security.
	2. Review Agenda
	3. Lesson Activity
	• The Luck of the Draw
	4. Checking Out What We've Learned
	Whole-Group Debriefing
	5. Closing (optional)
	Choose any closing activity from appendix A.

Gathering (optional)

Ask students to write on any of the following topics:

- Write about what it means to have personal security. Would your definition be the same as your parents'? Why or why not?

- Write about a time when you experienced complete safety and security. What was special about this experience? What made you feel so safe and secure?

- Write about an experience in which you felt completely unsafe. What made the situation so unsafe? Was there anything you could do to reduce the danger? What happened? How did you come out of it okay?

- Think about the conditions a child needs to feel secure growing up. Which ones would be on your "top 10" list?

- What kinds of situations or conditions create the most insecurity for young people?

- What conditions in your neighborhood or community threaten your security the most?

Invite students to read their writing or discuss any of these questions.

Review Agenda

Write the agenda on the board and review it with the class.

The Luck of the Draw

Materials: Several bags of peanuts in the shell (or another type of treat); one basket or tray for each group of five or six students. Each group should have about 75 peanuts.

Make copies of the Who's Secure in the United States? handouts (p. 281). Make one set of copies for each group of five or six students. Cut out the cards and place each set face down in a tray or basket.

Divide the class into groups of five or six students. Have each group arrange their chairs in a circle. Ask two students from each group to volunteer to be the "game directors." Each pair of game directors will sit on the floor in the center of the circle. One director's task is to pass the basket to the person who needs to draw a card. The other director is the peanut distributor.

Explain to students that the basket will be passed around the circle and students will each pick a card and read it out loud. Each card describes the life situation of an individual or family and the student holding it will be allowed to collect 0 to 20 peanuts. The peanut distributor will take the card and give the student holding it the appropriate number of peanuts. Students may not eat their peanuts during the activity. Students continue picking cards and reading them, going in sequence around the circle.

As they listen to the stories on the cards, ask students to think about the conditions that make life insecure and risky for some families and individuals as well as the conditions that make life secure and safe for others. Allow 20 to 25 minutes for students to read cards in their groups.

Checking Out What We've Learned

Lead a discussion with the whole class, using the following questions:

- Did everyone get the same number of peanuts? Why or why not? What seemed to determine the number of peanuts people received?

- Did everyone who got peanuts earn them through hard work? Should anyone have gotten peanuts who didn't?

- Were there any situations that families faced that were beyond their control? What were they?

- What aspects of security seem to greatly improve an individual's life chances? What factors seem to diminish a person's chances for a healthy, productive life?

- If we accept that the cards represent a cross-section of individuals and families that live in the United States, do all U.S. citizens seem to have an equal chance at a good life? Why or why not? Is it possible for all U.S. citizens to have equal life chances growing up here? What would need to change for everyone to have equal life chances?

Closing (optional)

Choose any closing activity from appendix B.

STUDENT HANDOUT

WHO'S SECURE IN THE UNITED STATES?

Your house burned down in a fire and your family doesn't have home-owner's insurance. You lost everything your family owns.

Take NO treats.

Due to the efforts of the people in your neighborhood, you now have a community garden where neighbors can grow vegetables for their families.

Take ONE treat.

You just graduated from high school and were lucky enough to get a job. You are saving all your money so that you can train to be an electrician.

Take ONE treat.

Your mom got a scholarship to go to college and now has a very good job.

Take TEN treats.

Your mother worked for the airlines for 10 years. The airlines had to cut back on the number of people it employs. Your mother lost her job this year.

Take NO treats.

Your family owns a small grocery store in the neighborhood. Your parents made very little money this year because they couldn't keep their prices as low as the big chain supermarket that opened one mile away.

Take NO treats.

S T U D E N T   H A N D O U T

WHO'S SECURE IN THE UNITED STATES? (continued)

Kids are constantly spray-painting graffiti on the walls and sidewalks in your neighborhood, including the front of your family's garage. You have to spend Saturdays repainting your garage.

Take NO treats.

Your younger brother and sister were both diagnosed with lead poisoning from the paint in your apartment. Your family has no health insurance.

Take NO treats.

Your father's union just won a wage increase and guaranteed health benefits.

Take FIVE treats.

Last spring a volunteer worked with families in your neighborhood to improve basic nutrition. Your family now purchases food with more protein and less fat.

Take ONE treat.

Your brother receives a scholarship to attend college in another state. Everyone is happy for him, but it means you will have one less working adult to contribute to your family's income.

Take ONE treat instead of the TWO you took last year.

Your father cannot work because of an industrial accident. Your mother must work at a low-wage job even though she would rather stay at home with her young children.

Take NO treats.

S T U D E N T   H A N D O U T

WHO'S SECURE IN THE UNITED STATES? (continued)

Your family started a small construction company with two other close friends. For the first time in almost 10 years your father and older brother have had full-time work all year long.

Take ONE treat.

Your father works for a supermarket chain. He buys fresh produce and sells it to the supermarkets in the country. If the produce has not been sold after three days, he sells it to the supermarkets in the inner city.

Take TWO treats.

Your mom works for a business that provides day care for your little sister in the same building where your mother works. The company also encourages secretaries like your mom to take free classes to upgrade their skills.

Take TEN treats.

Your parents both work to try to keep up with the cost of living. Your mom doesn't have to stay home during the day because your brothers are enrolled in a Head Start program. Although your parents' wages are not high, they make sure you get what you need.

Take FIVE treats.

A chemical company is the major employer in your town. Toxic chemicals have been found in the ground water, and people in your town contract cancer at much higher rates than normal. Most people don't want to make trouble because the company offers good jobs.

Take NO treats.

Your family has lived in this neighborhood for three generations. Now the city wants to build a highway right through it. If you can't stop the highway, the government will buy your house for less money than it will cost for your family to buy another home.

Take NO treats.

STUDENT HANDOUT

WHO'S SECURE IN THE UNITED STATES? (continued)

You come from a close-knit African-American family where relatives have always helped each other out. Everyone in your family pitches in so that each child has the opportunity to attend college or vocational training. You are very proud of your family's accomplishments.

Take FIVE treats.

You have participated in a summer job program in which you helped to renovate 10 houses in the neighborhood. Because you were so good at this, you have been selected to participate in a carpenter's apprenticeship program.

Take FIVE treats.

Your mom inherited money from a relative this year and she invited everyone in your family to decide together what to do with the $25,000 she received.

Take FIVE treats as long as you give THREE of them to people who have none.

You live with two sisters who had babies when they were teenagers. They live hard lives, and one has abused her children. You have moved in with an aunt to get some peace and quiet. You want to finish high school, but it's scary to think about whether you have a real future.

Take NO treats.

You were out with friends on a Friday night and you were wounded in a drive-by shooting. You had been mistaken for a member of a rival gang. You are now afraid to go outside, especially at night.

Take NO treats.

Your father is president of a bank in your town. Your mother is an accountant, and you hardly see her during the tax season. You like your big house and all the stuff you have, but you'd like more attention from your parents. You feel like they hardly notice you're there.

Take TWO treats.

WHO'S SECURE IN THE UNITED STATES? (continued)

Your mother and father used to work in a car assembly plant. The company has moved the plant to Mexico where it can pay its workers less. Your mom cleans houses now and your dad found part-time work at the local gas station. Your family is under a lot of stress.

Take NO treats.

You live in a good home. You go to a good school. You've lived in the same safe neighborhood your whole life. Both of your parents are college-educated, and they both have good jobs. You feel like you can grow up to be anything you want to be.

Take TEN treats.

Your mom is a computer technician at night and your dad is a union truck driver during the day. Your family schedule is a little crazy, but your mom and dad share child care and household chores. They make sure that the whole family does something special together every week.

Take TEN treats.

Your parents are divorced but they still fight all the time over money and over you. You feel pulled in two directions all the time. You get depressed and have stopped doing your homework.

Take NO treats.

You were born into the Oglala Sioux tribe and live on a reservation. Your family is deeply committed to preserving your tribal heritage and makes every effort to honor and celebrate tribal traditions. Although you get bored sometimes, you're also proud of who you are.

Take FIVE treats.

Your dad is Mexican American and your mom is European American. Your complexion isn't very dark. You live in the Midwest where your school friends think all Mexicans are lazy. You're afraid even to mention your family's heritage. You think all the kids will make fun of you.

Take NO treats.

S T U D E N T   H A N D O U T

WHO'S SECURE IN THE UNITED STATES? (continued)

Your family's farm has been devastated by the flooding of a nearby river. It will take your family at least two years to recover the farm, if that's even possible. In the meantime you're living in a trailer camp without your dog, who got lost in the flood.

Take NO treats.

Your parents have good jobs, but they spend all of their extra income on private school fees so that you and your sister can get a good education. Your neighborhood school is not very safe and it seems like a lot of teachers there have given up.

Take ONE treat.

You went into the Air Force as an 18-year-old. When you left the Air Force, you used money from the G.I. Bill to pursue a degree in engineering. You now own a successful engineering firm. You are married and have two children who do well in school.

Take TEN treats.

You are a third-generation Chinese American. Your parents wanted you to join the family business and they have had a difficult time accepting your plans to teach English to new immigrants in your community.

Take FIVE treats.

Your father works at a printing shop. He and other workers have been asking the company to raise wages, which have not kept pace with the cost of living. The company says it can't raise wages and will fire employees who continue to complain.

Take only ONE treat.

Your grandparents established a trust fund of $500,000 that you will receive when you turn 21. You even have people who manage this money so that your trust fund keeps growing every year.

Take TWENTY treats.

S T U D E N T   H A N D O U T

WHO'S SECURE IN THE UNITED STATES? (continued)

You are a 25-year-old white male who didn't go to college. You know that the income of white males without a college education has declined more in the past 20 years than the income of any other group. What's the point of even looking for a job?

Take NO treats.

You have been physically abused at home. You ran away at age 15 and have lived on the streets for two years. You'd like to get off the streets but you don't know how, and you have no other place to go.

Take NO treats.

No one in your family has gone to college. A teacher at school has encouraged you to apply. You've been accepted but you will need to work to help pay for college.

Take FIVE treats.

You live in a big city. You go to a public school that's old and dirty. Kids fight a lot. You are really smart but you know it's very "uncool" to like school and get good grades. You don't feel like you can ever really be yourself.

Take NO treats.

Letting Go of Labels

OBJECTIVES

Students will:

- experience what it feels like to be labeled;
- become more aware of their "comfort zone" in social situations.

PEACEABLE CLASSROOM PRINCIPLES

- Affirmation and acceptance
- Appreciation for diversity
- Personal connections
- Building community

AGENDA

1. **Gathering (optional)**

   Brainstorm

2. **Review Agenda**

3. **Lesson Activity**

   - The Comfort Zone

4. **Checking Out What We've Learned**

   Whole-Group Debriefing on Labels and Comfort Zones

5. **Closing (optional)**

   Choose any closing activity from appendix B.

Gathering (optional)

Ask the class to brainstorm a list of some of the labels students and teachers use to describe people at school. Then ask whether any of these labels have positive or negative overtones. Are some labels perceived positively by some students and negatively by others? You might explore the connection between the teenage compulsion to label everyone and the need to belong as well as the need to define the "in crowd" and the "out crowd."

Review Agenda

Write the agenda on the board and review it with the class.

The Comfort Zone

Explore with the class the idea of each person having a social "comfort zone." When we interact with others we often gravitate to people that we think are like us and experience discomfort with people we don't know who seem different from us. Reassure students that feeling some discomfort around people who are different from us is natural. Ask students to make a list for themselves (no one else will see it) of three groups that they would feel most uncomfortable being with. Ask students to describe—without naming the groups—why it might feel more awkward to be with some groups than with others. Students might say, "Because I don't know what to say or do," or "I don't want to say the wrong thing and offend someone," or "I don't think they like me." Discuss the kinds of social barriers that separate people who are different from each other.

Copy and cut out the Headband Labels (p. 291).Place loops of masking tape on the back of each headband strip. (The headband labels included are most appropriate for older adolescents. For younger adolescents you may want to eliminate some and add others.) Explain to students that each of them will receive a headband that labels him or her as a member of a specific group or as an individual with a particular trait. Students will not be able to see what's written on their headbands, since the headbands will be stuck to their foreheads.

Begin placing labels on the forehead of each student. (You may want to ask a few students to help you.) After everyone has a headband, tell students that they have about 10 minutes to socialize with each other. Encourage students to mingle. They must, however, follow three rules:

1. Respond to each person as if the headband he is wearing is true for him.

2. Do not tell anyone what is written on her headband.

3. Talk to people whose headbands identify them as people who are in your social comfort zone. When you encounter someone who would not be in your comfort zone, you might want to ask her some questions, give her some advice, or simply walk away. You decide.

When 10 minutes are up say, "Freeze." Ask students to think about how people reacted to them. Did they feel that they got friendly, hostile, or confused responses from their peers? Ask all the students who think that their headbands had positive labels to stand on one side of the room. Ask all students who think they have negative labels to stand on the other side of the room. Ask students who felt they received both positive and negative responses to their labels to stand in the middle.

Ask several students from all three groups to explain what students said or did that made them feel that their labels were positive, negative, or a little of both. It's especially important to discuss how students reacted physically to others (facial expression and physical gestures). Remind students that a great deal of communication is nonverbal. We often give away what we're thinking about without saying a word. What comments or questions gave students clues about their labels? Ask if any student thinks that she knows what her label says. Ask her to guess, then take off her headband and read it. Then let the rest of the students take off their headbands and read them.

Checking Out What We've Learned

Use the following observations and questions to initiate a discussion of the headband activity.

- Although some of you may be embarrassed by or angry about the label you received, there are students here at school, probably even in this class, who share these same characteristics and are treated the way you were.

- What labels do you think hurt people the most or make people the angriest? Why?

- Did people with negative headbands hang out together? If so, why do you think that happened?

- What can you do personally, or through organizations at school, to help students stretch beyond their personal social comfort zones and get to know people who are different from them? To answer this question consider:

  - Where and with whom do you sit in class?
  - Who gets invited to participate in special projects at school?
  - Are there unspoken rules about who does what at school?
  - Are there many opportunities to talk with students who are different from you?

Closing (optional)

Choose any closing activity from appendix B.

HEADBAND LABELS

I get straight A's.

I'm a computer nerd.

I'm white and most of my friends are black.

I'm gay but I haven't told anyone.

I don't believe in God.

I'm very religious.

My family is very wealthy.

My family is poor.

I'm a football player.

HEADBAND LABELS

I'm a virgin.

I belong to a church youth group.

I'm African American and hang out only with African Americans.

I've been hospitalized for depression.

I'm black and have only white friends.

I'm sexually promiscuous.

I'm dyslexic and have trouble reading and writing.

My mother is often on welfare.

I'm a leader in school government.

HEADBAND LABELS

I've had an abortion.

I drink alcohol a lot.

I'm the head cheerleader.

I'm a basketball player.

I've been physically abused at home.

I'm pretty, smart, and popular.

I think abortion is murder.

I'm a recent immigrant to America and I don't speak English well.

I'm white and I don't want to get to know anyone who isn't like me.

HEADBAND LABELS

I don't wear a smile all the time.
You have to get to know me before I respond.

I'm very liberal.

I'm very conservative.

I'm a bully.

I'm a special education student.

I hang out with kids from lots of different groups.

I draw and write poetry, but people don't know it.

Some of my friends are gang members.

I'm a friendly person. I get along with just about everyone.

Crossing Cultures: A Simulation Game*

OBJECTIVES

Students will:

- observe another culture in order to understand its beliefs, habits, and social "rules;"
- discuss challenges to communication across cultures.

PEACEABLE CLASSROOM PRINCIPLES

- Appreciation for diversity

AGENDA

1. **Gathering (optional)**

   Choose any gathering activity from appendix A.

2. **Review Agenda**

3. **Lesson Activities**

   - Crossing Cultures
   - Whole-Group Debriefing or Written Reflection

4. **Checking Out What We've Learned**

   Cross-Cultural Microlab

   Note: This lesson takes at least two class periods, depending on the amount of time you spend debriefing.

5. **Closing (optional)**

   Choose any closing activity from appendix B.

---

* Adapted from *Games by Thiagi: Diversity Simulation Games*, by Sivasailam Thiagarajan, PhD, © 1995. Adapted with the permission of the publisher, HRD Press, Amherst, Mass. (413) 253-3488.

295

Gathering (optional)

Choose any gathering activity from appendix A.

Review Agenda

Write the agenda on the board and review it with the class.

Crossing Cultures

Materials: For the BUNO culture:

- **one die for each person**
- **2x2-inch squares of paper made from 10 different colors of paper (about 20 squares for each person**
- **envelopes (one for each person)**
- **colored markers**
- **clear plastic name badges (one for each person)**
- **blank index cards (one for each person; these will go inside the name badges)**
- **two to five badges with the word "Visitor" written on them**

For the PLUTI culture:

- **approximately 100 plastic beads**
- **string for the beads (one string for each person)**
- **a plastic bag or container for each person**
- **a magic wand or special object**
- **colored markers**
- **clear plastic name badges (one for each person)**
- **blank index cards (one for each person; these will go inside the name badges)**
- **a bag of candy**
- **two to five badges with the word "Visitor" written on them**

Explain to the class that they will be playing a game in which each student will take on the identity of a person in one of two fictional cultures, the BUNO culture and the PLUTI culture. Students will have time to learn about their cultures and will have time to practice the habits and rituals that are part of their cultures. Some students from each group will visit the other culture and report back to their own culture about what they observed.

Divide the class into two equal groups. The simulation works best if there are 12 to 25 people in each culture, although cultural groups can be as small as 8 people. You'll need to have two separate rooms available, one for each culture.

Ask one volunteer from each group to teach the culture to their group. This volunteer will read directions out loud and will do his or her best to demonstrate the rituals and behaviors that are part of the culture. Give the volunteer from the BUNO culture the BUNO Culture handout (p. 299). Give the volunteer from the PLUTI culture the PLUTI Culture handout (p. 301). Rehearse the rituals and behaviors with the two volunteers *before* you begin the simulation. Each volunteer will read directions out loud and will do his or her best to demonstrate the rituals and behaviors that are part of the culture.

Ask the groups to go to separate rooms to learn and practice their cultures with the two volunteers. Give students 20 or 30 minutes for learning and practice.

Each group needs to designate two to five people as visitors. These people need to put on badges that say "visitor." Once each group has mastered the rules of its culture, have the visitors go to the other culture. When the visitors arrive, students should be behaving as members of their culture. Point out that this means that no English should be spoken. Allow 10 minutes for this first visit, then send visitors home to describe what they observed about the other culture. Allow visitors five minutes to describe what they saw.

Send a new group of visitors back to the other culture for 10 more minutes, then have them return home again and spend five minutes describing what they observed.

Whole-Group Debriefing or Written Reflection

Bring both groups together. Ask members of the PLUTI culture to describe and interpret the BUNO culture. Remind students to distinguish observations from interpretations. For example, observations could begin, "I observed them ...," or "I saw them ..." Interpretations could begin "I imagine that they did that because ...," or "I assumed that this meant ..." It is important to differentiate between observations and interpretations because interpretations are often wrong. Behaviors can be easily misunderstood.

Ask members of the BUNO culture to describe their culture correctly, including its values, beliefs, habits, etc.

Then ask members of the BUNO culture to describe and interpret the PLUTI culture, reminding students to distinguish observations from interpretations. When these students have finished, ask members of the PLUTI culture to describe their culture correctly.

After allowing members of each culture to speak, choose several of the questions below to discuss or write about.

- As a visitor, how did you feel about the culture you were visiting?
- For the rest of the group, how did you feel about the visitors?
- What made it difficult for members of each culture to understand the other? What would have made it easier?
- Did anyone begin to feel that their fictional culture was better than the other fictional culture? Why do you think this happens?
- What was it like to be an insider? What made you feel that way?
- What was it like to be an outsider? What made you feel that way?
- When do you feel like an outsider or an insider in your own life?

Checking Out What We've Learned

Cross-Cultural Microlab: Divide the class into groups of four or five, ensuring that each group has students who were members of both cultures. Have each student respond to the following questions (each student has about two minutes to respond). Ask for one student in each group to record responses.

- What assumptions do we often make about groups that are different from our own?

- What makes communication across cultures challenging?
- How can we make those who are different feel more welcome?
- Where can we make better efforts to cross cultures in the classroom? In school activities? In the community we live in?

Ask the recorders to share responses with the whole class.

Closing (optional)

Choose any closing activity from appendix B.

BUNO CULTURE

1. **Cultural Values and Admired Character Traits:** Competitiveness, individualism (each BUNO person has his own personal shield in his name card holder and creates a special hand sign that is different from everyone else's), materialism and trade, autonomy, seriousness.

2. **Verbal Communication:** Verbal communication is highly valued. You repeat everything three times to make sure it was heard.

3. **Nonverbal Communication:** There is no touching in public in the BUNO culture.

4. **Introductions:** You begin every interaction in the same way. You say, "Oy-no" three times and give your personal hand sign. "Oy-no" means "I am unique," so you want your personal hand sign to reflect your own personality.

5. **Social Distance:** You stand at least three feet away from anyone with whom you are interacting.

6. **Affect or Emotional Expression:** You don't express emotions very much. Most of the time your facial expression says "Let's get down to business." There are three exceptions:

    - You get visibly angry with foreigners who don't follow the rules. You shout "Ba-kee" at them three times and walk away in disgust. "Ba-kee" means "Barbarian."

    - When you "win" a trade, you make fun of the other person, point your finger at him or her, and call him or her "Suk-kos" three times.

    - You look down and hide your head in shame when someone accumulates $1,000 because you have not worked hard enough to have acquired that much wealth and power.

7. **Trading Game You Play:** The object of your game is to collect cards of the same color. Each time you collect five cards of the same color, you can go to the bank and receive money. You must designate a male to be the banker.

    Directions for the game:

    This game is played in pairs. One of you begins the game by saying "Rah-tee" three times. For the first round the banker identifies which two numbers (1, 2, 3, 4, 5, or 6) will "win" each trading session.

    - The person who says "Rah-tee" rolls his die first; then another player rolls her die.

    - When either player rolls one of the winning numbers, the winner gets to take all the cards of one color from the other player. (Players have up to three rolls of the die with the same person. If no one rolls the winning number, players leave each other in silence and move on to play the game with someone else.)

S T U D E N T   H A N D O U T

BUNO CULTURE (continued)

- The winner makes fun of the loser by pointing her finger at him and saying, "Suk-kos" three times. Then the players leave each other and find new "trading" partners.
- When players have five cards of the same color, they take them to the bank and are given money and new cards in exchange.

Other rules:

- You may not turn in your cards until after you have completed a least one trade round with another person.
- When you go to the bank you must first say "Oy-no" three times and give your hand sign. Then you can turn in your five cards of the same color.
- Men will collect $500 and 10 more cards. Women will collect $100 and five more cards.
- When you have "earned" $1,000 you get to call out the next two winning numbers for the trade rounds.

8. **Special Ceremony:** When a person has collected $1,000, he or she calls out "Sah-tom" three times. The rest of the players stop what they are doing, go to a wall or corner of the room, and hang their heads in shame. Everyone says, "Yah-tee" ("I want your wealth") to himself three times. Then the $1,000 winner calls out the two new winning numbers for the next trade round. Trade resumes.

9. **Social Status:** The banker, men, and those who "win" the trading game consistently have high status in this culture and get more "goodies." There is no difference in status between the young and the old. Everyone participates in trade rounds at her own risk and struggles to win.

10. **What a Foreigner Needs to Do to Feel Welcomed and Accepted:** Foreigners need to say "Oy-no" three times and give a personalized hand sign to the banker. Then they will receive color cards to trade.

11. **Taboos and Consequences:** If anyone touches you, shout "Ba-kee" at them as you push them out the door.

PLUTI CULTURE

1. **Cultural Values and Admired Character Traits**: Group solidarity, cooperation, respect for elders, humor, loyalty, celebrations (especially including food) that unify the group.

2. **Verbal Communication:** Words are not as highly valued as other forms of communication.

3. **Nonverbal Communication:** Nonverbal communication is highly valued. You laugh at each other a lot. Physical touching is very important. In public you are encouraged to hug, pat people on the shoulder, and hold hands. All of these activities are permissible and encouraged within and between sexes. If you are a young person, you kneel and show respectful silence in front of the elders.

4. **Introductions:** When you meet someone who is not an elder, both of you face each other and use the following series of gestures to create a welcome sign. One gesture flows into the next one so that it looks like one continuous movement.

   • Press the palms of your hands together in a praying position with fingers pointing upward.

   • Point your "praying hands" toward the other person.

   • Release your palms and put your arms by your sides.

   • Form a circle with your arms in front of your body and clasp your hands.

   • Hug the other person.

   • Say, "Kah-zee-mah."

5. **Social Distance:** You interact with others within a close distance (only one or two feet from the person you're talking with).

6. **Affect or Emotional Expression:** You are very expressive and demonstrative. You laugh out loud when two of you win a game.

7. **Social Status:** You gain social status by being part of a family clan. Divide the culture into at least two or three clans. Each clan designs its name tag. Every clan member has a similar name tag. Men and women are treated equally. There are two chosen wise elders (one male and one female) whose status is superior to others. They are seated apart from everyone else.

8. **Game You Play:** The object of the game is for both of you to win the game and then collect beads from the elder to add on to your necklace. When you receive three beads, you can be "initiated" and wear your necklace. (At the beginning every group member receives a string and a bag for collecting beads.)

   Directions:

   • The game is played in pairs. You face each other and begin the game by greeting each other by saying "Kah-zee-mah."

   • Then you both count to three together out loud. On the count of three, you each hold up one, two, three, four, or five fingers. You both win the game if you each hold up the same number of fingers.

STUDENT HANDOUT

PLUTI CULTURE (continued)

- If you hold up a different number of fingers the first time, you get two more tries. If you don't "win" in three tries, you end your interaction with a hug or a pat on the shoulder and go to another person.

- If you win, you hug each other and then go to the elders and kneel. The elders open their arms, giving you permission to speak. You both say "Kah-zee-mah" and you each receive one bead from the elders to put on your necklace string.

9. **Special Ceremony:** When someone has collected three beads from the elders, she becomes an "initiate." The initiate claps her hands three times and says, "See-kee-la!" Everyone else freezes. The initiate then says, "Ooh-la." Then everyone gathers in a circle, standing next to fellow clan members for the necklace ceremony.

    The elders and the initiate stand in the middle of the circle. Everyone in the circle chants: "Kah-zee-mah" three times. While people are chanting the female elder touches the initiate with the magic wand (or special object) and the male elder places the necklace around the initiate's neck. Then the initiate passes out candy to everyone. Finally everyone hugs each other and then goes back to playing the game.

10. **What A Foreigner Needs to Do to Be Welcomed and Accepted:** A foreigner needs to learn the greeting sign; then he or she can play the game.

11. **Taboos and Consequences**: If a foreigner does not express the proper greeting, a native hugs the foreigner and then gently takes the foreigner by the hand and walks the foreigner to the outer edges of the room so that the foreigner can observe how the greeting is done. Then the foreigner should try the greeting again.

Taking Action on a Community Problem

OBJECTIVES

Students will:

- identify, describe, and analyze a problem that affects them, their friends, their families, or communities;
- explore how to bring about change.

PEACEABLE CLASSROOM PRINCIPLES

- Social responsibility

AGENDA

1. **Gathering (optional)**

   Choose any gathering activity from appendix A.

2. **Review Agenda**

3. **Lesson Activity**

   - Planning Action

4. **Checking Out What We've Learned**

   Presentation or Event

5. **Closing (optional)**

   Choose any closing activity from appendix B.

Gathering (optional)

Choose any gathering activity from appendix A.

Review Agenda

Write the agenda on the board and review it with the class.

Planning Action

Begin by brainstorming a list of community problems that students are concerned about. Divide the class into small groups. Distribute the Community Action Research Project handout (p. 305) to each group. Ask members of each group to agree on one problem that they would like the whole class to address. After each group has chosen one problem, have each group fill out questions 1-4 on the handout. Next, invite each group to present its community problem to the class. Use the following chart to list the problems that students have identified and the goals that they set to address the problem. (Sample answers are shown.)

The Problem	Desired Goal	Specific Outcome
There are not enough summer jobs for young people in our community.	Increase the number of summer jobs available to teens.	Double the number of jobs available for teens in the next two years.
There is too much crime in our neighborhood.	Identify and implement strategies, policies, and programs that will make our neighborhood safer.	Establish a community policing program that includes neighborhood safety and self-defense programs and better street lighting within the next year.
Our community doesn't have a public recycling program.	Develop recycling opportunities for a variety of materials.	Establish pilot curbside recycling programs in two neighborhoods in the next two years.

After hearing from each group, the class needs to decide how it will choose one problem to address. Students might choose the problem that receives the most votes (individual or group votes). When the class problem as been chosen, students can divide up into research teams to complete the rest of the questions on the Community Action Research Project handout.

Checking Out What We've Learned

Have students make a presentation to another group in school or in the community about what they'd like to accomplish and what they've learned about the problem, or have students create an event that would help achieve their desired goal.

Closing (optional)

Choose any closing activity from appendix B.

COMMUNITY ACTION RESEARCH PROJECT

1. What is the problem? (What isn't working? What needs are not getting met?)

2. What is your goal?

3. What action do you intend to take to achieve your goal? What specific outcome do you hope for and how soon do you expect to achieve it?

4. Why is this a good idea? Why would people in the community support this outcome?

5. What is the root cause of the problem? (Lack of resources; clash of values, beliefs, personalities, etc.)

6. Who is presently affected by the problem?

7. What evidence proves that the problem exists and that specific groups are affected by it?

8. Who else may be affected if the problem is not resolved?

Conflict Resolution in the High School

S T U D E N T   H A N D O U T

COMMUNITY ACTION RESEARCH PROJECT (continued)

9. What key individuals and groups need to be part of the problem-solving process? What key resources does each individual or group have that could help you? What decision-making powers do they have? Complete the chart below.

Key individual or groups who need to be involved in problem-solving process	Key resources and/or powers

10. What information do you need before you engage with others in a discussion about this problem?

11. How will you get the information you need?

12. Using the chart below, identify three key people or groups who could help you achieve your goal. List at least one common interest you have with each person or group.

Key individual or groups who could help you achieve your goal	Common interests

S T U D E N T   H A N D O U T

COMMUNITY ACTION RESEARCH PROJECT (continued)

13. Identify two key people or groups who could prevent you from achieving your goal. What would their objections be? Are there any common interests you have with these persons or groups? Write this information in the chart below.

People/Groups	Objections	Common Interests

14. What steps do you need to take before discussing the problem with key individuals or groups? (e.g., documenting the extent of the problem; developing a survey, proposal, or petition; preparing a presentation; interviewing people who could help you get the facts; publicizing a town meeting; identifying key decision-makers needed to approve the necessary changes.) Use the chart below to plan these steps.

Task to be completed	By when?	Who does it?

15. After you have discussed the problem with key individuals and groups, identify other steps your class can take to achieve your goal.

APPENDIX A Gathering Activities

Gathering Activities are five- to ten-minute activities that set the stage for conflict resolution lessons by giving students a safe and fun way to share with each other. Gathering activities are intended to be positive, community-building experiences. Use your judgment in choosing the activities you think are most appropriate for your students. In all activities, students should have the opportunity to pass if they so desire. Many of these gathering activities were developed by and are used with permission of New York Metro Educators for Social Responsibility and the Resolving Conflict Creatively Program.

Anger Ball-Toss

Find a soft ball. Have the class stand in a circle. Begin by completing the sentence, "I feel angry when ..." Ask for a volunteer who is willing to restate what you just said. Toss that student the ball. That student restates what you said, then completes the sentence for herself. She then tosses the ball to someone else, who repeats what she said, then completes the sentence for himself, and so on.

Concentric Circles

Divide students into two equal groups. Ask one group to form a circle facing outward. Then ask the other group to form a second circle around that one, facing inward. Each person in the inner circle should be facing a partner in the outer circle. Tell students that they will each have about 45 seconds to share with their partners their responses to a question you will pose. All pairs of partners will speak simultaneously. Identify whether the inside partners or the outside partners will speak first. After the first partner has had a chance to share, signal that the other partner should begin speaking. When both partners have answered the question, ask students to move one, two, or three spaces to the right and pose another question to the group. Have students change partners for each new question.

Sample opening questions:

- Talk about the neighborhood in which you grew up as a kid. Where was it? What did it look like? What was something you liked about growing up there?
- What is the best present you've ever received? Why was it special?
- What's one thing you really dislike about high school? What's one thing you really like about high school?
- What do you think makes life hard for kids growing up right now?
- What do you think are the qualities of a good friend?
- What's something special that's been passed down in your family (a story, an object, an event or tradition)?
- Who is the most interesting adult outside your family that you've ever known?
- What is one thing your parents do or say that you don't want ever to do or say?
- If you became a parent, what is one thing you'd want to teach your children?
- What troubles you most about the world we live in today?

- If you could change one thing about your neighborhood or town, what would it be?
- If you were the principal of the high school, what is one change you would make to make the high school a better place for all students?

Feelings Check-In

Pass out markers and 5x8 index cards. Ask each student to write on the card in large letters one word that describes how he or she is feeling right now. Then ask students to hold up their cards and look at the variety of responses. Point out how rare it is for different people to bring the same feelings to an experience or situation. Invite students to share why they wrote down the words that they did.

Feelings Echo

Ask students to form a circle. Choose a feeling word for the activity such as angry, peaceful, upset, happy, or scared. Begin by completing the sentence "I feel [*feeling word*] when ..." Use a soft ball or special object to pass to a student who would like to go next and complete the sentence. Ask that student to toss the ball or pass the object to another student.

Go-Rounds

A Go-Round gives every student a chance to respond to a statement or question. Ask students to sit in a circle. Introduce the topic of the Go-Round in the form of a statement or question. Students then take turns responding, going around the circle. A person always has the right to pass when it's his or her turn to speak. After everyone has spoken, you can go back to those who passed to see if they have thought of something they want to contribute. The topic can be a general one that most students will be able to comment on (for example, "What is something you enjoyed about yesterday's lesson?") or it can be a way to introduce the content of the lesson. Some opening Go-Round topics include:

- What is something that makes you feel happy?
- What is one of your most treasured possessions?
- What do you usually do when you see a fight?
- Something I do differently than I used to is ...
- A time I helped out a friend or relative was ...

Group Clap

Ask everyone to close their eyes and begin to clap in whatever way they want. You can tell them that at first it will seem like a mess, but to stick with it and they will notice something happening. (Usually this begins very chaotically, but then gradually students start to synchronize the sounds they are making.)

Group Juggling

Get eight to ten soft balls that are three to five inches in diameter. Ask students to form a circle. If you have more than 15 people, you might want to split the group in half and have one facilitator for each group. Say to the group, "We're going to establish a pattern of tossing and catching the balls. I will say a student's name and then toss the ball underhand to her. That student will then say another student's name and toss the ball to him. You need to remember who tossed the ball to you and who you tossed the ball to. You will always catch the ball from the same person and always throw to the same person. We will do this a couple of times using one ball to get the pattern." After you've practiced with one ball, tell students that you are going to steadily add more balls. The goal is to see how many balls the group can juggle. Stop the activity and start over when too many balls are dropped. Remind students to say the name of the person they are throwing their balls to.

When the activity is over, take a few minutes to discuss the activity. What did you like about the activity? What didn't you like? What kinds of skills did you need to be successful? Was there anything we could have done as a group to be more successful? What made this activity challenging? Can you make any connections between being successful at this activity and being successful academically?

Guessing Box

Place an object into a box that you can close. The object should be something that in some way represents conflict or conflict resolution. Ask students to guess what's in the box. The guesses can be as wild or silly as they choose. Reveal the object, and ask a few volunteers how they came to think of the objects they guessed.

"I'd Like to Hear ..."

Have students say something positive they'd like to hear another person say about them. For example: "I'd like to hear someone say I'm a great dancer."

"I Got What I Wanted ..."

Have students complete the following sentence: "A time I got something I wanted was when ..."

"I Like My Neighbors Who ..."

This activity is a variation on Musical Chairs. Have students arrange their chairs in a circle and sit down. Stand in the center of the circle and complete the sentence "I like my neighbors. I especially like my neighbors who ..." (insert something that you like to do). Any students who also like to do what you've stated should stand up, leave their chairs, and try to move into another empty chair. At the same time you will try to find an empty chair to sit in. Whoever is left standing will complete the sentence, "I like my neighbors. I especially like my neighbors who... " and continue the game.

Initials

Have each student say his or her full name and then say positive adjectives using his or her initials. For example, George Frost—generous, friendly.

I Represent Conflict

Place yourself in the middle of the room and say, "Imagine that I represent conflict. Think about how you usually react when you experience a conflict personally or witness a conflict happening nearby. Then place yourself, in relation to me, somewhere in the room in a way that indicates your first response to conflict or disagreement. Think about your body position, the direction that you're facing, and the distance from conflict."

Once students have found a position relative to you in the room, ask individuals to explain why they are standing where they are. You might also want to ask, "If this represents your first reaction, what might your second reaction be, after thinking about the conflict?"

Mirroring

Have students work in pairs. One person is Person A, the other is Person B. Partners should stand facing one another. First Person B reflects all movements initiated by Person A, including facial expressions. After a short time, call, "Change," so that positions are reversed. Then Person B initiates the actions and Person A reflects. Have students discuss what it was like to mirror another person's actions.

Name Game with Motion

Have the group form a circle. Ask students to say their names and make a gesture that goes with their name. After each person says his or her name and makes a gesture, everyone in the group repeats the name and the gesture. Model the activity first, then go around the circle.

New and Good

Have students comment on something new and good that is happening in their lives. It can be anything—a good movie, a good time with a friend or family, a new idea, finishing a project for class. Model the activity for the class by speaking first.

Nonverbal Birthday Line-Up

Challenge students to line themselves up according to the month and day of their birthdays without talking. You will need to tell them where the line begins and where it ends. When the line is completed, ask them to say their birthdays aloud.

Putting Up a Fight

Go around the group and have students answer: "What is something you have that you would put up a serious fight for—even risk your life for—if someone tried to take it away?" (This can be a material thing, like a gold chain, or something intangible, like a good reputation.) Then ask: "Why is this so important to you?"

Something Beautiful

Ask each person to say something interesting or beautiful that he or she has seen lately and how that made them feel. Before anyone speaks, however, he or she must paraphrase what the previous student said. You can begin modeling the activity.

Standing Up

Have students describe a time they felt they were being taken advantage of and they stood up for themselves.

Strong Feelings

Ask students to describe a strong feeling they have been having in the last week and some reasons for that feeling.

What Color is Conflict?

Cut up a large quantity of 4x4 construction-paper squares in a wide variety of colors. Be sure to have plenty of red, black, brown, and gray. Ask each student to choose a color or group of colors that she thinks represents conflict. Either in the large group or in smaller groups of five or six, have participants share the colors they chose and why they chose them. (If you split up into smaller groups, come back together at the end and have volunteers share with the whole group which colors they chose and why.)

"What Would You Do ...?"

Go around the group asking each student to respond to this question: "If you saw a fight starting in the street between two people you didn't know at all, what would you do?"

What's Important in a Friend?

Ask students: "What do you think are the most important qualities in a good friend?"

"When I'm in a Conflict ..."

Go around the group, asking each student to complete the sentence, "When I get into a conflict, I usually ..."

Whip

A whip is a positive, incomplete statement that is completed in turn by each person in a circle. It goes quickly with each person answering in a short phrase. Some possible whips are:

- Something I'm good at that ends with "-ing"
- I feel good about myself when ...
- Something I like about my cultural or ethnic background is ...
- A hiding place I had when I was a child was ...
- Something that usually makes me happy is ...
- One word that describes how I feel today is ...
- One word that describes a strength of mine is ...

"You Like, I Like ..."

Give students a question they can answer briefly. Going around the circle, each person must repeat what the student before them said in response to the question before making their own statement. For example, if the question is, "What are your favorite things to wear?" and the first person who speaks says, "I like to wear jeans and big shirts with hoop earrings," the next person would say, "She likes to wear jeans and big shirts with hoop earrings, and I like to wear patched overalls and leather jackets."

Closing Activities

Closing Activities celebrate the time the group has spent together and conclude the lesson's activity on a positive note. Like Gathering Activities, they are good for building community in a classroom and bring a sense of closure to the lesson. Many of these Closing Activities were developed by and are used with the permission of New York Metro Educators for Social Responsibility and the Resolving Conflict Creatively Program.

Appreciation

Set the timer for three minutes. Tell the students they have the opportunity to say something they appreciated about the class today or about the group. Model by speaking first, then say that whoever is moved to speak may do so.

Closing Connections

Put the following statements (or others that you develop) on a poster or an overhead. Invite students to share their responses to any of the statements. Set a timer for three to five minutes and ask students to share their thoughts "popcorn style."

Sample statements:

- As I began this activity, I felt ... At the end of this activity I felt ...
- One thing that surprised me was ...
- As we worked together, I kept thinking about ...
- Now I'm more aware of how important it is to ...
- I liked this activity because ...
- I would have changed this activity by ...
- One thing that was fun, challenging, or eye-opening was ...
- After participating in the activity I realized ...
- Thinking about our classroom, it would be great if we could ...
- I found it really difficult to ...
- I found it easy to ...
- This helped me to learn more about ...
- I can take what I learned from this and apply it to ...
- I want to remember this experience the next time I ...

Encouragement Cards

Distribute index cards. Ask students to write anonymously one sentence expressing words of encouragement they might offer another student in the class. Collect the cards and redistribute them for a go-round of reading.

Feelings Check-In

Pass out markers and 5x8 index cards. Ask each student to write in large letters on the card one word that describes how he or she is feeling right now. Then ask students to hold up their cards and look at the variety of responses. Point out how rare it is for different people to bring the same feelings to an experience or situation. Invite students to share why they wrote down the words they did.

Goodbye/Hello

Ask students what behaviors or thoughts they would like to say goodbye to and what new behaviors or thoughts they would welcome. Go around with each student completing the blanks in the statement, "Goodbye ..., hello ..."

Go-Rounds

Closing Go-Rounds are like the Gathering Activities. Ask students to form a circle. Introduce the topic of the Go-Round in the form of a statement or question. Students then take turns responding, going around the circle. A person always has the right to pass when it's her turn to speak. After everyone has spoken, you can go back to someone who has passed to see if he has thought of something he wants to contribute. The topic can be a general one that most students will be able to comment on (for example, "What is something you enjoyed about today's lesson?") or it can be a way to review the content of the lesson. Some closing Go-Round topics include:

- What qualities could you share with the group that would help us work together more easily?
- What's a new idea or awareness that came to you today?
- What quality do you have that would make you a good negotiator?
- What quality do you have that would make you a good mediator?
- What's a time when someone has helped you or another person?

Group Yes!

Ask students to stand in a circle and hold the hands of the people on either side. Everyone bends over, hands almost touching the floor. Start saying "Yes" together softly and get louder and louder as you slowly straighten up, exploding into a loud, energetic "Yes!"

"If I Had a Wish ..."

Take turns sharing a wish, hope, or dream.

"I Used To ..."

Have students complete the blanks in the following statement: "I used to think (feel) ..., but now I think (feel) ..."

Rainstorm

The goal of this activity is to simulate the sound of a rainstorm. Have the group sit or stand in a circle. One person is the facilitator, who begins by rubbing hands together in front of one person in the circle. That person imitates the motion. Then the facilitator continues around the circle until everyone is rubbing hands together.

The second time around, the facilitator clicks fingers in front of one person. Everyone else should continue to rub hands together until the facilitator comes around with clicking fingers. As the facilitator passes by, he stops rubbing hands and starts clicking fingers.

The third time around the facilitator makes a loud pattering sound by slapping his thighs. The fourth time around the facilitator gets all participants stamping their feet. This is the height of the rainstorm.

Next the facilitator directs the subsiding of the storm, going around and changing stamping to pattering to clicking to hand rubbing to silence.

Telegram

Distribute index cards. Ask students to write on the cards one thing they would like to remember about today's lesson if they forget everything else. Collect the cards and redistribute them to be read in turn or, if time is short, select and read a few.

Closing Quotes

Cut out the following quotes and place them on a table for students to read. Each student selects one that speaks to him or her. Each student then reads the quote to the group.

"I have a dream ..."

—Martin Luther King, Jr.

"Never doubt that a small group of thoughtful, committed citizens can change the world; indeed, it's the only thing that ever has."

—Margaret Mead

"All humanity is one undivided and indivisible family, and each one of us is responsible for the misdeeds of all the others."

—Mahatma Gandhi

"The only thing necessary for evil to triumph is for good men to do nothing."

—Edmund Burke

"We must accept finite disappointment, but we must never lose infinite hope."

—Martin Luther King, Jr.

"The ultimate measure of a man is not where he stands in the moments of comfort and convenience, but where he stands in times of challenge and controversy."

—Martin Luther King, Jr.

"I was taught that the world had a lot of problems; that I could struggle and change them; that intellectual and material gifts brought the privilege and responsibility of sharing with others less fortunate; and that service is the rent each of us pays for living—the very purpose of life and not something you do in your spare time or after you have reached your personal goals."

—Marian Wright Edelman

"You gain strength, courage, and confidence by every experience in which you really stop to look fear in the face ... You must do the thing you think you cannot do."

—Eleanor Roosevelt

"If you have made mistakes ... there is always another chance for you ... you may have a fresh start any moment you choose, for this thing we call 'failure' is not the falling down, but the staying down."

—Mary Pickford

"There's no use in trying," she said. "One can't believe impossible things."

"I dare say you haven't had much practice," said the Queen. "When I was your age, I always did it for half an hour a day. Why, sometimes I've believed as many as six impossible things before breakfast."

—Lewis Carroll

"To love without roles, without power plays, is revolution."

—Rita Mae Brown

"If folks can learn to be racist, then they can learn to be antiracist. If being a sexist ain't genetic, then, dad gum, people can learn about gender equality."

—Johnnetta Betsch Cole

"One can never consent to creep when one feels the impulse to soar."

—Helen Keller

"The desk is a dangerous place from which to watch the world."

—John Le Carré

"The tough-minded respect difference. Their goal is a world made safe for differences."

—Ruth Fulton Benedict

"It just seems to me that as long as we are both here, it's pretty clear that the struggle is to share the planet, rather than to divide it."

—Alice Walker

"My definition of a free society is a society where it is safe to be unpopular."

—Adlai E. Stevenson

"If a man hasn't discovered something that he will die for, he isn't fit to live."

—Martin Luther King, Jr.

"Heaven is living in your hopes, and Hell is living in your fears."

—Tom Robbins

"A child educated only at school is an uneducated child."

—George Santayana

"You can't hold a man down without staying down with him."

—Booker T. Washington

"We have to dare to be ourselves, however frightening or strange that self may prove to be."

—May Sarton

"Those who profess to favor freedom, and yet depreciate agitation, are men who want rain without thunder and lightning."

—Frederick Douglass

"If you don't know where you are going to, you will end up somewhere else."

—Lewis Carroll

"Ain't nothin' to it but to do it."

—Maya Angelou

Grouping Strategies

Matching Activities for Forming Pairs

1. Make a set of conflict resolution cards by writing a conflict resolution "buzzword" on each card and then cutting it in half. (Sample buzzwords could include two-word phrases such as conflict resolution, problem solving, appreciate diversity, anger triggers, and so forth.) Give each student half a card and have students match words to find their partners.

2. Cut laminated postcards or pictures in half and have students find their "other halves." Or use two identical sets of trading cards, such as baseball cards, and ask students to find another person who has the same card.

3. Ask each student to find a partner who is wearing at least one piece of clothing that is the same color or style as yours. Variations: Find a partner who shares at least one of your physical characteristics; who has at least one initial that is the same as yours; or whose home phone number has at least three digits that are in your phone number.

Forming Groups of Three, Four, or More

1. Count off. If you have a group of 30, count off 1 to 5 for groups of 6; count off 1 to 6 for groups of 5; count off 1 to 8 for groups of 4; count off 1 to 10 for groups of 3.

2. Use playing cards to divide students into groups of four. Give each student a card and ask him or her to find three other students that have the same number or face card.

3. Create laminated puzzles from calendar pictures and photographs. For 30 students, cut 8 puzzles into 4 pieces each or 6 puzzles into 5 pieces each. Pass out one piece to each student. Students can solve the puzzles to form groups.

4. Ask students to form groups of four or five that include at least (choose four or five of the following categories):

   - one person who is male
   - one person who is female
   - two people who are of different racial or ethnic origins
   - one person who is an oldest sibling
   - one person who is a youngest sibling
   - one person who was born between January and June
   - one person who was born between July and December
   - two people who were born in different cities/states
   - one person who owns a pet and one who doesn't
   - one person who _____ (make up your own)

5. Cut out and laminate various images that are repeated on a sheet of patterned

wrapping paper. Give each student a cutout and ask all students with cutouts of the same object to form a group.

6. Use an assortment of wrapped penny candies to divide students into groups. Give each student one piece and ask all students with the same type of candy to form a group.

7. For any size group, keep a basket of student's names. Draw names randomly to create groups.

Grouping Strategies Based on Academic Content

Create groups of cards based on different subjects. Students can match the cards to form groups.

Math:

- pairs: two equations that share the same answer
- groups of three: three equations that share the same answer
- groups of three: a drawing of a geometric figure, a written description, and the degree of the angles associated with the figure
- groups of three: fraction, percentage, and decimal equivalents

English:

- pairs: antonyms and synonyms
- groups of three: words that are the same parts of speech (verbs, nouns, adjectives, prepositions, etc.)
- groups of four: sets of four characters associated with the same play or story

Social Studies:

- pairs: match cities and states, landmarks and countries, famous people and cultures, leaders and countries, events and dates, etc.
- groups of three, four, or five: groups of cities located on different continents, groups of famous people who lived in the same time period, objects and art associated with different countries, etc.

Science:

- pairs: names of chemical elements and their symbols
- groups of three, four, or five: groups of animals and plants that belong to the same scientific genus or species

Guidelines for Role-Plays

What is Role-Playing?

Role-playing is temporarily taking on a role and acting out a situation for the purpose of learning new skills or exploring new ways of relating to others.

In conflict resolution, role-playing lets students practice and experiment with new skills and behaviors to see how they feel, how the behavior "works," and what problems come up. It gives you, the teacher, the opportunity to give feedback and assess how well the student is acquiring and using new skills and understandings.

Types of Role-Plays

All of these types of role-plays can be scripted ahead of time or improvised on the spot by students.

Small Groups: Three or four students per group, with students taking turns as actors and observers.

Hassel Lines: The class forms two lines facing each other. Each actor in one line role-plays with the actor facing her in the opposite line. The role-plays take place simultaneously. Everyone in each line plays the same role.

Demonstration: The teacher and one or two students rehearse a role-play before class and perform the role-play for the class.

Whole Group: The class is divided into two or more groups. Everyone in the group speaks from the perspective of one assigned role. The teacher facilitates by calling on students.

Role-Play Techniques

Role Reversal: Actors switch roles halfway through the role-play.

Fish Bowl: The audience forms a circle around the actors and comments on the action or motivations of the actors.

Replacements: As the actors role-play, observers from the audience may tap them on the shoulder and replace them.

Role-Play Rules

- Stop everything when the teacher says "Freeze!"
- No booing or hissing from the audience.
- No swearing.
- No physical fighting—real or pretend.

The Teacher's Role

The teacher sets up the role-play and explains the rules. The teacher also facilitates the discussion at the end of the role-play. This discussion is very important, for this is where students receive feedback on their use of a particular skill.

To do this you need to:

- teach the class how to give appropriate feedback;
- demonstrate feedback skills;
- praise students when they give appropriate feedback.

Try to model the following feedback behaviors. You may also need to point out to students what you are doing, so they will learn to give similar types of feedback.

- Talk about the behavior, not the person. Role-plays are designed to promote behavioral skills, so it is important that feedback be directed at the behavior. For example, instead of saying: "You sounded like you wanted to solve the problem," say: "You said 'Let's work it out' and that let the other person know you wanted to solve the problem."

- Be specific. Tell students exactly what they are doing right or what could be improved. For example, instead of saying: "That was good," say: "You asked the other person what he or she wanted in the situation."

- Emphasize what was done well and suggest improvements for next time. For example: "You did a good job of looking her in the eye. Speaking up a bit more might be helpful next time."

- Suggest choices rather than giving instructions. Explore the consequences of the new choices. For example, instead of saying: "Ask her when she'll be finished with the tape recorder," say: "What do you think would happen if you asked her when she would be finished with the tape recorder?"

Questions for Processing the Role-Play

The types of questions you ask will influence the kind of feedback you get. Ask each actor:

- How did you feel playing the role?
- What did you notice yourself doing?
- How did the other person(s) respond to your actions?
- What do you think you did well?
- What might you have done differently or better?

Ask the observers:

- How did you feel as you watched the role-play?
- How did the conflict develop? How did it escalate?
- What stands out about how the actors talked/behaved?
- Why do you think they behaved as they did?
- What did they do that made the conflict better or worse?
- What might they have done differently?

For everyone:

- Have you ever been in a situation like this one?
- How did you handle it? How did it turn out?
- What might be another way to handle this situation?

End the discussion by summarizing the major issues. Tie these issues to the purpose of the role-play.

Facilitating Role-Plays

1. Explain the purpose of the role-play, such as practicing problem solving, trying new ways of communicating in conflicts, or practicing mediation. To learn from the role-play, students need to know why they are doing it.

2. Describe the role-play situation and the characters, as well as the type of role-play it will be.

3. Review the role-play rules.

4. Assign roles to players, taking care not to choose someone who might over-identify with the part. Give the roles fictional names.

5. Brief the actors; make sure they understand what the conflict is.

6. Brief the audience. As observers, what should they look/listen for?

7. Start the action. Intervene or coach only if absolutely necessary.

8. If the role-play doesn't come to a natural end, cut it off gently.

9. Thank the role-players, using their real names.

Once students are experienced with simple role-plays, they can begin to develop their own role-plays:

1. Have the class brainstorm situations

2. Choose one situation and flesh out the underlying problem or issues involved.

3. Develop the specific roles: their ages, gender, names, characteristics. How do the characters feel about each other? The situation?

4. Develop the background: What events led up to the current situation?

5. Decide on any supporting or secondary characters and develop them, defining their roles in the situation.

6. Choose a beginning point for the role-play.

Sample Infusion Lesson

The Israeli–Palestinian Conflict:
Complicating Our Thinking Through Perspective Taking

OBJECTIVES

Students will:

- research the Israeli-Palestinian conflict from the perspective of a group involved in the conflict;
- do an opinion walk-about from the perspective of their groups;
- step out of these perspectives to try to develop win-win solutions to the conflict.

PEACEABLE CLASSROOM PRINCIPLES

- Apreciation for diversity
- Cooperation and collaborative problem-solving
- Managing and resolving conflict

AGENDA

1. **Gathering (optional)**

   Choose any gathering activity from appendix A.

2. **Review Agenda**

3. **Lesson Activities**

   - Overview and Research
   - Opinion Walk-About
   - From Win-Lose to Win-Win

4. **Checking Out What We've Learned**

   Have each group share its solution with the class.

5. **Closing (optional)**

   Choose any closing activity from appendix B.

Gathering (optional)

Choose any gathering activity from appendix A.

Review Agenda

Write the agenda on the board and review it with the class.

Overview and Research

The state of Israel and occupied territories of Gaza, the West Bank, and the Golan Heights comprise a tiny geographical area. Every event and every step of the peace-building process affects Arab and Jewish Israeli citizens as well as Palestinians living in East Jerusalem and the occupied territories. One way to deepen awareness of the Israeli–Palestinian conflict is to explore the perspectives of various groups impacted by the peace process. In this set of activities each student will view events and consider the effects of possible peace-building steps through the eyes of one group.

You might begin by asking students to generate a list of various groups in Israel and the occupied territories who would have significantly different opinions and positions regarding the peace process.

Give each student a number and divide the class into groups that correspond to the percentages of group populations in Israel and the occupied territories. For example, if you have a group of 30 students you can divide the class in this way (populations are rounded):

> 1 through 8 (1.9 million): Israeli citizens who consider themselves religious Jews; generally politically conservative.
>
> 9 through 17 (2 million): Israeli citizens who consider themselves secular Jews; generally politically liberal.
>
> 18 through 20 (700,000): Israeli citizens who are Muslim Arabs.
>
> 21 (150,000): Israeli citizens who are Christians (Arab and European) and Druze.
>
> 22 and 23 (270,000): Jewish settlers who are citizens of Israel, but choose to live in the occupied territories.
>
> 24 through 30 (1.5 million): Palestinians living in East Jerusalem, Gaza, West Bank, and the Golan Heights who are not citizens of Israel.

After the class is divided into groups, give students time to find out about their groups. Begin by setting aside one period to provide an overview of the conflict using videos, maps, and current articles. Next, spend a period in the library so that students can do their own research. You might also consider inviting individuals and organizations from the local community who can share the perspectives of various groups with your class.

It is important during the overview and research stages to explore the relationships among the groups. Consider the following questions:

- Are groups unequal in power, status, financial resources, influence, and allies?
- What institutions play a major role in either precipitating the conflict or resolving the conflict and implementing a solution?
- Are there any groups that benefit from continuation of the conflict?
- Which groups are most interested in resolution? Are there any groups that could be allies?
- Which groups seem farthest apart or closest together regarding what they want?

- Do the people most deeply affected or harmed by the conflict have a voice in the decision-making process? If they don't, are more powerful groups committed to resolving the conflict? If not, why not?

Have students write journal entries imagining that they are living in Israel or the occupied territories as a member of their assigned group.

Have each group meet to discuss and agree on: (1) three of the most important concerns of the group; (2) three things they want other students to know about their group's experience; and (3) two or three things they need for a peace process to be acceptable. Have each group share its perspective with the whole class.

Opinion Walk-About

Try this exercise to explore further and share the group perspectives represented by the students. Ensure that there is time for a least one person from each group to share her thoughts, feelings, and reactions to each statement that you will read.

Post large signs around the room with the following words or group of words on each poster: outraged; fearful/threatened; justified/satisfied/affirmed; hopeless/powerless; concerned; optimistic/hopeful; alienated/ignored; ambivalent/uncertain; suspicious/hostile; reassured/more secure; doesn't matter to me.

Read a series of statements to the class that describe recent events and policies. Ask each student to listen to the statement from the perspective of his assigned group and move to the word that best describes his reaction upon hearing the statement. Invite students from each poster place to share their thoughts and feelings about the event or policy from their group's perspective.

Sample statements:

1. The check points and security inspections for Palestinian drivers coming to work from the West Bank into Jerusalem mean delays of up to two hours for those workers. If these checkpoints are closed, a person might not get to work or see family members for days or even weeks.

2. Thousands of Israeli Jews live in a 20-mile-wide strip of land that is bordered by the Mediterranean Sea to the west and the Green Line to the east. (The Green Line is the border of the West Bank.) The Green Line would become the western border of the independent state that Palestinians desire. As a result, these Israeli Jews would be positioned on a very small piece of land between the sea and a predominantly Arab and Muslim country.

3. Thousands of Palestinians who fled Israel in the late 1940s remain in refugee camps with inadequate shelter and public services.

From Win-Lose to Win-Win

Finally, ask students to step out of their assigned group perspectives to discuss possible solutions, considering the needs and concerns of all groups affected by the peace process.

Invite the students to consider that even in the best solutions to protracted conflicts there are groups that feel like winners and those that feel like losers. Realistically, different peace-building steps will likely benefit some groups more than others in the short term, given that all changes cannot be implemented at the same time. Peace building is slow and arduous and requires a deep commitment to a shared vision of a more just and peaceful future. When groups feel like losers, it's hard for them to invest in that shared vision.

Have the students form new groups. Make sure that each group contains at least one member from each of the original groups. Explain that students are now to step out of their assigned group's perspective. Give each group a question to work on. Sample questions:

1. If Israel were to relinquish the Golan Heights to Syria, what would Israeli Jews need to feel like winners?

2. For Jewish settlers to agree to leave Hebron, what would they need to feel like they haven't lost everything?

3. Compare a two-state solution with a one-state solution. What would both sides win in each case? How could either proposal result in a Win-Win solution?

Ask each group to think about possible solutions to the question by considering which groups might feel like losers and asking, "What might this group need to feel like a winner?"

Checking Out What We've Learned

Have each group share its question and its solutions with the class.

Closing (optional)

Choose any closing from appendix B.

Course Assessment Questionnaire

There are several ways that you can use these assessment questions with students:

- Choose five to ten of these questions for a written assessment.
- Give students the whole series of questions and invite students to select five to ten to answer.
- Select some questions for discussion in small and large groups (you might want to tape-record responses) and select some questions for written reflection.
- Give students the whole series of questions and select a few that you want all students to answer. Invite students to select a few additional questions that they would like to answer.

1. What are three things you want to remember most from this course?

2. What are two of the most important things you've learned in this course?

3. What's a skill you've learned and used that has changed your relationship with someone?

4. Describe what you now know about anger and anger management that you didn't know before.

5. How has learning more about cultural diversity changed your ideas and feelings about people who belong to different cultural groups than you?

6. List some of the things you do or say to yourself that help you defuse your anger in healthy ways.

7. What conflict style(s) did you use the most when you started this course? What new ones have you learned to use? Describe how you have used them successfully.

8. Has this course changed your ideas and feelings about prejudice and discrimination? How?

9. Has the meaning of any of these words changed for you during this course? How?
   - Respect
   - Community
   - Conflict
   - Listening
   - Violence
   - Peacemaking
   - Nonviolence

10. Describe one thing you've learned about yourself that surprised you.

11. What new questions do you have about conflict resolution and intergroup relations that you'd like to discuss and think more about?

12. In what ways was this course taught differently than other courses? Describe three learning activities that were new for you.

13. What aspect of the course, what issue, or what activity in the course was most challenging? Was there something in the course that was difficult for you to do or hard for you to confront?

14. What two or three activities did you like the best? Least? Why?

15. What two or three issues and/or activities do you wish all students in your school could experience? Why would you recommend these issues or activities?

16. In thinking back on this course, what images and experiences stand out the most for you? Why?

17. What's one way that learning negotiation and mediation skills might change your relationships with your family, friends, teachers, or employers?

18. Describe a conflict that you handled differently because of something you learned in this course.

19. Did this course make it easier for you to get to know other students? Explain.

20. Did you feel safe enough in this course to take the risk of being open and honest and sharing your stories with others? Why or why not?

21. Are there any changes you would make in this course to make it more effective?

22. If you were to summarize what this course was about to another student, what would you say? Use two or three sentences.

23. If you were to give advice to teachers about what's most important to keep in mind about teaching this class, what would you say? Use two or three sentences.

24. Do you think this course will change the rest of your time in high school? How? What might you be more aware of or do differently because you took this course?

25. What's one attitude or skill you hope students in this class will take with them when they leave?

Ballin, Amy, with Jeffrey Benson and Lucile Burt. *Trash Conflicts: A Science and Social Studies Curriculum on the Ethics of Disposal*. Cambridge, Mass.: Educators for Social Responsibility, 1993.

Benson, Jeffrey and Rachel Poliner. *Dialogue: Turning Controversy Into Community*. Cambridge, Mass.: Educators for Social Responsibility, 1994.

Berman, Sheldon. *Children's Social Consciousness and the Development of Social Responsibility*. Albany, N.Y.: SUNY Press, 1997.

Cecil, Nancy Lee with Patricia L. Roberts. *Raising Peaceful Children in a Violent World*. San Diego, Calif.: Lura Media, 1995.

Cohen, Richard. *Students Resolving Conflict: Peer Mediation in Schools*. Glenview, Ill.: Scott, Foresman and Co., 1995.

Creighton, Allan, Battered Women's Alternatives, with Paul Kivel, Oakland Men's Project. *Helping Teens Stop Violence*. Alameda, Calif.: Hunter House, Inc., 1992.

Fisher, Roger and William Ury. *Getting to Yes: Negotiating Agreement Without Giving In*. New York, N.Y.: Penguin, 1981.

Goleman, Daniel. *Emotional Intelligence*. New York: Bantam, 1995.

Gross, Fred, with Patrick Morton and Rachel Poliner. *The Power of Numbers: A Teacher's Guide to Mathematics in a Social Studies Context*. Cambridge, Mass.: Educators for Social Responsibility, 1993.

Kreidler, William. *Conflict Resolution in the Middle School*. Cambridge, Mass.: Educators for Social Responsibility, 1997.

Lantieri, Linda and Janet Patti. *Waging Peace in Our Schools*. Boston, Mass.: Beacon Press, 1996.

Lewis, Barbara A. *The Kids' Guide to Social Action: How to Solve the Social Problems You Choose and Turn Creative Thinking into Positive Action*. Minneapolis, Minn.: Free Spirit, 1991.

Lieber, Carol Miller. *Making Choices about Conflict, Security, and Peacemaking, Part I: Personal Perspectives*. Cambridge, Mass.: Educators for Social Responsibility, 1994.

O'Malley, Marion and Tiffany Davis. *Dealing With Differences*. Chapel Hill, N.C.: Center for Peace Education, 1995.

Rohnke, Karl. *Silver Bullets: A Guide to Initiative Problems, Adventure Games, and Trust Activities*. Hamilton, Mass.: Project Adventure, 1984.

Ury, William. *Getting Past No: Negotiating With Difficult People*. New York, N.Y.: Bantam, 1991.

---

* These titles are available from ESR. To order call 1-800-370-2515.

About the Authors

Carol Miller Lieber has worked as an educator for 30 years. She has been an elementary and secondary school teacher, a principal, and a university professor and was the cofounder of Crossroads, an independent secondary school in St. Louis, Mo. She is currently the director of professional services for Educators for Social Responsibility in Cambridge, Mass. Her work in conflict resolution, intergroup relations, and creating Peaceable Classrooms has focused on developing models for successful implementation of comprehensive, school-based programs. She is also author of the secondary-level curriculum *Making Choices About Conflict, Security, and Peacemaking*, available from ESR.

Linda Lantieri is the cofounder and director of the Resolving Conflict Creatively Program (RCCP) National Center in New York City. She has coordinated RCCP for the New York City Public Schools for eight years. She is the recipient of many awards, among them the Richard R. Green Distinguished Educator Award. She is coauthor of *Waging Peace in Our Schools*, published by Beacon Press.

The Resolving Conflict Creatively Program, an initiative of Educators for Social Responsibility, is a comprehensive, school-based program in conflict resolution and intergroup relations. One of the largest and most successful programs of its kind, RCCP works to reduce violence and promote caring and cooperative school communities.

Tom Roderick has been executive director of Educators for Social Responsibility Metropolitan Area (ESR Metro) since 1983. He cofounded the Resolving Conflict Creatively Program with Linda Lantieri in 1985. He has played a key role in developing RCCP over the years through his pioneering work in curriculum development, program development and implementation, and evaluation.

ESR Metro, located in New York City, is nationally known for its school-based conflict resolution programs, including the Resolving Conflict Creatively Program. ESR Metro also works with schools and community-based organizations in the areas of intercultural understanding and countering bias. ESR Metro has developed conflict resolution programs for children in bilingual classrooms, including Spanish, Mandarin Chinese, and Haitian Creole, as well as an Early Childhood Project to help preschool-age children develop emotional and social skills. In collaboration with the National Center for Children in Poverty, ESR Metro conducted a major research program to assess the impact of the Resolving Conflict Creatively Program on children in the New York City public schools.

About ESR

Educators for Social Responsibility seeks to make social responsibility an integral part of education in our nation's schools. We create and disseminate new ways of teaching and learning that help young people to develop the convictions and skills to build a safe, sustainable, and just world.

Our programs and products present divergent viewpoints, stimulate critical thinking about controversial issues, teach creative and productive ways of dealing with differences, promote cooperative problem-solving, and foster informed decision-making. We help young people develop a personal commitment to the well-being of other people and the planet and encourage participation in the democratic process.

ESR's Professional Development Services

"More than any other class, workshop, or in-service, this week has helped me grow as a person and as an educator."

—Institute participant

Comprehensive School-Wide Programs in Conflict Resolution, Violence Prevention, and Intergroup Relations

ESR offers specific conflict resolution and intergroup relations programs for middle and high schools, as well as elementary school programs.

Our comprehensive middle and high school programs include needs assessment, consultation with key school leaders, a three-day training for staff members, and continued staff development on site.

Training Formats to Meet Your Needs

ESR offers a wide range of training opportunities to meet the needs and budget of your school or organization.

Our formats include introductory workshops, one- to three-day seminars, week-long summer institutes and university courses, school-based model programs, consultation, and speakers on selected educational topics.

Our highly engaging workshops utilize a range of approaches from role-plays and simulations to small-group discussions and reflective writing.

For more information, call ESR Professional Services Department at 1-800-370-2515.

Also Published by ESR

Dialogue:
Turning Controversy Into Community

Jeffrey Benson and
Rachel A. Poliner

What would a controversial discussion look like
if it incorporated creative thinking and conflict
resolution skills? It might be cooperative rather
than competitive, and it might build rather than
fracture community. This new curriculum paints
a portrait of nonadversarial dialogue through
the story of Centerville, a fictional town caught
in a controversy over whether or not to
mandate school uniforms. The story that
unfolds provides a rich case study in how to
resolve public, as well as interpersonal, conflict.

Teachers will learn techniques and structures
for helping students build skills such as
listening, managing their anger, researching
issues, uncovering bias, understanding and
appreciating different perspectives, and creating
solutions.

Dialogue has 10 skill-focused chapters which
open with a scene from Centerville, followed by
activities for teaching, practicing, and assessing
skills. This unit is especially suited for social
studies and English teachers and student
government and debate team advisors.

Field Test Version
Grades 7-12
142 pages, ESR 1997
DIALOG
$16.00 Nonmembers,
$14.40 Members

Conflict Resolution
in the Middle School:
A Curriculum and Teaching Guide

William J. Kreidler

The highly acclaimed *Conflict Resolution in the
Middle School* features everything you'll need to
help students address the conflicts that come
with adolescence. Newly revised and
expanded, the curriculum features 28 skill-
building lessons and more! Additions to the
curriculum include:

- new sections on creating a classroom
  environment for teaching conflict
  resolution, developing staff and parent
  suport, and assessing student learning
  (including written tests);

- seven different implementation models
  with an exploration of each model's
  advantages and disadvantages;

- new skill lessons that explore personal
  power and responsible decision-
  making;

- an expanded infusion section that
  includes lessons on infusing conflict
  resolution into math and science;

- a section on adolescent development
  exploring gender and race;

- a new structure to make the guide easier
  to use.

REVISED AND EXPANDED EDITION!
Grades 6-8
384 pages, ESR 1997
CONMID
$38.00 Nonmembers,
$34.20 Members

The Power of Numbers:
A Teacher's Guide to Mathematics in a Social Studies Context

Fred Gross, Patrick Morton, and Rachel Poliner

The power of mathematics lies in its use as a tool not only for computing, but for making decisions, communicating, and predicting. This middle school math and social studies curriculum integrates goals and strategies, consistent with the National Council of Teachers of Mathematics *Standards*, to help students create mathematical questions; conduct research; record, interpret, and discuss results; and learn about the uses and misuses of math in real-world decision making.

Students learn to identify bias in questions and samples, construct graphs using data relevant to their lives and interests, and identify the complex societal issues underlying public policy planning and decision making using the Census and polling as connecting threads. These activities are an effective way of examining the elections within the context of a math course.

The guide includes numerous lesson plans and activities appropriate for heterogeneously grouped classes, suggestions for assessment, an appendix on cooperative-learning techniques, and a chart correlating the curriculum activities to NCTM *Standards*. The lesson plans may be used sequentially or selectively. For ease in photocopying, unbound, student handout masters for *The Power of Numbers* are available.

Grades 6-9
271 pages, ESR 1993
POWNUM
$38.00 Nonmembers,
$34.20 Members

**Unbound student handout masters
for photocopying
POWPAC**

**$12.00 Nonmembers
$10.80 Members**

Trash Conflicts:
A Science and Social Studies Curriculum on the Ethics of Disposal

*Amy Ballin
with Jeffrey Benson and Lucile Burt*

Trash Conflicts promotes deeper understanding of the impact of waste production and disposal. It goes beyond awareness and increasing students' appreciation of natural resources to initiating critical thinking, decision making, responsibility, and empowerment.

The curriculum starts where children are and moves them through a careful analysis of a complex series of interrelated issues, which include technology, economics, power, race, and class.

Through science-based experiments, research and analysis, role-plays, and discussions, students learn about the nature of garbage, disposal methods, consumer behavior, toxic waste, and the political process surrounding trash disposal.

This comprehensive teacher's guide incorporates a variety of activities, student handouts, and readings that help teachers integrate environmental education across subhect areas, including science, English, and social studies. As a self-contained or team-taught unit, it can be used in a variety of educational settings ranging from schools to community centers.

Grades 6-8
220 pages, ESR 1993
TRASHD
$28.00 Nonmembers,
$25.20 Members

Making History:
A Social Studies Curriculum in the Participation Series

*Boston Area Educators for
Social Responsibility
Sheldon Berman, series coordinator*

Making History helps teachers prepare students for democratic participation in society. Students are encouraged to use their own experiences to assess controversial issues. Activities explore the meaning of empowerment, both in the community and in the nation at large. Students review case studies of community action, learn about various models for decision making, and discuss strategies for creating change.

Grades 7-12
90 pages, ESR 1984
MAKHIS
$19.00 Nonmembers,
$17.10 Members

ESR Journal: Educating for Democracy

The ESR Journal continues to offer K-12 and postsecondary educators practical strategies and great ides for making social responsibility a reality in the classroom and in children's lives. The ESR Journal is a reservoir of resources on promising practices in the field of education for social responsibility, highlighting what works and why.

106 pages, ESR 1992
JOUR02
$13.00 Nonmembers,
$11.70 Members

Videos!

Everybody Rejoice: A Celebration of Diversity

29th Street Video Production/ESR

This video adds a new and engaging dimension to school conflict resolution and multicultural/diversity programs. An ethnically diverse group of high school students from the Public School Repertory Company present a collage of performances and perspectives that pay tribute to their individual and ethnic differences.

An uplifting, entertaining experience as well as an effective demonstration of how working together toward a common goal can positively effect students' sense of self, their awareness and appreciation of diversity and individuality, and their efficacy as members of a community working toward a common goal.

Video comes with a two-page users' guide complete with pre- and post-viewing discussion

questions. Produced by Tony De Nonno; coproduced by David Wallace.

Grades 9-12
26-minute videotape (1/2 VHS),
ESR 1991
EVBODY
$25.00 Nonmembers,
$22.50 Members

Waging Peace in Our Schools

This moving video offers you a chance to experience the in-depth components of the Resolving Conflict Creatively Program (RCCP), an initiative of Educators for Social Responsibility. You'll see conflict resolution skills being taught and students engaged in peer mediation, as well as hear the testimonies of children, teachers, parents, and administrators who have worked to change their schools. Dramatic positive changes are possible when an entire school community wages peace. Produced by Peter Barton.

26 minutes
WAGEPE
$39.95 Nonmembers,
$35.95 Members

An Eye for an Eye ... Makes the Whole World Blind

Alternative high school students, teachers, and their principal share the dramatic changes they have experienced in attitudes and behaviors in dealing with conflict in their lives, changes brought about as a result of their participation in RCCP. Produced by Peter Barton.

Grades 7-12
12 minutes
EYEFOR
$25.00 Nonmembers,
$22.50 Members

ORDER FORM

Call, mail, or fax your order
Tel. (800) 370-2515
Fax (617) 864-5164

esr

EDUCATORS
for
SOCIAL
RESPONSIBILITY

23 Garden Street
Cambridge, MA 02138
(617) 492-1764

Bill to: _____

Address _____

City, State, Zip _____

Phone _____

☛ Use street address for UPS delivery. Please allow two to four weeks for delivery. Rush service available, please call for details.

Ship to: _____

Street Address _____

City, State, Zip _____

Phone _____

☐ Enclosed is my check or money order in U.S. funds

☐ Enclosed is a purchase order

☐ Charge my order to ☐ MasterCard   ☐ Visa

Card # _____ Exp. _____

Signature _____

Phone _____

Qty.	Code	Description	Unit Price	Total Price

Remember to add 10% for shipping and handling ($3.50 minimum) for U.S. orders.

Subtotal	
S&H ($10%, $3.50 min)	
Total	